BUILDING TYPING SKILLS

SECOND EDITION SI METRIC

JEAN M. McCONNELL · WILLIAM L. DARNELL

McGraw-Hill Ryerson Limited

TORONTO, MONTREAL, NEW YORK, ST. LOUIS, SAN FRANCISCO, AUCKLAND, BEIRUT,
BOGOTA, DÜSSELDORF, JOHANNESBURG, LISBON, LONDON, LUCERNE, MADRID,
MEXICO, NEW DELHI, PANAMA, PARIS, SÃN JUAN, SAO PAULO, SINGAPORE,
SYDNEY, TOKYO

BUILDING TYPING SKILLS, Second Edition, SI METRIC

Copyright © McGraw-Hill Ryerson Limited, 1978, 1973.
All rights reserved. No part of this publication may be
reproduced, stored in a retrieval system, or transmitted,
in any form, or by any means, mechanical, electronic, photo-
copying, recording or otherwise, without the prior written
permission of McGraw-Hill Ryerson Limited.

ISBN 0-07-082676-5

234567890 BP 765

Printed and bound in Canada

Canadian Cataloguing in Publication Data

McConnell, Jean M., 1918-
    Building typing skills

ISBN 0-07-082676-5

1. Typewriting.   I. Darnell, William L., 1915-
II. Title.

Z49.M32 1978   652.3'02   C77-001807-6

Preface

The Purpose of this Book

The typewriter is the most common machine used in modern business establishments, and it is becoming an increasingly popular writing instrument in the home. The purpose of this book is to help the student of typewriting to use the machine effectively and efficiently. To do this, the student must master a variety of skills and must be given the opportunity to apply the skills in a variety of meaningful situations.

How the Book is Organized

In building any complex skill, it is essential that good work habits and correct techniques should be learned from the beginning, and that they should be practised continuously throughout the learning process. To establish and maintain the proper techniques most effectively, this book is organized on the "cycle" plan. Good techniques are introduced early, and at regular and frequent intervals, they are reviewed and reinforced. A corollary benefit of the cycle plan is that the student is never required to apply his typing skill to a situation that is beyond his probable level of achievement. As his skills increase, so does the complexity of the situation in which he must apply them.

The learning cycles in *Building Typing Skills* each consist of twenty-five lessons. In the first five lessons of each cycle, the student devotes all his efforts to building and consolidating his general typing skill. In the next five lessons, the student applies his skill to meaningful situations involving the production of manuscripts and properly arranged display work. In the third group of five lessons, the student uses his skill in the production of well-arranged letters and envelopes. The fourth group of lessons instructs the student in proper tabulating techniques and introduces him to common business forms. In the concluding five lessons of the cycle, the student reviews the new elements that have been introduced in the cycle, and in the final lesson, is given a test whereby he may assess his progress.

The Lesson Plan

For convenience of instruction and learning, *Building Typing Skills* has been lesson-planned. Each lesson contains enough material for the normal 45-50 minute typing period. A variety of material is provided in each lesson to sustain the student's interest and to provide the short, intensive spurts of practice which have proved to be so effective in skill building.

The *Review Warmup* sections of each lesson contain drills which review, consolidate, and build the skills which have been initiated in previous lessons. These drills always require some practice on the top row of keys. In an age when numbers are playing an increasingly important part in business and personal documents, it is imperative that typists have complete mastery of this area of the keyboard.

In the *Job* sections of each lesson, provision has been made for the individual differences which will be found among typing students. Sufficient material is provided so that the more skillful student need not mark time but can extend his skills with meaningful practice.

Preface to the Second Edition SI Metric

In this Second Edition of Building Typing Skills, the number of lessons has been increased to 150. Among the new topics covered are the Canadian Postal Code, carbon copies, spirit masters and stencils, telegrams, and job applications. In addition, throughout the book, considerably more attention is given to composing at the typewriter. From Lesson 10 on, most lessons contain an exercise headed THINK AS YOU TYPE, to provide students with regular and interesting practice in creative typing. Today's trend away from "copy-typing" is also recognized by the inclusion of an expanded amount of rough-draft and hand-written copy.

If an orderly conversion to the metric system of measurement is to be achieved, typists must know the correct symbols for the SI units and must be aware of the conventions that govern their use. In this revision of the second edition, all measurements are expressed in metric units and the latest conventions for expressing them are illustrated. Other new usages such as the 24-hour clock for expressing time and numeric dating are also illustrated and used in this revision. This edition is designed to reflect the best typing practice in the current business world.

Index

Contents

Of the many parts of a type-writer, you need to know the location and use of only these 14 parts at the start of your typing course:

1. **"Carriage"** . . . the top, mov-able part of the machine . . . carries the paper . . . moves horizontally to right and left.

2. **"Carriage-position scale."** . . . counts the spaces across the cyl-inder.

3. **"Carriage release"** . . . frees carriage so it can be moved eas-ily by hand to right or left . . . one at each end of the carriage. When you depress it, hold the adjacent cylinder knob firmly.

4. **"Carriage return"** . . . used to return the carriage and to space up the paper for the start of a new line of typing. On some

electrics, it is a large key at the right-hand side of the keyboard instead of the lever shown in the drawing.

5. **"Cylinder"** . . . the long roller in the carriage around which the paper turns . . . paper and cylinder turn each time you return the carriage or turn one of the cylinder knobs.

6. **"Cylinder knob."** . . . the large knob at each end of the cylinder.

7. **"Line-space regulator."** . . . controls the distance that the paper spaces up when the car-riage is returned by key or lever.

8. **"Margin sets."** . . . devices used to adjust the margin stops that control the margin area on each side of the paper.

9. **"Paper bail."** . . . clamps the paper against the cylinder . . .

10. **"Paper guide."** . . . used to guide the paper uniformly into the carriage.

11. **"Paper release"** . . . loos-ens the paper for straightening or removal.

12. **"Paper rest"** . . . the paper rests on it . . . so does the paper guide.

13. **"Printing point"** . . . the V-shaped slot where the type bars come up to strike and print on the paper.

14. **"Printing-point indicator"** . . . a line or mark or arrowhead pointing to the space on the carriage-position scale to which the carriage has moved and at which the machine is ready to print.

See how quickly you can find these parts on your typewriter:

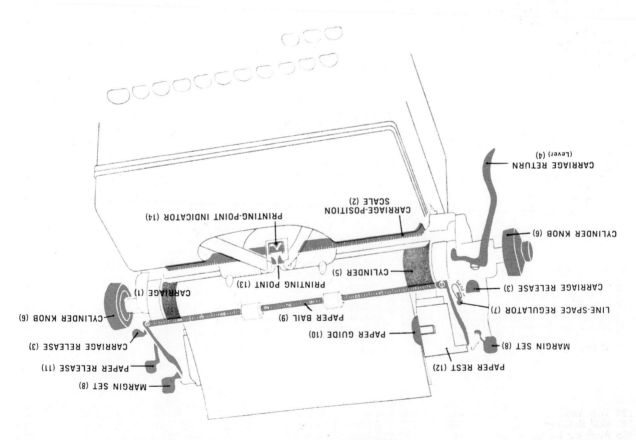

CARRIAGE RETURN (Lever) (4)

PRINTING-POINT INDICATOR (14)

CARRIAGE-POSITION SCALE (2)

CYLINDER KNOB (6)

CARRIAGE (1)

PRINTING POINT (13)

CYLINDER (5)

CARRIAGE RELEASE (3)

LINE-SPACE REGULATOR (7)

CYLINDER KNOB (6)

PAPER BAIL (9)

PAPER GUIDE (10)

MARGIN SET (8)

CARRIAGE RELEASE (3)

PAPER RELEASE (11)

PAPER REST (12)

MARGIN SET (8)

Getting Ready to Type

1. CHECK THE
   PAPER GUIDE

The paper guide should be set so as to centre the paper at 50. Directions are given on page 12.

2. SET LINESPACE
   REGULATOR

In all lessons, the opening drills are to be typed in single spacing.

3. SET MARGINS AS
   DIRECTED

Your machine has a left margin stop and a right margin stop. Set them separately, one at a time, as directed by your instructor.

4. PULL PAPER BAIL
   OUT OF WAY

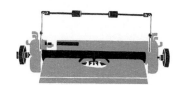

Pull bail toward you, or lift it up straight, out of the way of the paper you will be inserting.

5. INSERT PAPER

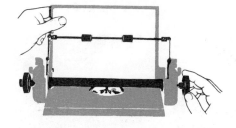

Hold the paper in your left hand and place it behind the cylinder, against the edge of the paper guide. With your right hand, turn the cylinder **knob to draw the paper into the machine. Turn up several line-spaces of paper.**

6. CHECK PAPER
   IS STRAIGHT

The top and bottom of the left edge should line up at the paper guide. If they do not, loosen paper (use paper release), straighten it, and return the paper release to its normal position.

7. RESET BAIL

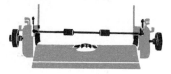

Adjust rolls to divide paper approximately into thirds; then place the bail snugly against the paper.

8. ADJUST FOR
   TOP MARGIN

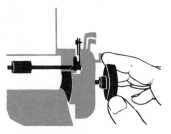

Turn the paper back down (use the cylinder knob) until only about two line-spaces or so of paper show above the top of the paper bail.

The ready-to-type position

Place your book on the right side of your machine, your paper and pencil on the left side.

Sit with your head erect, turned to face the book. Keep your back straight, your shoulders level, and your elbows in at your sides.

Your body should be centered opposite the J key. Lean slightly forward from the waist but sit well back in the chair.

Your feet should be braced flat on the floor, slightly apart.

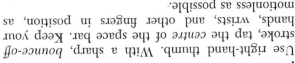

HOME KEYS

The home-key position

Each finger darts up and down from a "home key" on which it remains when not busy.

Left finger tips on ASD and F keys. Draw the left thumb in close to the forefinger.

Right finger tips on JKL and ; keys. The right thumb extends out above the space bar.

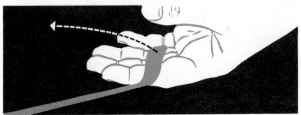

Curve your fingers correctly

On a manual typewriter, curve your fingers *tightly* (as though grasping a handle bar) and let the fingers rest lightly on the home keys, without pressure.

On an electric machine, curve the fingers *slightly* and hold them as close to the home keys as you can without quite touching them.

Striking the space bar

Use right-hand thumb. With a sharp, *bounce-off* stroke, tap the *centre* of the space bar. Keep your hands, wrists, and other fingers in position, as motionless as possible.

SPACE BAR

Returning the carriage

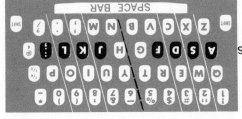

On a manual typewriter, in one quick, continuous sweep of your left hand: (a) place the forefinger and next two fingers against the carriage-return lever; (b) *flip* the lever with a toss of your wrist, returning the carriage to the margin stop; and (c) *dart* your left hand back to its home-key position. Make this motion without watching your hand.

On an electric typewriter, in one quick, smooth motion: (a) extend the little finger of your right hand to the carriage-return key; (b) lightly flick the key, causing the carriage to return automatically; and (c) *zip* the finger back to its home key — all without moving the J-finger from above its home key. Make this motion without watching your finger.

Lesson 1

HOME-ROW KEYS

1 f ff fff j jj jjj fff jjj ff jj f j f j

2 d dd ddd k kk kkk ddd kkk dd kk d k d k

3 s ss sss l ll lll sss lll ss ll s l s l

4 a aa aaa ; ;; ;;; aaa ;;; aa ;; a ; a ;

5 a; sl dk fj dk sl a; a;sl dkfj fjdksla;

WORDS

6 lad lad sad sad fad fad add add dad dad

7 lads lads fads fads adds adds dads dads

8 lass lass fall fall alas alas lass fall

9 a as ask asks flask lad lads alas salad

PHRASES

10 ask dad; dad asks; ask a lad; ask a dad

11 a sad lad; all sad lads; ask a sad lad;

12 a lass; a sad lass; ask a sad lass; ask

13 dad falls; all lads fall; sad lads fall

14 alas a salad; ads add a flask; sad fad;

Job 4.

Suggested time: 15 minutes
(a) Type the following letter in the style of your choice.
(b) Address a large envelope for it.

Ashley and Cooper Ltd., Suite 116 Granite Bldg., 10654 Jasper Avenue, Edmonton, Alberta T2V 6A9 Attention: James Panton. Gentlemen: Our firm is considering the extension of its operations, and one of the suggestions is the establishment of a branch plant in Edmonton.

So that this suggestion can be evaluated properly, we require information about the availability of industrial land and buildings in the Edmonton area. Our real estate advisor, Mr. John Rankin, has recommended your firm to us and has told us that we can rely on your judgment and discretion.

A list of specifications for the proposed plant is enclosed. We would appreciate receiving from you, before March 1, information about properties in your area that might accommodate it.
Very truly yours, William Reid, Vice-President.

Type a similar letter and envelope inquiring about a branch plant and land in Calgary. Address it to:
Western Realty Ltd., 1642 Seventh Avenue West, Calgary, Alberta T4B 7L6. Attention: Leslie Winters.

Job 5.

Suggested time: 10 minutes
Use each of the following words in a sentence to indicate its correct meaning. Consult your dictionary if necessary.

impel, monetary, comprehend, retrieval, caption, chronological, loose, tact, duplicate, site

Job 6.

Suggested time: 10 minutes
Compose, set up, and type a short letter to Room Reservations, Royal York Hotel, 100 Front Street W., Toronto, Ontario M5J 1E3. Request that a single room with bath be reserved for you on December 11. You will arrive via Air Canada on flight No. 702, scheduled to arrive at 16:40. You expect to remain for five days. Ask for a confirmation.

Lesson 2

WARMUP

1 aa ;; ss ll dd kk ff jj a ; s l d k f j

2 a as ask a ad sad dad fad lads all adds

NEW KEYS

3 j jh jh jjj hhh jhj had had has has hal

4 f fg fg fff ggg fgf gas gas gal gal gad

5 jag jag hag hag lag lag sag sag hal has

6 hall hall gash gash lash lash hags hags

7 j ju ju jjj uuu juj jug jug hug hug lug

8 d de de ddd eee ded leg leg fed fed see

9 egg egg hue hue sue sue dug dug age age

10 heal heal fuel fuel heel heel gulf gulf

LEFT HAND

11 deaf deaf safe safe fade fade sage sage

RIGHT HAND

12 hull hull hull hulk hulk hulk lull lull

WORD BUILDING

13 all; dull full gull hull lull dull full

14 ash; sash dash gash hash lash sash dash

SENTENCES

15 dad has a safe lease; all fuel has lead

16 elf had a jade seal; a dull leaf fades;

Suggested time: 15 minutes
Set up the following, properly displayed on a full sheet.

ARTICLE IV

DUTIES OF OFFICERS

SECTION 1.   THE PRESIDENT

The President shall chair the Board of Directors and shall preside at all meetings of the Society and of the Board of Directors. He/she shall present an annual report to the members and appoint the standing committees, except the Finance Committee, and such other committees as he/she may deem necessary. He/she shall sign all policies and perform such other duties as shall be assigned from time to time.

SECTION 2.   THE VICE-PRESIDENT

The Vice-President shall, in the absence or disability of the President, perform the duties of that office. The Board of Directors may designate from their own number one or more additional Vice-Presidents subordinate to the elected Vice-President.

SECTION 3.   THE SECRETARY

The Secretary shall keep a record of the votes and of the other proceedings of all General Elections and special meetings of the Society and of all meetings of the Board of Directors. He/she shall have the custody of the corporate seal and affix the same to all instruments required to be sealed, and shall perform such other duties as are required by the Board of Directors and the Bylaws of the Society.

SECTION 4.   THE TREASURER

The Treasurer shall: (a) have charge and custody of and be responsible for all funds and securities of the Society; receive and give receipts for monies due and payable to the Society from any source whatsoever, and deposit all such monies in the name of the Society in such banks, trust companies or other depositories as shall be selected and designated for such purpose by the Board of Directors from time to time; and (b) in general perform all of the duties incident to the office of Treasurer, and such other duties as from time to time may be assigned to him by the Board of Directors.

The books of accounts and records shall, at all reasonable times, be open to the inspection of the members of the Society. The Treasurer shall furnish to the Directors, whenever required by them, such statements and abstracts of records as are necessary for a full exhibit of the financial conditions of the Society.

Lesson 3

REVIEW

1 a;sldkfjgh ghfjdksla; a;sldkfjghfjdksla

2 elk fed egg hue hag dug sue hug due jug

NEW KEYS

3 k ki ki kkk iii kik aid fig jig did lie

4 f fr fr fff rrr frf fir are far jar rag

5 did did rig rig rid rid sir sir air air

6 rise rise ride ride fire fire hire hire

7 j jy jy jjj yyy jyj say day gay ray lay

8 f ft ft fff ttt ftf fat fit sat set sit

9 the the yet yet let let fry fry try try

10 gray gray tray tray trey trey stir stir

ONE-HAND WORDS

11 fate fate fare fare grad grad rate rate

12 kill kill hill hill jill jill hull hulk

BUILDING WORDS

13 ear; gear dear fear hear rear tear year

14 ate; sate date late fate hate gate rate

SENTENCES

15 the freight is high; the desks are red;

16 the red trailer is faster; day is here;

17 the fudge is hard; did he see the fight

Lesson 150

Test

Job 1.

Suggested time: 15 minutes
Type two 5-minute writings. Score and hand in the better one.

Canada can boast of possessing the longest paved highway in the 13
world. Eight thousand kilometres long, the Trans-Canada Highway 26
links Victoria, British Columbia with St. John's, Newfoundland. Al- 39
though the road has been officially opened for some time, it is being 52
added to and improved every year. Now most stretches of this high- 65
way are generally in first class condition, with only short links offer- 78
ing even minor motoring difficulties in most provinces. 90

As it spans the continent from the timbered slopes of the Pacific 103
coast to the rugged Atlantic shoreline, the road provides the motorist 117
with an infinite variety of scenes and experiences. It winds through 130
towering vistas of the Rocky Mountains, knifes across the broad, 143
flat stretches of the cattle and wheat country, and then threads its 156
way around the rugged northern shores of the Great Lakes. It bustles 169
through the industrial heartland of Ontario, roams through the old- 182
world charm of Quebec; and then weaves past the historic settlements 195
in the Atlantic provinces. To drive its length is to understand the 209
variety of scene and mood that is Canada. 218

Designated for safe, comfortable driving, Trans-Canada Highway 231
standards call for pavement seven metres wide, with three metre 244
shoulders. Curves are gradual, and grades are held to gentle slopes 257
that nowhere exceed six per cent. Driving is easy, and the view ahead 270
is always clear. Now it is a pleasant experience to drive across Canada. 285

Job 2.

Suggested time: 10 minutes
Set up in good tabular form on a half-sheet of paper.

Words Frequently Misspelled

absence	apparatus	decide	eighth	heroes
absurd	argument	definite	embarrass	imaginary
across	arrival	descend	excellent	independent
afraid	beginning	desirable	exercise	influence
all right	believe	describe	existence	library
already	biscuit	despair	familiar	marriage
always	brief	develop	fierce	messenger
amateur	business	disagree	foreign	mortgage
anxiety	cafeteria	divide	frivolous	muscle
anxious	courtesy	easily	governor	necessary

Lesson 4

WARMUP

1 a;sldkfjghfjdksla;sldkfjghfjdksla;sldkf

2 the try like jar fur stray is this thus

NEW KEYS

3 s sw sw sss www sws saw sew was wad wag

4 l lo lo lll ooo lol how who low dog foe

5 tow tow row row how how low low who who

6 tows tows owed owed woke woke word word

7 a aq aq aaa qqq aqa que qui qua quo quo

8 ; ;p ;p ;;; ppp ;p; pat par pad pap pop

9 quip quip quit quit quid quid quad quad

10 peep peep past past part part pipe pipe

SENTENCES

11 who were the two girls; look at the ewe

12 the first part of the paper was so good

13 all the older pupils will quit at four;

14 ask her to show you the last order too;

15 we shall try to ship your orders today;

16 do look at the queer old pepper holder;

17 we will get the litre of pulp for paper

18 it was a quiet day for all the quitters

This has not always been so. When plans for the building of the
Canadian Pacific Railway were announced, many responsible individuals denounced the scheme as sheer folly. An editor of a popular
English magazine warned his readers not to invest their money in
what he termed, "this mad project." To support his argument, he
pointed out that, "the Canadian Pacific Railway will run, if it is
ever finished, through a country frostbound for seven or eight months
in the year, and will connect with the western part of the Dominion,
a province which embraces about as forbidding a country as any
on the face of the earth." He went on to describe British Columbia
as "a barren, cold mountain country that is not worth keeping."

Fortunately for Canada and Canadians, there were people of vision
and foresight who saw the great potential in a united country and
supported the building of a transcontinental railway.

72
85
98
112
125
138
151
164
177
190
203
216
230

THINK AS YOU TYPE

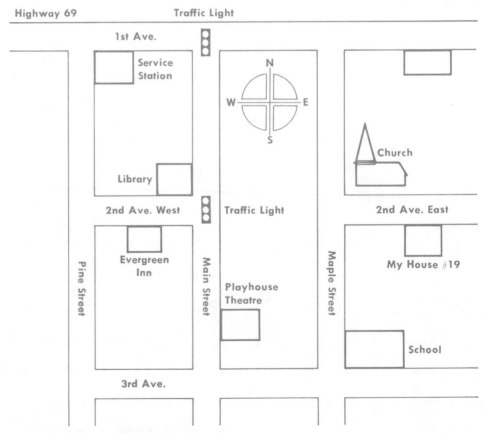

Compose and type detailed directions for

1. reaching the Playhouse Theatre from Highway 69,
2. going from the Playhouse Theatre to my house (#19 2nd Ave. East),
3. going from my house to the Evergreen Inn.

Lesson 5

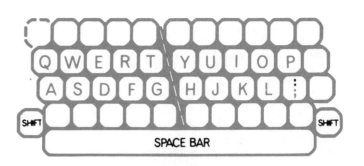

WARMUP

Rhythm	1	`a;sldkfjghfjdksla; a;sldkfjghfjdksla;sl`
Reaches	2	`juj ded frf kik ftf jyj sws ;p; aqa lol`
Words	3	`the how jug kit day tip low ask for qua`
Vowels	4	`iii kit ii sits ii fill ii ride ii pipe`
	5	`eee dew ee sell ee feel ee heed ee deed`
	6	`aaa hat aa hall aa last aa saga aa data`
	7	`uuu jug uu just uu drug uu hugs uu your`
	8	`ooo too oo foot oo root oo hook oo soup`

To Make Capital Letters for Left-Hand Keys

1. Use the little finger of the right hand to depress and hold the right shift key while you —

2. Strike the left-hand key to be capitalized.
3. Quickly, return the little finger from the shift key to the ";" key.

SHIFTING FOR LEFT-HAND KEYS

9 `fF; dD; sS; aA; rR; eE; wW; qQ; gG; tT;`
10 `Sue Gus Ted Ada Roy Faye Doug Ella Will`
11 `Fred Ruth Rita Terry Allie Garry George`
12 `Tuesday Thursday Friday Saturday August`

To Make Capital Letters for Right-Hand Keys

1. Use the little finger of the left hand to depress and hold the left shift key while you —

2. Strike the right-hand key to be capitalized.
3. Quickly, return the little finger from the shift key to the "a" key.

SHIFTING FOR RIGHT-HAND KEYS

13 `jJa kKa lLa ;:a uUa iIa oOa pPa hHa yYa`
14 `Joe Kay Rae Iris Larry Harry Ollie Pete`
15 `Jed Kit Harry Keith Lewis Harold Louise`
16 `July Ottawa Orillia Laurel Joseph Peggy`

Lesson 149

Rhythm the and for man siz pay sit sot wit aid lay pen nap die sod

Alphabet exile queen grave blaze joint dough weary frame space break

Top Row $100 $1 320 $1.28 $1 584.92 $385.05 $66.66 $892 $3 204 $500

Job 1.

Type the following interoffice memorandum. Prepare a carbon copy.

To: Gerald Baxter
    Accounting Department

From: Ronald Gilbert
    Vice-President

Subject: New Investors

Date: 19-- 06 01

The following new investors have purchased shares in our Canada First Retirement Fund in the amounts indicated.

Mrs. Roxanne Moreau 832 Niagara Blvd. Welland, Ontario N4C 1E2	Certif. No. 2578	$1 200
Mr. Maxwell Humber 891 Assiniboine Rd. Winnipeg, Manitoba R2S 8C6	Certif. No. 2592	1 000
Mr. Frederick Lyon 1467 Angus Blvd. Regina, Sask. S2X 4A5	Certif. No. 2599	850

Please forward to each of our new investors a proper certificate with an appropriate covering letter.

urs

R.G.

Job 2.

Mr. Baxter has asked you to compose and type a letter to be sent to each of the new investors mentioned in Job. 1. In your letter, welcome the new investor, mention that the certificate is enclosed, and suggest that additional investments could be beneficial. Make a carbon copy and address an envelope for each letter.

TIMED WRITING

Although our railways no longer play the vital role that they once   13
did in communication and in the transportation of goods and passen-   26
gers, their importance and economic value are not disputed. Every-   39
one recognizes their usefulness and acknowledges their contributions   52
to the development of this country.   59

Lesson
6

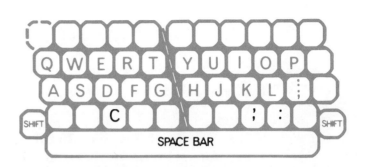

WARMUP

Rhythm 1   a;sldkfjghfjdksla; a;sldkfjghfjdksla;sl

Words 2   for the kid lid did hid aid say day lay

Shifting 3   Fred Luke Gail Hugh Sara Karl Ella Jake

NEW KEYS

4   d dc dc ddd ccc dcd cod cad cud ice cap

5   k k, k, kkk ,,, k,k at, it, to, do, so,

6   l l. l. lll ... l.l i.e., e.g., c.o.d.,

Spacing After Punctuation

1. Leave one space after a comma.
2. Leave one space after a semi-colon.
3. Leave one space after a period that indicates an abbreviation.

4. Leave one space after a capitalized letter and a period that indicate an initial or abbreviation.
5. Leave two spaces after the period at the end of a sentence.
6. Leave two spaces after a colon.

PRACTICE

7   Tea, coffee, cocoa, are for sale there.

8   cute, kick, lick, face, ice, act, pick,

9   Alta., Sask., P. S., Apr., Aug., Sept.,

10   These are shorter: Tues., Wed., Thurs.

PARAGRAPH

Dear Peter: We had a trip to Calgary. The weather was fair all the way. Our car pleased us, too. If you take that auto trip this year, you will like it. If you wish, take our car.

Job 1.

The Huron Steel Company, 18 Lakeshore Drive, Hamilton, Ontario N2X 4T3 Attention: Mr. R. E. Lavers, Plant Superintendent, Gentlemen:

On Thursday, October 22, which has been designated Community Studies Day, the senior classes of our school will devote the afternoon to a study of the principal industries in our community. The purposes of the study are to gain a better understanding of the organizations that contribute to the economic stability of our city and to learn something about the job opportunities that exist in these organizations.

It would help to make our Community Studies Day a success if you or one of your colleagues could speak to a group of our students at 1.30 p.m. You will be given one hour for your presentation, and we hope that at least fifteen minutes of that time will be devoted to answering questions from your student audience. The students will meet you in room 211 of our school.

We would appreciate your letting us know whether or not you can accept our invitation by checking the appropriate responses on the enclosed card and returning it to us before October 1.

Sincerely yours, John T. Maynard, President, Students' Council.

Job 2.

The Atlas Oil Company, 1922 Main Street, Hamilton, Ontario N2V 4A6 Attention: Director of Public Relations. To speak at 2.30 p.m. in room 214.

Job 3.

Simcoe Stores Limited, 14 Mountain Drive, Hamilton, Ontario N2R 3S2 Attention: Miss M. Boyer, Personnel Manager. To speak at 1.30 p.m. in room 220.

Job 4.

Canadian Motors Company of Canada Limited, 2673 Burlington Boulevard, Hamilton, Ontario N2P 1B3 Attention: Mr. Ralph Kinder, Director of Personnel. To speak at 2.30 p.m. in room 312.

THINK AS YOU TYPE

Type a character sketch of some person who has made an impression on you. It may be a friend, a parent, a teacher, a figure in public life, etc. Choose three characteristics and describe each with an incident to help the description.

Lesson 7

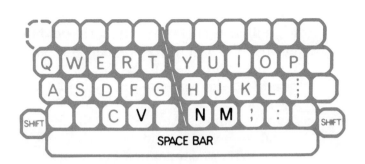

WARMUP

Rhythm 1   aa ;; ss ll dd kk ff jj gg hh fjdksla;s
Words 2   cap cat cut cup car cur cue coy cow cot
Shifting 3   Carl Eric Dale Jack Earl Dick Kate Cora

NEW KEYS

4   jjj jmj mmm jmj jam may rim mad him mum
5   mm make mm them mm more mm came mm maim
6   fff fvf vvv fvf vie vim via vat vet viv
7   vv live vv very vv have vv love vv save
8   jjj jnj nnn jnj can ran fan man not now
9   nn main nn nine nn then nn send nn cent

SENTENCES

10   Ninety funny men gave Nan nine pennies.
11   Vince favoured having very vivid views.
12   Mary and Marvin may come home in March.

PARAGRAPH

Gentlemen: We have offices in Toronto,
Montreal, Vancouver, Regina and London.
We consider it a privilege to serve you
at any one of them. Please call in and
see us when you wish to start a plan to
save money for the future.

Bill and I left the city early on Friday afternoon. We wanted to   13
avoid the heavy traffic that was bound to develop later, and we   26
wanted an early start for the restful weekend that we had been plan-   39
ning for the past month.   44

The highway out of the city was busy but not crowded, and within   57
a few minutes we were out in the country. The weather was warm   70
and sunny, the road was good, the car was performing perfectly,   83
and every omen pointed to two days of peace and relaxing quiet.   95

At the turn-off to the lake, a police car was parked beside the road,   109
but neither Bill nor I paid any particular attention to it. Our minds   122
were occupied with thoughts of fish waiting to be caught, of fish   135
being caught, and of fish frying in the pan. If only we had displayed   148
some curiosity about the presence of the police car, we might have   161
avoided the night of terror and pain that lay before us.   172

As we pulled up in front of the cottage, I noticed some fresh tire   185
marks in the dusty roadway. They caused me no concern because   198
I knew that Joe, the local handyman, often stopped by to perform the   211
minor chores that we had entrusted to him.   219

THINK AS YOU TYPE

Set up and type a tabulated list of at least twenty important Canadians. On the left, give the person's name and on the right, the position or occupation. Some people that you might name are: The Governor General, the Lieutenant Governor of your province, The Prime Minister of Canada, the Premier of your province, some important cabinet ministers, an outstanding educator, some churchpeople, an inventor, a scientist, medical researchers who have made important discoveries, etc.

Lesson 148

WARMUP

Rhythm   `a;qpa;slwosldkeidkfjrufjghtygh fjrufjdkeidkslwosla;qpa;slwo`

Alphabet   `A judge will quiz the boy on the price of the mixed knives.`

Top Row   `Jones & Quince earned a dividend of 4.6% ($1.25) this year.`

Jobs 1 to 4.

For each Job, type the form letter given below using today's date and changing the copy as indicated for Jobs 2 to 4. Use the full-blocked style, and prepare an envelope to accompany each letter.

Lesson 8

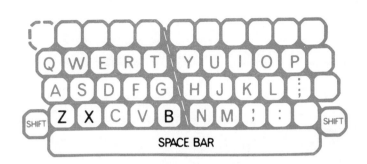

WARMUP

Rhythm 1   a; sl dk fj gh fj dk sl a;sldkfjghfjdks

Words   2   man mat may mad men new not nor non now

3   vane vain very vote vary vase veto view

NEW KEYS

4   fff fbf bbb fbf fib fob bid bed bad bud

5   bb bulb bb bomb bb barb bb baby bb blob

6   sss sxs xxx sxs six sex fix mix fox box

7   xx flux xx exit xx axle xx axis xx taxi

8   aaa aza zzz aza zoo zip zig zag zee zoe

9   zz fuzz zz zinc zz quiz zz zero zz size

SENTENCES

10   Barbara bought a baby a big bright bib.

11   Six boxers fix axles at the next exits.

12   Lazy dog dozed; he had no zip, no zest.

13   Alberta, British Columbia, Nova Scotia.

PARAGRAPH

A lazy man is a mighty poor risk on any
job. He dozes when things are quiet as
he has no wish to excel. When he calls
it quits before his tasks are finished,
he leaves his chore to the next fellow.

Job 2.

On a spirit master or stencil, arrange and type the following to be duplicated on the appropriate machine. Double space the material so that it looks well on a full sheet of paper. Run off 15 copies, if possible.

COMMONWEALTH PRODUCTS
known throughout the nation
_____

Date

NOTICE TO ALL SALES STAFF

The quarterly sales meeting will be held on January 5 and 6, at the Fort Garry Hotel, Winnipeg. A copy of the agenda for the conference is enclosed. It is requested that you study the program carefully and that you make whatever preparations are necessary in order to contribute to the program discussions and activities.

The company will reimburse you for all necessary living expenses incurred during the period of January 4-6, up to the limits of a daily allowance of $45. Room reservations have been made for you at the Fort Garry Hotel. The daily rate will be $28.50. Louis J. Wilson:urs

AGENDA, SALES CONFERENCE, 19-- 01 05 and 06
NOTE: All meetings will be held at the Fort Garry Hotel, Winnipeg, Manitoba. You are requested to be on hand at 09:00 each day of the Conference; meetings will be held in Room 1650 of the hotel.

January 5

09:00 — 09.45	Get Acquainted — Coffee Hour
09:45 — 10:00	Introduction of McKenzie & Campbell Executives
10:00 — 10:30	Address by Mr. Alan R. Stevens, President
10:30 — 11:45	"What We Have Done and What We Plan to Do in Sales." Mr. Louis J. Wilson, General Sales Manager.
11:45 — 13:00	Lunch
13:00 — 13:30	Discussion of New Products
13:30 — 14:15	"Opening Closed Doors." A 25-minute film on the techniques of salesmanship.
14:15 — 15:00	"Selling Our Products." A panel discussion by Messrs. Watson, Pullen, Anderson, and Johnson.
15:00 — 16:00	A session on an Examination of New Markets for our Products.

Lesson 9

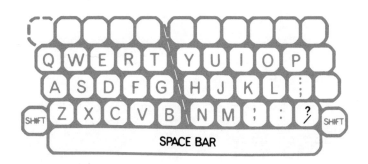

WARMUP

Rhythm 1 a;sldkfjghfjdksla; a;sldkfjghfjdksla;sl

Words   2 bib big bit bob boy box bat bad but buy

3 flax flux next text exit exam axis oxen

4 zero zest zone zinc fuzz buzz fizz jazz

NEW KEYS

5 ;;; ;/; /// ;/; you/him she/you him/her

6 // and/or // he/she // you/we // me/him

7 ;;; ;/; ;?; ??? ;?; who? why? how? you?

8 ?? what? ?? when? ?? where? ?? whither?

More Spacing After Punctuation
Leave two spaces after a question mark.

9 C/O means, in care of. A/C is account.

10 Who are you? Will she come? May I go?

PARAGRAPH

Do you remember your first visit to the
zoo? Do you recall a thrill at peering
upon so many queer, exotic animals that
first time? It is quite probable that,
like most children, you were amazed and
excited by all the things that you saw.
Were you not just bursting with the joy
of making new discoveries?

Lesson 147

WARMUP

Rhythm a b c d e f g h i j k l m n o p q r s t u v w x y z abcdefg

Alphabet A perky fox is the main objective of a dog's zealous quest.

Top Row Do you know that 8 is $12\frac{1}{2}$% of 64, 25% of 32, and 50% of 16?

Job 1.   Set up the following in an attractive manner, on a full sheet of paper.

BIBLIOGRAPHY AND FOOTNOTES COMPARED

The facts set out in a bibliography entry are the same as those given in a "complete" footnote, with the following differences:

1. Author's Name. The bibliography places the surname of the author first in the entry; the footnote places the given name first.
2. Periods. The bibliography uses a period instead of a comma in several places:
    (a) at the end of the author's name
    (b) at the end of the title
    (c) at the end of the facts of publication
3. Facts of Publication. The bibliography does not use parentheses to enclose the facts of publication for books, which is the practice followed in footnotes; in articles, however, parentheses continue to enclose the date and sometimes the city of publication.
4. Page Numbers. The bibliography gives the inclusive page numbers of an article, essay, or book (if it gives them at all) at the end of the entry; the footnote gives the specific page number referred to in the manuscript.
5. "Translated by". This phrase is written in full when it occurs in a bibliography; it is abbreviated to "trans." when it occurs in a footnote.

EXAMPLES OF ENTRIES

Listed below are examples of the same references, (a) as footnotes, (b) as bibliography entries.

(a)   [1]Allan E. Sparling, Canadian Record Keeping Practice, 2nd Edition (Toronto: McGraw-Hill Ryerson Limited, 1972), pp. 84-86.
    [2]W. L. Morton, Manitoba: A History (Toronto: University of Toronto Press, 1957), P. 186.

(b) Sparling, Allan E. Canadian Record Keeping Practice, 2nd Edition. Toronto: McGraw-Hill Ryerson Ltd., 1972.

Morton, W. L. Manitoba: A History. Toronto: University of Toronto Press, 1957.

Composition at the Typewriter

Creative Typing

The use of the typewriter is not confined to the business office. It has become the personal writing tool of people in all walks of life. Most professional writers create their work at the typewriter; newspaper reporters write their stories on the typewriter; students type their assignments (and thereby earn better grades); and men and women all over the world compose their personal and social correspondence seated in front of a typewriter.

The noted Canadian writer, Pierre Berton, composes at the typewriter.

Think as You Type

If you wish to use your typewriter as you would a pen or pencil to put down words to express your thoughts and ideas on paper, you should build this skill as you build your finger skill. Each day you should perform some "type as you think" exercises, moving from easy letter insertions to words and phrases, then to the more difficult expression of ideas into sentences. Eventually you will find it easy and natural to express your ideas in whole paragraphs.

Some people can write legibly at 25 to 30 words per minute at top speed. You have been developing this skill ever since you learned to read and write. Good typists can write their thoughts using their machines at 50 to 80 words per minute. As you increase your manual skill in typing, you can develop your skill in using the typewriter as your personal writing tool.

Where Do You Look?

You are learning "touch" typing; therefore, you do not want to watch the keys as you strike them. When doing your own "writing with the typewriter", you have no copy to fasten your eyes upon. "Where will I look?" you ask.

That is a good question!

The answer is different for each person. Perhaps you will feel most comfortable looking out the window while you see "with your mind's eye" the word you wish to type. Perhaps it may help you to look at the paper to see what you are getting down on it as you think of words to type. You may feel more inspired with your eyes closed.

Try to find the best way for you. Enjoy yourself. Teach your fingers to spell. Teach yourself to communicate words and ideas by using the typewriter as your writing tool.

Job 1.

Insert the proper punctuation marks in the following sentences.

1. Is June 3 July 8 or July 19 best for the companys meeting
2. Are the footnotes placed correctly on the page she asked him
3. Jules Brooksbank the clubs accountant designed its new form
4. When Susans folder was returned she noticed two Xs on the cover
5. When if ever will the war end

Job 2.

Insert the proper capitalization and punctuation in the following.

1. When he was in regina saskatchewan he visited the diefenbaker building
2. He interviewed dean tucker at mount allison university
3. He practised scuba diving in the caribbean the mediterranean and the english channel
4. The oceanography school is located at woods hole on cape cod
5. He gave his social insurance number to the foreman of the jury

Job 3.

Add a prefix to each of the following words to change it to one with negative meaning. Use each of your newly constructed words in a sentence.

E.g.   polite   impolite   It is considered impolite to whistle at the table.

mature, adequate, mobile, responsible, relevant, literate, rational, capable, legal, divisible.

Job 4.

Type the following sentences correcting the spelling errors.

1. A new goverment course in tayloring is being ofered.
2. The Wenesday meeting was most revelant to our situation.
3. It is inconvient to obtain the brocher for the docter.
4. The perquisites for the job are inconsistant with company polisy.
5. The Personel Manager was truely sorry to have missed the fourtieth interview.

THINK AS YOU TYPE

You have been invited to attend a congress of young people at which representatives from countries all around the world will be present. You have been warned that you will be expected to speak for about one minute on each of the following topics:

1. Why I am proud to live in Canada.

2. Some of Canada's contributions to world development.

Type approximately 120 words on each topic.

Lesson 10

WARMUP

Rhythm 1   `a;sldkfjghfjdksla;sldkfjghfjdksla;sldkfjghfjdksla;s`

Alphabet 2   `a b c d e f g h i j k l m n o p q r s t u v w x y z`

Shifting 3   `Jake Jan John Joe June Joy Jane Jean Jack Jay Joyce`

The Backspacing Key

On your typewriter there is a key, which, when depressed firmly, will move the carriage back one space at a time. Find the location of the BACKSPACING KEY on the key bank. If it is in the upper right-hand corner, it may be operated by the little finger on the right hand. If it is in the upper left-hand corner, it may be operated by the little finger on the left hand. However, if you wish to depress the key more than 3 or 4 times, you should use your thumb for firm, expert manipulation.

TYPE YOUR NAME at the top of each page of work from now on. By expert use of the Back-spacing Key, your name will end even with the right margin of your work:

Elizabeth Mundell

Move your carriage over to the end of the line (on the right-hand side of the page). Starting at this point, depress the backspace key *once for each letter and space* in your full name. Now, type your name.

SPEED SPURTS

4   `so do of go or to he me an am if it is by us no on`

5   `as at in we be on my up he ha pa re ah ho la ti to`

6   `due rue rut rid men hay sow key pay pat pot dot dog`

7   `dug pen jam man wit fit fix fox tab tub hem lay six`

8   `the are she did was and you see for not his him her`

9   `this that then them they when what were will from`

10   `that they, what they, when will, this will bring.`

THINK AS YOU TYPE

Type the following sentences inserting appropriate words for the drawings

2:30 p.m. Miss Munroe called to remind you of dental appointment Friday morning at 10 o'clock.

3:10 p.m. Mr. Criss, lawyer, returned your call of yesterday. Contract is ready for you to sign.

3:35 p.m. Mr. Knowles, Star Builders, called regarding increased prices on recent invoice. Please call him at 690-4856.

3:45 p.m. Air Canada called advising no first class accommodation on Flt. #424 to New York, May 30. They are holding one economy reservation

4:15 p.m. Mr. Yuri of Easy Rite called. Please phone 624-8010.

4:30 p.m. Mr. Lefebvre of Juno's Garage called. He recommends a valve job. Please call 238-7506.

THINK AS YOU TYPE

Compose a letter to be sent to Miss Winnifred Coulter who phoned today requesting a job interview. Mr. Carver will see her Tuesday, June 3, at 10:30 a.m. Ask her to bring her Data Sheet to the interview and to be prepared to take your employment pretest. Miss Coulter's address is 60 Thayer Avenue in your town. Supply all necessary letter parts.

Prepare a sample typing exercise which Miss Coulter will be expected to type as part of her employment pretest.

Lesson 146

WARMUP

Rhythm   `a;sldkfjghfjdksla;sldkfjghfjdksla;sldkfjghfjdksla;sldkfjghf`

Alphabet   `Byron Davies Grant Foley Black Wiley Quamme Zaph Jones Roux`

Top Row   `weepy 23306 worry 29446 write 24853 twerp 52340 piper 08034`

Lesson 11

WARMUP

Rhythm 1 `a;sldkfjghfjdksla;sldkfjghfjdksla;sldkfjghfjdksla;s`

Alphabet 2 `cab dog fin hut jaw keg lay map que res vow zoo fix`

Shifting 3 `Ron Ross Roy Robb Rab Rena Reg Rick Rene Rona Robin`

WORD FAMILIES

4 `one, done gone lone hone cone bone tone zone none`

5 `ore, fore sore gore core wore pore bore more lore`

6 `all, fall gall hall tall wall ball pall call mall`

EASY PHRASES

7 `of the to the in the at the by the on the so the`

8 `see the, are the, can the, for the, put the, the`

9 `they were they must with them for them what were`

SENTENCES

10 `Has none of the boys in the zone gone for a cone?`

11 `They wore more of the clothing before night fell.`

12 `A ball in the hall made us all fall by this wall.`

How to Plan and Set Margins

A. Establish the Centre Point

To plan and set margin stops for equal margins on the sides of the paper, we must know at what point on the carriage-position scale the centre of the paper will come. Follow these steps to get a centering point.

1. Choose an easily remembered centre point. Most machines are best suited for 50, but some are better at 45 or 40.

2. Set the carriage at that point on the scale.

3. Crease a sheet of paper down the centre.

4. Insert your paper and move it to the right or left until the crease appears at the centre of the V-shaped printing point. You will have to loosen the paper by using the paper release to do this.

5. Move the paper guide to the right or left until its edge is against the edge of the paper.

6. Make a note of the exact position of the paper guide. In future, check to see that it is always in that position before you begin to type. If you do this, you will always be certain that the centre of the paper is at the centering point you have chosen.

B. Set the Margin Stops

1. Determine the length of line you need. For example: The paragraph that follows requires a 50-stroke line as indicated.

2. Calculate *half* that line length, because you will *always* plan to have half the typing on one line to the left of the centre point and the other half to the right of the centre point. For example: In a 50-stroke line, half the strokes (25) will be on each side of the centre point.

3. For your left margin stop, subtract the number representing half the line (e.g. 25) from the centre point (e.g. 50). For a 50-stroke line, with centre at 50, your left margin will be at $50-25 = 25$ on the carriage position scale.

4. For the right margin, add the number representing half the line (e.g. 25) to the centre point. Your right margin would then be at $50+25 = 75$. We add 3 extra strokes on the right to allow for variations in length of the last word on the line. So, always move your right margin an additional 3 strokes to the right. This would place your right margin at 78.

9:35 p.m.   Mr. Posta of Acme Steel called regarding new steel prices. Please call him at 921-6242.

10:05 a.m.   Mr. Klatter of Superior Sales called for an appointment to show their new line. Suggested he phone back tomorrow.

10:30 a.m.   Miss Coulter called requesting job interview. She will phone back tomorrow for appointment.

10:40 a.m.   Mr. Tyler of Lindsay Electric called confirming tomorrow's luncheon date.

11:10 a.m.   Miss Normanden of ABC Advertising phoned requesting you be guest speaker at next month's dinner meeting. Please confirm. Her phone: 624-3210.

11:45 a.m.   Mr. Yates of Butler Steel wishes copy of new price list. Mailed today.

11:50 a.m.   Mr. Quigley of Quigley Construction phoned to cancel appointment with you tomorrow.

1:05 p.m.   Mr. Yakamoff of Niagara Steel called to advise new tender deadline of June 3.

1:30 p.m.   Miss Pinter of Allied Bus Company wishes you to call her at 629-5728.

1:35 p.m.   Mrs. Schmidt of Bell Canada called regarding new display in directory. Please call 555-1511.

1:50 p.m.   Mr. Joyce of Block Construction wishes you to visit new building site Friday afternoon. Please confirm by calling 621-9030.

Type the following paragraph on a half sheet of paper, using a 50-stroke line. Before you begin, insert your paper so that the top edge is just visible. Use your carriage return lever to move down to the 13th line-space. Begin to type.

```
Dear Fred:  Mr. John Gray of our head office will
be in your county early next week.  He would like
to have the pleasure of seeing you so that he can
tell you about our new product.  Will you be able
to meet John sometime Monday, during the morning?
```

THINK AS YOU TYPE

Type the following paragraph inserting appropriate words for the drawings.

```
The         and the         made the trip by        .
If they went by        , the trip would take 2
long.  They were able to take their         and
             with them but had to leave their
at home.  They each read a         on the plane,
and they saw the         come up over the         .
```

Lesson 12

TYPE SMOOTHLY AND RHYTHMICALLY

WARMUP

Rhythm   1 a;sldkfjghfjdksla;sldkfjghfjdksla;sldkfjghfjdksla

Alphabet 2 aqua debt face edge nigh jinx mock love zest wary

Shifting 3 Alan Ivan Emma Kent Gwen Lucy Carl Mark Dave Neil

SPEED SPURTS

4 he me and big got end had met men new use she did

5 us to aid cut the rid sir yet for key owe dog pen

Lesson 145

Speed   I know that you will do what you can to help me on the job.

Top Row $1 327.60, $500, $69.35, $12.98, $25.00, $1 000, $80 950.00

Attention   Use the correct spelling in the following sentence.

It will b eze 4 u 2 wait 2 days 4 them 2 b ¢.

Internal Office Forms

Typical of the forms that are prepared in every office and duplicated for internal use, is the Cheque Requisition form illustrated below.

CHEQUE REQUISITION

Amount $ 250 _____

Payable to

Name   Mr. Fred Gorchinski _____

Address   85 Euclid Avenue, Toronto, Ontario _____

Charge to Account No. E 47 _____

For   Watering and cutting lawns May 15 - May 31

Requisitioned By _____

Approved By _____

Date   19.. 05 31 _____

Job 1.   Copy the Cheque Requisition form illustrated above.

Job 2.   Ms. Carver is absent from the office today. You are taking her telephone calls and you have received the following messages. On a full sheet of paper, prepare a form and type in the information about the telephone calls which you received.

9:30 a.m. Mrs. Kiboe of Standard Press called requesting an interview for a newspaper article. She will call back tomorrow.

6 ill, bill fill hill kill mill pill sill till will

7 ame, came dame fame game lame name same tame same

8 to the, to this to them to that to those to these

9 The mill on the hill will send a bill for a sill.

10 The same name has been given to a very tame game.

Type and complete the following sentences.

11 The first month of the year is----------------.

12 I was born in the month of----------------.

13 The last month of the year is----------------.

14 This is the month of----------------.

15 The month after July is----------------.

The Tabulator for Paragraphing

To indicate the beginning of a new paragraph, we usually *indent*, or start in 5 spaces from the margin. Your machine has what is known as a tabulator (called a TAB BAR or KEY) for this purpose. Locate on your machine the TAB BAR or KEY, the TAB SET KEY and the TAB CLEAR KEY. Follow these steps to indent a paragraph.
1. Set margin stops for the line needed.
2. There may be tab stops already set. Clear these — on some machines, there is a "Total Clear" key; on other machines, move the carriage to the *end* of the line and then return the carriage while holding down the TAB CLEAR KEY.
3. To set a tab stop — space in 5 strokes from the left margin, and then press the TAB SET KEY.

4. To indent from the left margin — press the TAB BAR or TAB KEY. The carriage will jump to the place where the tab is set. Be sure you hold the key or bar until the carriage has stopped moving.

NOTE: TO START A NEW PARAGRAPH
1. If the material being typed is double spaced, indent the first word 5 spaces, using the tabulator.
2. If the material is single spaced, *leave a blank line between paragraphs*. The first word may be indented or not (BLOCK STYLE) as desired. In your timed writings, you are allowed a one word credit for making each paragraph indention.

Job 1. Copy the following information on the Monthly Attendance form.

BECKERTON PRODUCTS COMPANY
MONTHLY REPORT
EMPLOYEE ATTENDANCE
MAY, 19..

Name	No.	Position	Days Present	Days Absent	Times Late
ARSENAULT, Hardy	4290	Accountant	22	0	0
AZZARO, Paula	4291	Stenographer	20	2	1
BIJAK, Marcia	4292	Stenographer	22	0	0
CAMILLETII, Arno	4293	Typist-Clerk	21	1	0
FINKELSTEIN, Nathan	4294	Filing Clerk	18	4	2
FLEWELLING, Remi	4295	Keypunch Operator	21	1	0
IVANIC, Win	4296	Accountant	22	0	0
LUISETTO, Maria	4297	Typist	22	0	1
McKEOWN, Muriel	4298	Mail Clerk	21	1	0
MINTEX, Max	4299	Computer Operator	20	2	1
PLANTE, Paul	4300	Shipping Clerk	22	0	0
PITZ, Cathy	4301	Receptionist	22	0	0
PRYER, Kent	4302	Duplicating Operator	21	1	0
PUGLIESE, Tony	4303	Programmer	22	0	0
RAE, Donna	4304	Switchboard Operator	19	3	1
RALPH, Garry	4305	Keypunch Operator	21	1	2
SNIEDER, Rhonda	4306	Typist	20	2	1
SMYTHE, Marlene	4307	Stenographer	22	0	0
TYRRELL, Julianne	4308	Filing Clerk	21	1	0
WELKOVICS, Linda	4309	Programmer	20	2	2

Job 2. Devise and prepare a form that might be used for rating employees. At the top of the form, provision should be made for entering the employee's name, number, position, and department. The body of the form is to provide for rating the following qualities: skills, reliability, attitude towards work, ability to get along with people, appearance, attendance, and punctuality. Each of the qualities is to be rated as excellent, good, average, or poor. The form is to be signed by the head of the department in which the employee works.

Job 3. On the form you prepared in Job 2, enter your own name as an employee and then rate yourself on the qualities listed.

THINK AS YOU TYPE In a paragraph, described three qualities that you feel have been developed or strengthened in you because of your typing course. Typing courses aim to develop qualities like neatness, accuracy, the ability to organize, concentration, productivity, and so on. How well has your course succeeded in attaining its aims?

Before you begin, follow the steps given above to set your tabulator for indenting. Use a 50-stroke line.

```
        One of the keys to becoming a good typist is
to acquire a perfect stroke early in your course.

        Each stroke should be a crisp, sharply dealt
blow aimed with precision at the centre of a key.

        Think of each one of the keys as feeling red
hot; that might help you to strike them properly.
```

Lesson 13

TYPE SMOOTHLY AND RHYTHMICALLY

WARMUP

Rhythm 1 `a s d f g h j k l ; asdfghjkl;asdfghjkl;asdfghjkl;a`

Shifting 2 `Alice Joyce Betty Linda Carol Karen Elaine Patricia`

Alphabet 3 `Five or six big white jet planes zoomed by quickly.`

WORD PATTERNS

4 `fab fad fag fan far fat fit fix fir fin fig fib fob`

5 `fog fox foe for fur fun gun gut got gob gab gad gag`

WORD FAMILIES

6 `ay, bay day gay hay jay lay may nay pay ray say way`

7 `ent, bent cent dent tent rent sent lent went advent`

Job 1.   Prepare a telegram for your Sales Manager, Mr. James R. Watson, to be sent to Mr. Michael O'Toole, General Manager of the western division of Canadian Manufacturers Limited, 132 West 14th Avenue, Victoria, B.C. V6A 9T4. Advise Mr. O'Toole that Mr. Watson will be arriving in Victoria on October 16, Flight AC #268 at 22:50 and wishes to be met at the airport. Make your message brief but complete.

Job 2.   Prepare a Happy Birthday telegram for a friend of yours who lives in another part of Canada or the U.S.A.

TIMED WRITING

Only a few years ago, the use of the typewriter was confined to the business office, and even there it was used chiefly to type letters. Today, typewriters are found in almost half the homes in Canada, and they are used in all departments of our business establishments. The typewriter is no longer a special business machine, it is another writing instrument like the pencil and the pen.   13 26 39 52 65 74

Because the use of the typewriter is so widespread, typing instruction should not be limited to those who are planning careers in the business world. Everyone should learn to type fast and efficiently. Knowing how to type has personal values as well as career values.   87 101 114 126

The ability to type is likely to be useful in many kinds of situations. Therefore, typing skills should be wide and varied. It is not sufficient to be able to type only from printed copy. In addition to this skill, the modern typist must be able to compose at the typewriter, to type from rough, handwritten copy, and to set up all kinds of information in pleasing form.   139 152 165 178 191 194

You may be sure that the ability to type well will be of benefit to you throughout your lifetime. You will find almost daily opportunities to put your skills into practice, and the ability to seize these opportunities will be most rewarding.   208 221 234 242

Lesson 144

WARMUP

Speed   When more cash is paid into the new fund it will grow fast.

Top Row   Scherer & Neal billed us for $4 756.32 less a 4½% discount.

Attention   Correct the spelling errors:

The pretentous accomodation caused me much embarasment.

EASY
PHRASES

8 in the, in that, in them, in this in those in these

SENTENCES

9 They say you may have a gay day sailing on the bay.

10 She went to fix the vent that was bent in the tent.

THINK AS
YOU TYPE

Type and complete the following sentences.

11 Four words that rhyme with bay are ---, ---, ---, ---.

12 Four words that rhyme with ball are ---, ---, ---, ---.

13 Four words that rhyme with cap are ---, ---, ---, ---.

14 Four words that rhyme with can are ---, ---, ---, ---.

15 Four words that rhyme with book are ---, ---, ---, ---.

PARAGRAPHS

These paragraphs are to be typed with single spacing in the blocked style. Paragraphs are not indented, but a blank line is left between paragraphs.

To type well, you should sit erect with your eyes fixed on the copy from which you are typing.

For proper balance, your feet must be braced flat on the floor and should be placed slightly apart.

You should sit well back in your chair, with your body centered opposite the J key on the home row.

You should lean slightly forward from your waist, and your elbows should hang loosely at the sides.

Your copy from which you type should be placed to the right of the typewriter at a slight angle.

Telegrams

One of the common methods of communication between business offices and individuals is the telegram. As a typist, you may be called upon to prepare telegrams for submission to the telegraph company.

Most telegrams are phoned into the telegraph office. However, it is essential that a written record of the message and other pertinent details – the date of sending and type of telegram – be kept for filing. A telegram should be typed double spaced, unless the length of the message necessitates single spacing. Since there are two classes of telegraph service, you must indicate (usually with an X) the class of service that is desired.

The charge made for transmitting a telegram is based on the number of words in the message portion of the telegram. For this reason, you should be familiar with some of the rules observed by telegraph companies when counting chargeable words.

1. Dictionary words are counted as one word each, regardless of length.

2. Each part of a hyphenated word is counted separately.

3. An abbreviation or contraction of a word is counted as a complete word.

4. Common abbreviations and trade names, such as OK, AM, PM, FOB, COD, are counted as one word each, provided that the letters are written together.

5. Each figure of a number is counted as one word; e.g., 12 (2 words), 500 (3 words). If these numbers were written out as words — e.g., twelve (1 word), five hundred (2 words) — there would be less chance of error in transmission, and the word count would be lower and more economical.

6. Suffixes to numbers count as separate words: e.g., 3rd (2 words. If these are written as words — e.g., third (1 word) — the word count is less, and the likelihood of error is lessened.

7. Normal punctuation marks are transmitted free of charge. However, if a word is written for any punctuation mark — e.g., STOP for a period —that words is chargeable.

8. The special characters $, &, #, /, and —, are counted as one word each.

CANADIAN NATIONAL • CANADIAN PACIFIC
TÉLÉCOMMUNICATIONS
CANADIEN NATIONAL • CANADIEN PACIFIQUE

send this message subject to the terms on back
dépêche à expédier aux conditions énoncées au verso

Mr. John Marceaux
2641 Garden Avenue
Victoria, B. C.
V4A 7P9

Effective July one all prices increase ten percent. Advise you submit summer orders prior that date. New pricelists available May thirty.

Peter Stravinsky
Sales Manager

check / mots		full rate / plein tarif	X	night letter / lettre de nuit	tolls / coût
charge account no. / numéro du compte	9275	cash number / numéro de caisse			
sender's name for reference only / nom de l'expéditeur pour référence seulement		People's Jewellery Co. Ltd.			
address and telephone / adresse, téléphone	300 Birch Street, Toronto, ON		M3T 6L5	814-1266	6106B(7-68)

Lesson 14

WARMUP

Rhythm	1	a;sldkfjghfjdksla;sldkfjghfjdksla;sldkfjghfjdksla
Shifting	2	Edith Myrna Diane Molly Faith Hazel Sandra Judith
Alphabet	3	jack bolt high view quiz dust next form copy tape

WORD PATTERNS

4 good mood food foot feet feed feel fell fall fill

5 bond band bank bark bard bird bind bend bent belt

WORD FAMILIES

6 ate, date fate gate hate late mate pate rate sate

7 ead, bead dead head lead mead read dead head lead

EASY PHRASES

8 for the for them for this for that for him for it

9 for these for those for which, for what, for her,

SENTENCES

10 What is good for them is best for what they want.

11 That for which they came is for her and for them.

THINK AS YOU TYPE

Type the following paragraph replacing the numbers with the proper word form.

Carl was 12 years of age and had lived
there for 5 years. He had 3 brothers and
4 sisters and, of course, 2 parents. From
the age of 9, he had had a paper route which
covered 15 blocks. Carl rose up at 6 each
morning to deliver his 70 papers. Usually
he was through by 8. He earned between 9
and 11 dollars a week for his work.

AIR TRAVEL SCHEDULE

Date	Flight	Times	
October 16	CPA # 2	lv. Toronto	10:35
		ar. Vancouver	11:50
	AC #268	lv. Vancouver	13:30
		ar. Victoria	13:50
19	AC #271	lv. Victoria	18:00
		ar. Vancouver	18:20
24	AC #505	lv. Vancouver	16:40
		ar. Calgary	18:45
28	PWA #433	lv. Calgary	07:30
		ar. Edmonton	08:25
November 2	AC #507	lv. Edmonton	14:45
		ar. Saskatoon	16:50
10	PWA # 16	lv. Saskatoon	18:00
		ar. Regina	19:00
14	AC #505	lv. Regina	20:50
		ar. Winnipeg	21:55
20	AC #107	lv. Winnipeg	14:00
		ar. Toronto	16:35

Job 3. Type a letter to each of the hotels on Mr. Watson's itinerary requesting a reservation for a large single room.

Lesson 143

WARMUP

Speed **He is busy at his desk but he will take time to talk to me.**

Top Row **His 45¢ and 47¢ trips sold faster than the 28¢ or 39¢ ones.**

Attention Unscramble the following sentence.

They paid bill the when came they back from last that trip.

Lesson 15

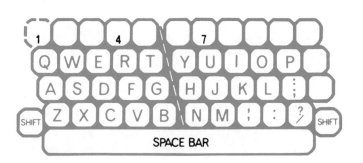

WARMUP

Rhythm 1   a; sl dk fj gh fj dk sl a; a;sldkfjghfjdksla;sldk

Alphabet 2   Brown Moore Green Jones Black Lewis Taylor Miller

Shifting 3   vine tack quit exam busy raze sigh half jade plow

The small letter "l" is used to represent the number 1 on most typewriters. (Some machines have a special 1-key located at the extreme left end of the top row. The A-finger is used to strike such a 1-key.)

NEW KEYS

4   jjj ju7j ju7j j7j j7j 777 171 717 177 77 17 71 77

5   The 7 girls sold 777 books to 77 boys in 17 days.

6   fff fr4f fr4f f4f f4f 444 141 414 144 44 14 47 74

7   The 4 girls sold 444 books to 44 boys in 14 days.

SPEED SENTENCES

8   There are 7 days in every week; is this not true?

9   And, there are always 4 full weeks in each month.

10   You should know that 7 and 7 always add up to 14.

PARAGRAPH

Please send us 47 copies of the new book you advertise on page 4 of your new catalogue. These books are needed for our senior class and we hope that they will reach us before May 17.

THINK AS YOU TYPE

Type the paragraph replacing, wherever possible, words with numbers.

He asked seven hundred and seventeen people to come to the four meetings to be held during the first four weeks of June. There were four hundred and seventy-four people who said that they would come to all four meetings. Only seventy-one people refused to come to any meetings.

Job 2.

To Mary Corrigan, Training Division. From John Harper, Marketing Director. On the subject of Training Conference.

I have just learned that Queen's University is sponsoring a three-day conference for senior sales executives. The conference will commence on March 15, and the subject is Exploring Canadian Markets. (P) Since we are planning to extend our marketing activities, it might be useful to have two or three of our sales executives attend this conference. (P) Please obtain complete information about the conference, and submit it with your recommendations before February 1.

JH urs cc. Mr. Morrisey.

Job 3.

To Gordon Hunter, Order Service Department. From Graham Welsh, Personnel Department. On the subject of Promotion of Helen Punter. The Personnel Director has approved your recommendation that Miss Punter be promoted to the position of Supervisor of Inventory Records. The promotion is to be effective April 1. (P) Also effective April 1, Miss Punter's salary will be increased to $215 per week. At the end of a 3-month probationary period, her salary will be reviewed to determine whether a further increase is merited. (P) Please convey to Miss Punter our appreciation of her good work and our congratulations on her promotion.

GW urs cc. Payroll Department.

Lesson 142

WARMUP

Speed   I also like the item that you want and shall order it soon.

Top Row   A bill for $5.40 and one for $36.80 must be paid by May 27.

Attention   .deeps ruoy tsoob nac uoy ,revo dna revo enil a epyt uoy fI

Jobs 1 and 2.

Your Sales Manager, James R. Watson, is preparing for a trip through western Canada and asks you to type up the following information.

ITINERARY

Date	City	Hotel
October 16	Victoria	Empress
19	Vancouver	Vancouver
24	Calgary	Palisser
28	Edmonton	Macdonald
November 2	Saskatoon	Bessborough
10	Regina	Saskatchewan
14	Winnipeg	Fort Garry
20	Toronto	At home

Lesson 16

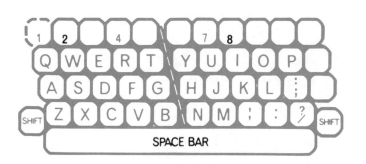

WARMUP

Rhythm 1   a ; s l d k f j g h f j d k s l a;sldkfjghfjdksla

Shifting 2   knew five text gyro jazz must quip glad high back

Alphabet 3   White Parry Giles Yates Scott Major Davies Oliver

NEW KEYS

4   kkk ki8k ki8k k8k k8k 888 181 818 188 88 18 84 87

5   The 88 letters must be typed for them in 8 hours.

6   sss sw2s sw2s s2s s2s 222 121 212 122 22 12 18 17

7   Can you send us 222 boxes of cards within 2 days?

SPEED SENTENCES

8   Can she bring all 78 bags rather than 21 of them?

9   There will be 2 extra boxes to put in the 2 cars.

10   Don Lewis lives at 128 Rose Street, Regina, Sask.

PARAGRAPH

      Their annual meeting will be held on May 12. They expect 874 delegates to attend and they will require at least 22 meeting rooms. Already, they have 78 resolutions that have been drawn up to be presented to the assembly.

THINK AS YOU TYPE

Type the paragraph replacing, wherever possible, words with numbers.

At our last meeting we had four hundred and seventy-two people. They all attended our final dance on the twelfth of the month. The band had twenty-four members and seventeen different band instruments. We awarded eighteen prizes for four-teen spot dances. The two door prizes were drawn at twelve.

Lesson 141

Speed A better outlook is a sure way of getting better attention.

Top Row Invoice #608, amounting to $138.72, received a 5% discount.

Attention Insert capitals where necessary:

Mr. jean degaulle, president of belle motors, was honoured.

Interoffice Memos

In all but the smallest offices, communication in written form is necessary between persons within the office. For this purpose, a special form called an interoffice memo is used. The style and size of the form will vary from office to office, but usually it will contain the information illustrated below.

                    INTEROFFICE MEMO

     To: John R. Stevens   From: Frank S. Willis
          Personnel Dept.   Sales Dept.

     Subject: Annual Sales Meeting   Date: November 6, 19--

          Tentative plans have been made to hold our annual
          sales meeting on December 17. It is anticipated
          that 23 or 24 people will attend the meeting this
          year.

          Would you reserve a suitable meeting room for us
          at the Westview Country Club? The accommodation
          that we had last year was excellent, and, if
          possible, we would like to have the same room
          again.

                                        F.S.W.

     urs
     cc. Mr. Macdonald

Job 1.   Make a copy of the interoffice memo illustrated above.

Jobs 2 and 3. Using the current date, type the following memos:

Lesson 17

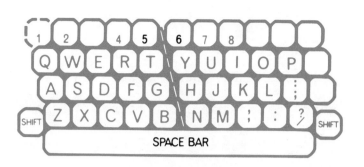

WARMUP

Rhythm 1 a;sldkfjghfjdksla;sldkfjghfjdksla;sldkfjghfjdksla

Alphabet 2 zone hymn lynx view quad take rest jump gift crab

Shifting 3 Allen Lloyd Smith Young Clark Haley Rogers Murphy

NEW KEYS

4 fff f55f f55f f5f f5f 555 151 515 758 45 25 52 58

5 Send 575 cartons of paper to 54 East 55th Street.

6 jjj jy6j jy6j j6j j6j 666 161 616 768 46 26 65 62

7 On June 6, we shall send Order No. 5665 to Pelee.

SPEED SENTENCES

8 The 15 boys and 6 men caught 25 pike and 65 bass.

9 Our team made a score of 16; the other scored 25.

10 John added 4 and 5 and 6 and 7; his answer is 22.

PARAGRAPH

The coach reported that the squad would need 65 pairs of shoes before September 15. The shoes should range in size from 4 to 7. So the manager prepared order form number 267 and said the shoes would be bought on August 25 when he paid a visit to the city.

THINK AS YOU TYPE

Type the sentences substituting the appropriate number for the ■.

2 and 4 make ■ .   2 and ■ make 7.   2 and ■ make 8.

2 times 4 is ■ .   2 times 6 is ■ .   2 times 8 is ■ .

If I take 7 from 12, I leave ■ ;   8 from ■ leaves 6.

Lesson 140

WARMUP

Speed   If I send the goods next week, we shall be able to use them.

Accuracy   Brad jumped to fix a zero mark on the viewing scale quickly.

Top Row   Bob's dad said, "I <u>must</u> pay the bill of $90 at 4% interest."

Job 1.

Using the full-blocked style with open punctuation for greater speed, complete as many jobs as possible in the time allotted to you.

Miss Muriel Renton, 722 Lavender Road, Toronto, Ontario M7T 4A9
Dear Miss Renton:

Thank you for submitting an application for summer employment at Echo Lodge. The qualifications and personal history outlined in your letter have impressed us favourably, and we should like to discuss them further during a personal interview.

Mr. Roger Stanton, our Assistant Manager, will be in Toronto next week to conduct such interviews. He has scheduled a meeting with you for 10:30 a.m. on Monday, June 12, in Suite 507 of the Amherst Arms Hotel. If it is impossible for you to keep this appointment, will you please telephone Mr. Stanton at the Amherst Arms Hotel between 9:00 and 10:00 a.m. on Monday, June 12, so that a more convenient time may be arranged.

It would be appreciated if you would fill out the enclosed application form and bring it with you to the interview.

Very truly yours, John R. Wagner, General Manager

Job 2.

Mr. Ronald Hargen, 618 Richvale Blvd., Toronto, Ontario M6S 5B3 appointment: 1:00 p.m., Monday, June 12.

Job 3.

Miss Grace Connelly, Apartment 608, Armour Heights Terrace, 1721 Wilson Avenue, Toronto, Ontario M5V 2L8 appointment: 2:30 p.m., Monday, June 12.

Job 4.

Mr. Fred Renton, 1806 Chesley Dr., Willowdale, Ontario N4P 9R2 appointment: 9:30 a.m., Tuesday, June 13.

Job 5.

Miss Nora Jamieson, 1621 Kingston Road, Toronto, Ontario M5D 8T6 appointment: 11:00 a.m., Tuesday, June 13.

Lesson 18

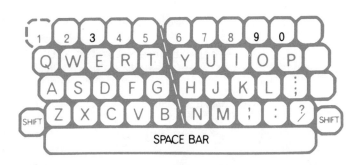

WARMUP

Rhythm 1 a ; s l d k f j g h f j d k s l a ; s l d k f j g

Alphabet 2 zero oxen many wave back jolt quit high flip does

Space-Bar 3 weak keen need damp part time exit took kept tame

Drills 4 Tom came. He ran. Tom fell. He won. Tom went.

NEW KEYS

5 ddd de3d de3d d3d d3d 333 131 313 738 53 63 36 35

6 The 3 meetings were held in room 1343 on April 3.

7 lll lo9l lo9l l9l l9l 999 919 749 839 69 59 93 96

8 Between 1959 and 1969, school population doubled.

9 ;;; ;p0; ;p0; ;0; ;0; 000 101 010 740 830 50 9003

10 We need 20 or 30 girls to sort out 10 000 papers.

SPEED SENTENCES

11 We will meet between 10:30 and 11:30 at my house.

12 Address his mail to 190920 Queen Street, Toronto.

PARAGRAPH

The matches will be played between May 7 and May 28. If your score is 89 or less, you will be playing in group 1. If your score is 90 or more, you will be playing in group 2. The winners from each group will play two final matches during the field day which is to be held on June 6.

THINK AS YOU TYPE

13 Type the odd numbers from 1 to 27

14 Type the even numbers from 2 to 28

15 Continue 3, 6, 9, . . . to 42

Job 1.

Type the following letter which accompanies the Data Sheet in Lesson 128.

2413 LaSalle Blvd., Cornwall, Ontario K3P 7D9   Current date

General Builders Limited, 102 Pleasant Street, Cornwall, Ontario K5T 9N7 Attention: Mr. Gerrick Marsters, Personnel Manager, Gentlemen:

Please consider my application for the position of mail clerk in your firm. The Placement Officer in our school advised me that there will be an opening for this type of work in your firm in June.

Information concerning my education and experience is outlined on the enclosed Data Sheet. I am very much interested in the Business Education subjects which I have taken in Secondary School and I plan to continue my studies in this field at Night School. I believe that my courses and work experience will help me to carry out successfully the duties of mail clerk and any general office tasks I may have the opportunity to perform.

May I please have a personal interview? You may reach me by letter or call me at 358-7391 any time after 4:00 p.m.

Yours sincerely, Lorraine DesRosiers

Encl.

Job 2.

Compose an application letter in which you will enclose the Data Sheet you prepared in Lesson 129. You are applying for a position as general office worker at Mobile Manufacturing Ltd., 732 Transit Street in your town. The job was advertised in your local paper today.

Job 3.

Address a large envelope for the letter in Job 2.

THINK AS YOU TYPE

Answer the following questions concerning your job interview.

1. Why is appearance important in a job interview?
2. How would you dress if you were applying for the following jobs: auto mechanic, electrical apprentice, sales clerk, mail clerk, general office job?
3. Why do employers look with suspicion at "job hoppers"?
4. What can you do?
5. What kind of work are you looking for? What is wrong with the answer, "Anything"?

Lesson 19

SIT ERECT; BE ALERT!

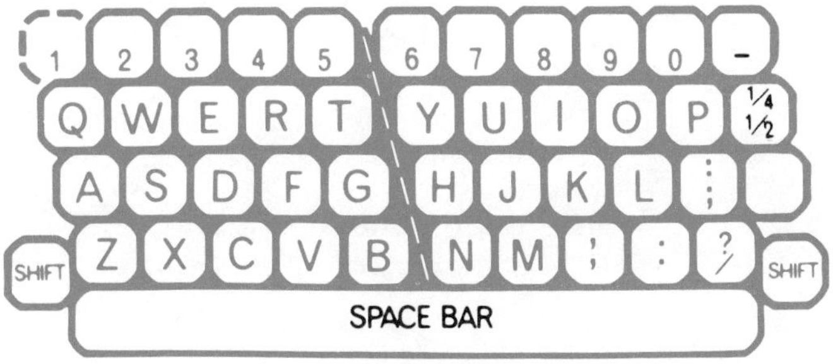

WARMUP

Rhythm 1 a;sldkfjghfjdksla;sldkfjghfjdksla;sldkfjghfjdksla

Alphabet 2 yacht razor index bluff equal given jumps unknown

Stroking 3 all fall hall shall ash dash lash flash slash ask

NEW KEYS

4 ;;; ;½; ;½; ½½½ 1½, 2½, 3½, 4½, 5½, 6½, 7½, 8½ 9½

5 The silver stock opened at 27½ and closed at 31½.

6 ;;; ;½¼ ¼¼¼ ½¼½ 1¼, 2¼, 3¼, 4¼, 5¼, 6¼, 7¼, 8¼ 9¼

7 He knows that ½ of ½ is ¼. Then, what is ½ of ¼?

8 ;;; ;-; ;-; --- full-page, half-sheet, two-thirds

9 Two-thirds of the in-laws were there at the show.

NUMBER DRILLS

10 we 23 to 59 it 85 or 94 up 70 pi 08 re 43 wet 235

11 it 85 wit 285 pit 085 writ 2485 write 24853 et 35

SPEED SENTENCES

12 Send me 6½ dozen Grade A large eggs at 54½ cents.

13 I can buy 2½ times the amount for only 13¼ cents.

14 Her daughter-in-law drives a two-tone sports car.

PARAGRAPH

The dash is sometimes used in place of other forms of punctuation. To make the dash, type two hyphens one after the other, with no space before or after. For example: Her daughter-in-law--not her son-in-law--is buying a 10-room house.

THINK AS YOU TYPE

Type words that rhyme with:

bay, bar, bun, bed, bid, bad, bag, ban, bat, beg
card, tall, port, cart, corn, bone, ripe, camper

Job 2.	Send the same letter in the same style to:
	Mr. Raymond Borrell, Director of Secretarial Studies, Capital Business College, Stoney Creek, Ontario N7D 4G3
Job 3.	Send the same letter in the same style to:
	Miss Janet Handley, Head of the Commercial Department, Lakeshore High School, Oakville, Ontario N6H 2J5
Job 4.	Address large envelopes for each of the letters in Jobs 1, 2, and 3.
THINK AS YOU TYPE	List three letter styles. Which style do you prefer? Why?

Lesson 139

WARMUP

Speed   Telling that odd riddle seems to leave the men in a muddle.

Alphabet   Six jovial antics of Beth quite amazed a large happy crowd.

Top Row   The 4's are faulty on model #87906; the 8's on model #4253.

Letter of Application

An application letter is prepared by a person who is applying for a job. Usually a Data Sheet similar to the one in Lesson 128 is also prepared and accompanies the letter of application. The letter itself follows the style of a personal business letter. It should be set up in an attractive manner and typed as neatly as possible. Your prospective employer will receive the first impression of you through your letter of application.

Timed Writings to Measure Your Skill . . .

One of the means by which you check your progress in acquiring typing skills is the timed writing. By taking a timed writing, you can measure your rate of typing, or "typing speed." To determine "typing speed," count every five strokes (letters or spaces) as one word. Your speed will be the number of 5-stroke words you can type in 1 minute, i.e., *words per minute, or wpm.*

To Take a Timed Writing . . .

Your teacher will probably use signals such as these to guide your practice in your timings:

1. "Goal." Set yourself a goal.

Example: Today, you are going to try to type two lines in one minute.

2. "Practise." Glance over the copy and select the words that you feel might be difficult to type. Practise each of them two or three times.

3. "Timing" — Return the carriage quickly.

4. "Ready . . . Type!" Type as much of the paragraph as you can before the teacher calls time. At first you will be timed for 1 minute; later, your timings will be for 2, 3, and 5 minutes.

5. "Time!" Stop. Return the carriage, and inspect your work. Note how close you came to your goal.

6. "Ready to repeat . . . Type!" Type for another minute starting from the beginning of the same paragraph. You should get more done this time.

7. "Time!" Stop and inspect your work.

8. "Practise." Type two or three times each word that caused any difficulty. Repeat the above steps as often as time permits.

Before You Start . . .

Have you ever seen a young child run too fast and then suddenly fall over his own feet? It can happen in typing too — with your fingers of course! This will not happen to you, if you remember a few simple things to do before starting your timed writing and while typing.

First. Check your posture. Good posture helps you to type well.

Second. Try to relax and enjoy yourself as you work towards reaching the goal you have set yourself.

Third. Keep your eyes on the copy from the time you start typing until the teacher calls "Time!"

Fourth. Sharp, snappy stroking of the keys prevents key-jams. Use your best key-stroking all the time.

Fifth. Try to keep your key-stroking at a smooth and regular pace. Keep the carriage moving steadily.

REMEMBER — This is not a race. It is a timed writing to see how far you can type at a steady pace for a given amount of time.

To Determine Your Speed . . .

When you have completed your timed writing you will want to know your rate of typing, or "typing speed."

1. Find the number of words you have typed. There is a scale to the right of the timed writing to help you do this quickly. The numbers tell you how many 5-stroke words you have typed from the beginning of the exercise to the end of any given line.

If you did not complete your last line of typing, but you did complete more than half the line, include the full number of 5-stroke words for the line. If you completed up to half the line, add half the number of 5-stroke words given for the line to the number of words shown in the scale for the last complete line you have typed.

2. Divide the total number of words typed by the number of minutes timed. This will give you "words per minute" (wpm).

Error Tolerance . . .

If you are making more than an average of two errors per minute during your timed writing, you may be (1) typing too fast; (2) using incorrect typing techniques. Aim for fewer than two errors per minute on a timed writing during the first few months of your typing course, and no more than one error per minute by the end of the year. The number of errors you should tolerate is one per minute. This is called your error tolerance.

Recording Your Rates . . .

So that you can measure your progress from day to day and from week to week, you should record your best rate on each timed writing. Your record can be a simple chart showing the date and the rate you achieved. Better still, you can record your results in the form of a graph, which will demonstrate visually the progress you are making. Your instructor will probably suggest an effective method for recording the rates that you achieve. It is important that you constantly strive to increase your rate on timed writings. Each time you type, you are competing with yourself and your own record.

Type a paragraph entitled "My Next Vacation." Where are you planning to go and when? Why did you choose that particular place? How do you plan to travel? What type of clothing are you going to take with you? How much money do you think you will need?

Lesson 138

WARMUP

Speed   If I send the goods next week, will you be able to use them?

Alphabet   A judge will quiz the boys on the price of the mixed knives.

Top Row   12 m 38 kg 600 km 4 cm² 0.01 m³ 200 mL 300 mg 10 t 15 mm 8 g

Job 1.

Using today's date, set up the following letter in the full-blocked style.

Mr. Edward Humphrey, Principal, Lakefield Collegiate and Vocational School, 1819 Collingwood Crescent, Lakefield Centre, Ontario N9C 8F2
Dear Mr. Humphrey   Subject: Spelling Contest

The Hamilton chapter of the National Business Club is again sponsoring a spelling contest in the greater Hamilton area. We hope, Mr. Humphrey, that some of your students will be able to participate.

As in previous years, the contest is based on a list of one thousand words carefully selected by a committee of business people and educators. To be eligible for an award, participating students must make a perfect score on two tests. Each test consists of one hundred words that are to be dictated to the students. The tests will be marked and scored by your own teachers and only the names of those students making a perfect score will be forwarded to the National Business Club.

We would appreciate it, Mr. Humphrey, if you would pass on to the appropriate member of your staff the enclosed pamphlet. It contains full information about the contest and suggests efficient procedures for conducting it in your school.

Very truly yours

John Harrington, Chairman, National Business Education Committee.

WARMUP

Rhythm   1   a; sl dk fj gh fj dk sl a; a;sldkfjghfjdksla;sldk

Alphabet   2   quiet dozes might black field vixen enjoy wrapped

Stroking   3   bus bush busy burn burnt box born bow bowl butter

NUMBER REVIEW

4   we 23 up 70 it 85 to 59 or 94 pi 08 wet 235 it 85

5   we 23 were 2343 wet 235 wry 246 wit 285 writ 2485

6   Add 7 to 1, 6 to 2, 8 to 3, 9 to 4, 10 to 5 and 1

WORD FAMILIES

7   ire, dire fire hire mire sire tire wire quire ire

8   elt, belt celt felt melt pelt welt belt felt pelt

9   ell, bell cell dell fell jell sell tell well yell

ACCURACY SENTENCES

10   Mix the vapid frozen soup quickly in a brown jug.

11   Lazy Jack is quite vexed by a power machine gift.

SPEED SENTENCES

12   A class of 27 was divided into 3 teams of 9 each.

13   In 1959, there were 48 high schools in this area.

14   We gave 10$\frac{1}{2}$ to her and 6$\frac{1}{4}$ to her daughter-in-law.

TIMED WRITING

Most of us like the fall. It is the time of 10
year when the air is crisp and clear, and the sun 20
is almost sure to shine each day. It is the time 30
for long walks in the woods, for corn roasts, and 40
for the sweet taste of fresh ripe fruit. Old and 50
young seem to get a new zest for life in the fall 60
of the year. 63

Lesson 137

WARMUP

Speed   Will we be able to send them the goods they want next week?

Alphabet   exile queen grave blaze joint dough weary frame space break

Top Row   Water freezes at 0 °C and boils at 100 °C.   Today it is 25 °C.

Job 1.

Using today's date, set up the following letter in the full-blocked style.

Mr. Tom Prosser, Personnel Manager, Huntley-Eastman Steel Co., 2742 Burrard Street, Vancouver, British Columbia V3T 7A2 Dear Mr. Prosser

We are revising our training program in an effort to increase the efficiency of our office workers. One of the innovations that we want to make is to provide each member of our office staff with a Style Manual.

The Style Manual would contain facsimile models of all our business forms properly filled out. It would also contain sample letters properly set up on letter-size paper. A reference section at the end of the manual would list proper forms of address, useful postal information, and rules for indexing all types of correspondence.

We have been informed that your firm recently compiled a similar Style Manual and that you have been using it with excellent results. We should appreciate receiving a copy of your manual and any suggestions you might care to make about using it effectively.

Very truly yours, J. Harrington Smith, Training Director

Job 2.

Send the same letter to:

Mr. Frank Lawson, Imperial Cable and Wire Limited, 1862 7th Avenue West, Calgary, Alberta T4B 5L8

Job 3.

Send the same letter to:

Miss Eileen Mayer, Office Manager, Central Drug Products, Limited, 1426 Oxford Street, London, Ontario N6C 9E2

Job 4.

Address "small" envelopes for each of the letters in Jobs 1, 2, and 3.

Lesson 21

WARMUP

Rhythm 1 `a b c d e f g h i j k l m n o p q r s t u v w xyz`

Stroking 2 `car care cat cart caw cow cot cote coat copy cope`

Numbers 3 `up 70 upper 70034 out 975 outer 97534 rip 480 480`

WORD FAMILIES

4 `ice, dice lice mice nice rice twice advice police`

5 `orn, born corn horn morn worn thorn forlorn shorn`

6 `ock, block clock flock smock knock pock rock sock`

PHRASES

7 `as is, as if, as the as they as he as she as they`

8 `when he when she when they when it when that when`

ALPHABETIC SENTENCES

9 `He will make a quick visit to the big zoo on Monday just to see a fox imported recently.`

10 `A man perched on the queer box while he told his wife and children an amazingly clever joke.`

11 `Did you realize how quickly government taxes jumped just after the war began?`

12 `Five or six dozen cartons of juniper berries will be quite enough for my candied pickles.`

THINK AS YOU TYPE

13 Type the days of the week.

14 Type the months that start with J.

15 Type the months that start with A.

16 Type the months that start with M.

17 Type the remaining months.

TIMED WRITING

`I do hope that you can come to our camp this` 10
`year. It is a very easy drive from your house to` 20
`the camp, and all the routes are paved. The main` 30
`lodge was built near the lake, and every room has` 40
`a view of this water. Our friends come back year` 50
`after year. They claim that the food, the rooms,` 60
`and the sports are as good as can be found.` 69

Commonwealth Products

KNOWN THROUGHOUT THE NATION

Executive Offices . . . .   220 Berkeley Street, OTTAWA, ONTARIO K2L 8D4

February 16, 19--

Mr. Lorne Standish
468 Cypress Avenue
Ottawa, Ontario   K3M 9E5

Dear Mr. Standish

This letter is typed in a full-blocked style which
is the most modern of letter styles. It is gaining
in popularity in Canadian business offices.

In this style every line begins at the left margin.
Because you do not have to indent at all, it is the
fastest letter to type. You will find this a most
useful style when a large quantity of letters must
be produced in the shortest possible time.

Some people do not use this letter setup because it
tends to give an unbalanced appearance to the finished letter. However, its practical advantages far
outweigh this small flaw.

Very truly yours

T. R. James

T. R. James, Supervisor
Staff Training Division

urs

> FULL-BLOCKED
>
> open punctuation

Lesson 22

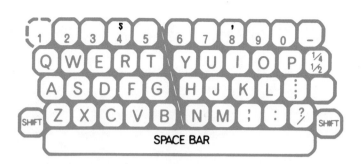

WARMUP

Rhythm 1   a;sldkfjghfjdksla;sldkfjghfjdksla;sldkfjghfjdksla

Alphabet 2   Back High Glad Quip Must Jazz Gyro Text Five Knew

Numbers 3   we 23 pry 046 wore 2943 your 6974 pop 090 top 590

NEW KEYS

4   fff f4f f$f f $50 $60 $70 $80 $90 $10.28 $1 000

5   Only $26.50 is still owing on the bill of $83.79.

6   Pay Bob $25, Jim $37, Ron $48, and pay $69 to me.

7   kkk k8k k'k k'k 'k' 'k' ''' 8' it's boy's girl's,

8   That isn't John's coat. It's Robin Brown's coat.

9   Cam's jump was highest in the school's high jump.

TIMED WRITING

Our visit to the zoo will surely be a joyous ₁₀
and exciting day. We shall see quiet animals and ₂₀
noisy animals. There will be creatures with such ₃₀
queer names as the lynx, zebra, llama, and quail. ₄₀
The exotic birds will thrill us as they strut and ₅₀
preen their feathers. The lazy camel will rub on ₆₀
the fence; the sly fox will slink into the corner ₇₀
while a fuzzy bear roves round and round his den. ₈₀

THINK AS YOU TYPE

Type the paragraph using the dollar sign and numbers to represent the amounts of money.

We had one hundred and twenty-eight dollars for
the party. The band cost seventy-two dollars,
decorations twenty-four dollars, and prizes eighteen
dollars. We were left with only fourteen dollars
for all the other expenses.

Job 1.   Copy the letter on page 216.

Job 2.   Using today's date, set up the following letter in the full-blocked style, using open punctuation.

Professor P. T. Monderer, Department of Geography, University of Western Ontario, London, Ontario N7R 4P9 Dear Professor Monderer

We were delighted to learn that you have agreed to collaborate with Professors Bridston and Kleppinger in the preparation of a book on the geography of Canada.

There is a great demand from the high schools of both Ontario and Manitoba for a new textbook suitable for their courses in Canadian geography. We believe that you and your co-authors can write a book that will satisfy that demand.

We would request that the material which you are preparing on the Canadian Northland be approximately 10 000 words in length and be submitted for editing not later than February 1.

We are looking forward to working with you.

Sincerely yours Stuart M. Massa, Editor-in-Chief

Job 3.   Prepare a small envelope for the letter in Job 2.

THINK AS YOU TYPE

1. Name at least five products of science. For each item state how it is helpful to people and how it can harm people.

> E.g. Aeroplanes are used to transport people.
> Aeroplanes are used to bomb people.

2. Explain how you feel when you listen to the following types of music. Mention the place where you last heard each type. How did the location affect your feelings?

> rock, classical, folk, religious, sitar.

Lesson 23

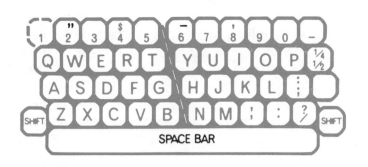

WARMUP

Rhythm 1   a;sldkfjghfjdksla; a;sldkfjghfjdksla; a;sldkfjghf

Alphabet 2   Does Flip High Quit Jolt Back Wave Many Oxen Zero

Numbers 3   er 34 err 344 were 2343 pout 0975 pot 095 put 075

NEW KEYS

4   sss s2s s"s "s" "s" "what?" "why?" "when?" "who?"

5   He said, "That number is 247." She asked, "Why?"

6   "Come along quickly," said teacher; "Time is up."

7   jjj j6j j_j _j_ _j_ 678 234, he must pay the $50.

8   This author makes that clear in Learning to Type.

9   A jacket of that quality will cost at least $125.

PARAGRAPH

An underscore, _, is the shift of the 6 key. To underscore: first, type the material that you wish to stress; second, move the carriage back to underscore each letter. If there are more than 5 strokes to be underscored, draw the carriage back by hand; otherwise, the backspacer should be used by the little finger, while at the same time your eyes remain fixed on the copy. It is good typing technique to handle the backspacer properly.

TIMED WRITING

The use of quotation marks is an interesting 10
study. Here, for example is a quotation within a 20
quotation: Mr. White, our leader, said, "We need 30
a man of strong will to proclaim when the time is 40
right, 'This is wrong; we desire no part of it.'" 50

We use quotation marks when naming the title 60
of an article, a chapter of a book, a short story 70
or a poem. The title of a book, however, must be 80
underlined when it is named. 86

Up to this time, there has been no mention made of the art of   13
erasing on typewritten work. We agree with one expert who claims   26
that in no other area of typing skill do students seem to do so well   39
with so little instruction. In fact, quite often students rely on an eraser   52
for accuracy once they have been permitted to use it. Students may   65
forget that the aim of this course is the building of typing skills,   78
not the building of erasing skills.   85

Of course there are times when erasing is in order. If your teacher   99
permits you to erase, please protect your machine by moving the   112
carriage as far as you can to the right or to the left so that the   125
shavings fall on the table and not into the machine. Use your margin   138
release if needed. Use only a clean eraser and make certain that   151
your work is spotless.   155

Lesson 136

WARMUP

Speed We shall be able to send them the goods they want next week

Alphabet quit jump race back cold from hang exit zest wave your quiz

Top Row 10 26 39 48 57 9 mL 26# $39 48% 57 & 10 & 26 (39) & (47) 10

In offices all across Canada there are workers who are bored with   14
their jobs. They are the country's biggest failures. They took their jobs   29
because they liked the pay or the hours or the location or because   42
they had a friend in the office. They have no interest in the firm for   56
which they work or in the products with which they deal, and so   69
they have no enthusiasm for the work they are doing. They do their   82
work in a dull and monotonous routine, keeping one eye on their   95
supervisors and the other on the clock. To them, every day seems   107
like an eternity.   111

The Full-Blocked Letter Style

The *full-blocked* (sometimes called the extreme-blocked) style for setting up letters is one in which *every* line in the letter begins at the left margin. Because it requires no tabulation, the full-blocked style is efficient to use. This style is not as popular as the blocked style but it is used in many Canadian business offices.

Lesson 24

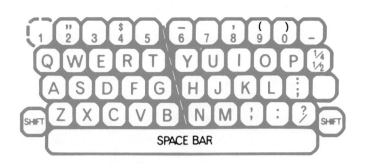

WARMUP

Rhythm 1   a b c d e f g h i j k l m n o p q r s t u v w xyz

Alphabet 2   Take Rest Jump Gift Crab Zone Hymn Flux View Quad

Numbers 3   to 59 too 599 toot 5995 top 590 tip 580 trip 5480

NEW KEYS

4   111 191 1(1 (1((1((12 (13 (45 (67 (89 (100 (289

5   The left parenthesis (is the shift of the 9 key.

6   ;;; ;0; ;););));) 12) 13) 45) 67) 89) 100) 389)

7   The right parenthesis) is the shift of the 0 key

8   We require (a) more time and (b) a new reference.

9   He said, "Miss Bone (our teacher) is coming now."

THINK AS YOU TYPE

10   Type the names of the four western provinces.

11   Type the names of the two central provinces.

12   Type the names of the four Atlantic provinces.

13   Type the names of four states of the United States.

14   Type the names of five Canadian cities.

TIMED WRITING

     We plan to go on a long trip this next year.   10
We now have a new car, and last month we bought a   20
new trailer. Four of us can sleep in the trailer   30
and one can sleep in the car. For the past three   40
months, we have been poring over maps from nearly   50
every part of Canada. We have now selected three   60
routes that seem to appeal to all of us. We hope   70
that nothing will spoil our well-laid plans.   79

so yearbook not distributed to students until fall. Book to include more spring activities. Grads can pick up book in fall or have it mailed for extra 50¢.

(d) Film Society — Profit made on last movie so film society to show another. Phil M. moved we okay showing "The Odd Couple" in March. Kathi A. seconded. Motion carried.

New Business

(a) Harlem Diplomats — Mr. Fiddes reported $302 on game. He suggested saving money for worthwhile project. Sue M. moved money be carried in the B.A.C.'s account until it is to be used. Keith K. seconded. Carried.

(b) Chess Club — Mr. Neck asked if any money could be spent on the club (1) possibility of small chess trophy (2) purchase of additional chess sets. Moved by Carolyn Jones that Chess Club find out cost of these items and report later. Seconded by Maureen Gray. Carried.

Adjourned 2:00 p.m. Next meeting Tuesday, Feb. 17, period 6, Rm. 314.

Lesson 25

Test

In each 25th lesson, you will be presented with material that is suitable for testing your progress to that point. The test material will incorporate all the skills that you should have acquired and will enable you to compare your skills with those of your classmates. **Practise the material,** and then ask your instructor to administer it to you under test conditions. Good luck!

Job 1.

Type two 2-minute writings. Score and hand in the better one. Suggested time allowance 10 minutes.

It takes time to learn a skill. A baby will 10
take many weeks just to learn the basic skills to 20
walk, feed himself and talk. The child will fall 30
quite a few times before he is able to run around 40
with any speed or grace. As he grows up, a child 50
will practise long hours to master a skill needed 60
to jump a rope, swim, skate or play a game. Thus 70
you cannot expect to be a very expert typist in a 80
day or even a month. You will need to practise a 90
great many hours to perfect each of the skills it 100
takes to make up the art of the speed typist. It 110
will take zeal and much effort. 116

Job 2.

Type the paragraph twice. Hand in the better copy. Suggested time allowance 10 minutes.

"How much do you want for Tom's book?" asked
the man, holding up a copy of THE SCARLET DAGGER.
"It's worth at <u>least</u> $25," I replied confidently.
The man (I never did <u>learn</u> his name) put down the
book and walked away.

Lesson 135

WARMUP

Speed   She was told to come as soon as she could.   She might come.

Numbers   weepy 23306 witty 28556 wrote 24953 wiper 28034 write 24853

Accuracy   The text gave sixty amazingly hazardous tricks for lizards.

Job 1.

You attended the February 10 meeting of the Students' Council. The Agenda for this meeting appears in Job 2, Lesson 134. The notes which you took at the meeting are printed below. From these notes prepare the Minutes of that meeting. Use the set up as suggested in Job 1, Lesson 134.

Frank Accomando called meeting to order at 11:05. Vera Balabon and Julie Bains were absent.

Business Arising Out Of The Minutes
(a) Buses – Haven't decided yet whether to pay $20 for third bus. The Principal offered to help – will call Mr. Cook at the street railway office.
(b) Presidents' Council – Sue M. wants names of anyone interested in questioning guests on the CHCH TV program.

Committee Reports
(a) Student Assemblies – Some students outside committee are interested. Sue M. moved that they be allowed to come on to this committee. Kathi A. seconded. Motion carried.
(b) Social Committee – Profit on Feb. 7 dance. An exact report to be presented at next meeting.
(c) Yearbook – New policy by publisher

Job 3.

Type the following paragraph twice. Hand in the better copy. Suggested time allowance 10 minutes.

Because of an extremely severe climate, only 14 different species of animals live in the whole of the Arctic region. The largest of the mammals living there is the polar bear. Polar bears live on the shores of the Arctic Ocean or on ice floes and some may have a mass of 800 kg. This area is the home of various kinds of caribou, all related to the reindeer. These animals migrate over long distances, moving north in summer and back to the bushland in winter. The mass of the caribou will vary from 75 kg to more than 200 kg; they feed on lichens, grasses, leaves, and twigs.

Job 4.

Type the paragraph inserting appropriate words for the pictures. Suggested time allowance 10 minutes.

A [image] named Jack owned a [image] which was painted [image]. He also owned a [image] and an [image]. He had thought of buying a [image], but was afraid that the [image] would not like the [image]. He also feared that the [image] might catch a [image] which would frighten the [image].

for these books. Jeff moved that the Students' Council should not support this cause since we contributed so much to the United Appeal. Steve D. seconded. Motion defeated.

Leslie Bone moved that we contribute $32, which will ship 36 cartons of books. Dean Hockey seconded. Motion carried.

TIME AND PLACE OF NEXT MEETING
The next meeting will be held on February 10, 19...... in Room 311, period 6. The meeting was adjourned at 4.30 p.m.

_____
President

_____
Secretary

Job 2.

On a full sheet of paper, attractively set up the following Notice and Agenda of the meeting of the Students' Council to be held on February 10, 19......

STUDENTS' COUNCIL

Notice of Meeting

Date: 19-- 02 10   Room: 311   Time: Period 6

Agenda

1. Approval of Last Meeting's Minutes

2. BUSINESS ARISING OUT OF MINUTES
   (a) Buses
   (b) Presidents' Council

3. COMMITTEE REPORTS
   (a) Student Assemblies
   (b) Social Committee
   (c) Yearbook
   (d) Film Society

4. NEW BUSINESS
   (a) Harlem Diplomats
   (b) Chess Club

5. DATE, TIME, AND PLACE OF NEXT MEETING

Lesson 26

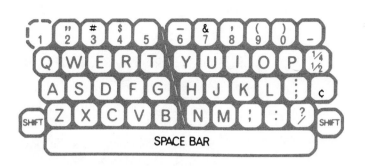

WARMUP

Alphabet 1   a b c d e f g h i j k l m n o p q r s t u v w xyz

Stroking 2   log lot lock locker lit litter lug luck late lust

Numbers 3 $32 76¼ 28½ $55 "96" $700.80 '45' (81) (63) $4.50

NEW KEYS

4   ddd d3d d#d #d# #d# #76 #32, #9 and #4 are ready.
5   Get me 3# of #1 grade, and 5# of #2 grade coffee.

6   jjj j7j j&j j&j &j& &j& &&& B & B, Black & Black.
7   He owes: $25 to Ford & Reid; $35 to Bate & Horn.

8   ;;; ;¢; ;¢; ¢;¢ ¢;¢ 10¢ 20¢ 30¢ 40¢ 50¢ 60¢ 70¢ 8
9   Potatoes are at 49¢, onions 27¢, and carrots 21¢.

PARAGRAPH

Do you use your space bar the right way? It
should be tapped twice after a period, a colon, or
a question mark. Only one space follows a comma.
Good neat spacing gives your typing a smart look.
Practise tapping the space bar correctly. Do not
lift your eyes from the copy while you strike it.

THINK AS YOU TYPE

Type the answer to each of the following questions using one word or a
phrase, not a sentence. Put each answer on a line by itself. Number your
answers to correspond to the questions.

1. What are the colours of our flag?
2. In what month is Remembrance Day?
3. What is the name of your favourite professional football team?
4. In what year were you born?
5. What is your favourite method of transportation?
6. Which country of the world would you like to visit?
7. What magazine have you read lately?
8. In what year did your province enter Confederation?
9. What colour are your eyes?
10. Who is the Prime Minister of Canada?

BUSINESS ARISING OUT OF MINUTES

Buses — Council was informed that one of the buses hired for the Sherwood-Southmount hockey game arrived late due to an accident. The bus dispatched in its place was authorized to be used one way by the H.S.R. Supervisor, and Council has been charged an additional $20 for this service. Mr. Britton is investigating. However, since such complications can arise, Council were asked to give serious consideration to the hiring of buses in the future.

COMMITTEE REPORTS

(a) Advertising Committee — Mr. Britton suggested that a list of the advertising committee members be made up as soon as possible. Frank Accomando moved that this committee be allowed to have a chairman who will sit in on the Council meetings. Kathi Aitken seconded the motion. All were in favour. Frank will check this procedure in the Constitution.

(b) Social Committee — Cathy Grant announced that the price of $250 for the "Illustration" was at a reduced cost due to the original plan of hiring two bands for the February 7 dance. She moved that the contract be revised to a price of $300. Frank Accomando seconded the motion. The motion was carried. Cathy's revised budget estimates a profit of $110.

(c) Foster Parent Plan — Leslie Bone read a short article which will be mailed to the Board office for publication in the "School Tie." She also read a letter to be mailed to Freddie. Leslie will arrange a bulletin board display in the main hall showcase. She is also preparing a P.A. announcement regarding the progress Council is making in sponsoring this child.

NEW BUSINESS

(a) Presidents' Council — Sue M. reported that Presidents' Council will be producing thirteen programs on Channel 11. Students who wish to appear on any of these programs should speak with Sue Maychak for further arrangements. Students will be allowed to interview the guest on the show. Students' Council members will pass this information on to their fellow students.

(b) Mr. Mastin has appealed to Council Presidents to ask their councils if they would be interested in financing the postage for books from the depository which will be sent to Africa. There is a library being set up in Ghana and money is needed to finance the postage

Lesson 27

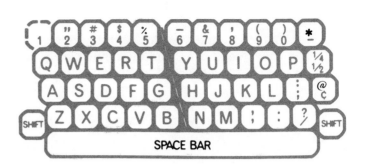

WARMUP

Rhythm 1   `a;sldkfjghfjdksla;sldkfjghfjdksla;sldkfjghfjdksla`
Alphabet 2   `Quip Gray Hall Lamb Zero Bump Oats View Jury Kind`
Numbers 3   `we 23 wet 235 were 2434 wit 285 wot 295 wore 2943`

NEW KEYS

4   `fff f5f f%f %f% %f% 55%, 45%, 2%, and 3%, and 4%.`
5   `The bank will charge 5½% discount or 6% interest.`

6   `;;; ;-; ;*; *;* ;-* 29* 30* 41* 56* 78* 10* 37***`
7   `Refer to Lewis* and Scott** for the right answer.`

8   `;;; ;¢; ;¢@ ;@; @;@ @29 @35 @47 @56 @85 @97 @10.9`
9   `Buy 35 ripe bananas @ 10¢; 14 doz. oranges @ 60¢.`

THINK AS YOU TYPE

Type boys' or girls' names starting with each letter of the alphabet in sequence. E.g. Anne, Bob, etc.

TIMED WRITING

The hush was broken in a quiet zone in front 10
of City Hospital by the wail of a police siren as 20
Car Number 28 sped to the scene where the jagged, 30
twisted mass marked the location of the accident. 40
They asked 5 witnesses to report to Station No. 6 50
at 07:30 to be queried and advise as to what they 60
had seen. Everyone agreed that the driver of the 70
green car had been at fault. He had been driving 80
at an excessive rate of speed and had not come to 90
a halt when the traffic light turned red. 100

THINK AS YOU TYPE

Compose a report which will be sent to each member of the staff of your school in advance of the staff meeting. Outline what you consider are important considerations for changes in your school's curriculum. If material and facilities permit, prepare a stencil of your report, run off copies on a duplicator, and distribute copies to the staff members.

Suggestion: If material and facilities are limited, form groups of four or five and prepare one report which will represent the ideas of your group. Each group will duplicate a report for distribution.

Lesson 134

WARMUP

Speed   If he does the jobs now, we can pay him more than they can.

Numbers   pure 0743 purr 0744 pore 0943 pout 0975 pyre 0643 poor 0994

Accuracy   The zoologist spoke eloquently on the life of the dinosaur.

Job 1.

Minutes of a Meeting

A report of what occurs at a formal meeting is known as the Minutes of the meeting. On a full sheet of paper, or on a stencil, make a copy of the following Minutes. Allow an extra 5 spaces for the left margin to permit storing of the Minutes in a loose-leaf binder. Allow a top and bottom margin of 6 line spaces. The heading for the second page of minutes of a meeting begins on line 7 and is as follows:

Students' Council Meeting   Page 2   February 3, 19.....

STUDENTS' COUNCIL MEETING

MINUTES, FEBRUARY 3, 19.. ..

The meeting was called to order at 3:00 p.m. by Sue Maychak. All members were present with the exception of Vera Balaban and Angus McCallum. The minutes of the previous meeting were read and approved.

Lesson 28

Alphabet	a b c d e f g h i j k l m n o p q r s t u v w xyz
Stroking	dog dot dock doctor dig digger dug duck deck dust
Numbers	$23 #67 #82 55% "69" 70 & 80 '45' (18) (36) $4.50

ONE-HAND DRILLS

Left	fed feed feeder feet seat wear wearer wet ware we
Right	hip hill mill pill poll pull jolly polly molly up
Left	test tested taste tasted brass vast waste greased
Right	noon union plum plump opinion lump lumpy onion on

Rules for the Division of Words

To be a good typist, one must learn to divide words at the end of a line when necessary. Learn the following rules so that you may apply them if you need to.

1. Divide a word only when you cannot avoid it.

2. Divide between syllables. For example: men-tion. A good typist keeps a dictionary handy and consults it when in doubt about the proper syllables in a word.

3. Divide as close to the middle of the word as possible. For example pronun-ciation, rather than pro-nunciation.

4. Divide after a prefix. E.g., contra-diction, rather than con-tradiction.

5. Divide before a suffix. E.g., reason-able. Where a consonant is doubled before adding a suffix, divide between the double consonants. E.g. ship-ping.

DIVIDING WORDS

Copy these words. They are divided as they would be if it were necessary to split them at the end of a line.

cour-teous dis-play chil-dren main-tain ship-ping
dig-nity win-ter man-ner mo-ment deal-ing in-tend

PARAGRAPH

Note how some words are divided at the end of lines to maintain an even right margin.

Do you have a hobby? A great many people do
have a hobby. One that is widely enjoyed is that
of taking pictures. Using a camera, one may keep
a unique record of friends and family from day to
day. Also, it is fun to study the art of photog-
raphy. One must expect the odd failure and a few
funny results to occur, but as time goes on, some
prize winning photos may be the ultimate achievement for all your efforts.

THINK AS YOU TYPE

Type as many words as you can using only those letters which are used to form the word "COMPUTER". E.g., me, met, come, etc.

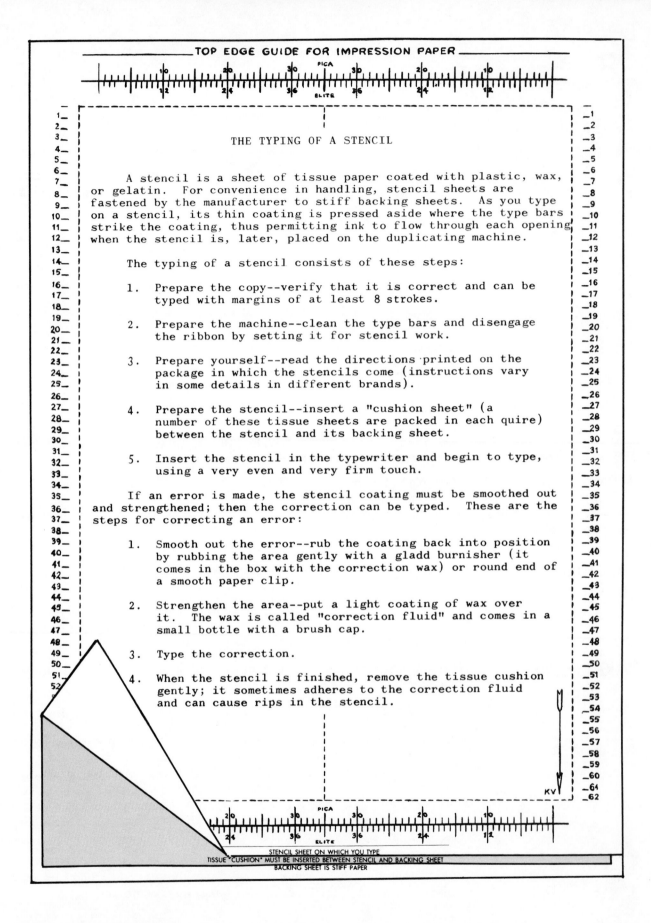

TOP EDGE GUIDE FOR IMPRESSION PAPER

THE TYPING OF A STENCIL

A stencil is a sheet of tissue paper coated with plastic, wax, or gelatin. For convenience in handling, stencil sheets are fastened by the manufacturer to stiff backing sheets. As you type on a stencil, its thin coating is pressed aside where the type bars strike the coating, thus permitting ink to flow through each opening when the stencil is, later, placed on the duplicating machine.

The typing of a stencil consists of these steps:

1. Prepare the copy--verify that it is correct and can be typed with margins of at least 8 strokes.

2. Prepare the machine--clean the type bars and disengage the ribbon by setting it for stencil work.

3. Prepare yourself--read the directions printed on the package in which the stencils come (instructions vary in some details in different brands).

4. Prepare the stencil--insert a "cushion sheet" (a number of these tissue sheets are packed in each quire) between the stencil and its backing sheet.

5. Insert the stencil in the typewriter and begin to type, using a very even and very firm touch.

If an error is made, the stencil coating must be smoothed out and strengthened; then the correction can be typed. These are the steps for correcting an error:

1. Smooth out the error--rub the coating back into position by rubbing the area gently with a gladd burnisher (it comes in the box with the correction wax) or round end of a smooth paper clip.

2. Strengthen the area--put a light coating of wax over it. The wax is called "correction fluid" and comes in a small bottle with a brush cap.

3. Type the correction.

4. When the stencil is finished, remove the tissue cushion gently; it sometimes adheres to the correction fluid and can cause rips in the stencil.

KV

STENCIL SHEET ON WHICH YOU TYPE
TISSUE "CUSHION" MUST BE INSERTED BETWEEN STENCIL AND BACKING SHEET
BACKING SHEET IS STIFF PAPER

Lesson 29

WARMUP

Rhythm   `a; sl dk fj gh fj dk sl a;sldkfjghfjdksla;sldkfjg`

Stroking   `ear earn eat east easter eastern elect erect exit`

Numbers   `67% $98 7 @ 10¢ 385 & 940 (7) (4) 34½ 86¼ $100.00`

Rules for the Division of Words

1. Do not divide:

(a) Words that are pronounced as one syllable. E.g., shopped, brought, string
(b) Words of four letters or less. E.g., copy, rely
(c) Contractions such as wouldn't, couldn't, etc.
(d) Abbreviations, proper names, numbers, or degrees. E.g., RCAMC, Macdonald, $962.05, M.Ed.

(e) Hyphenated compound words at any place other than the hyphen. E.g., self-control

2. Leave a syllable of at least two letters on the upper line. E.g., you may divide ad-mit, but not about or alone.

3. Carry a syllable of at least three letters, or two letters and a punctuation mark, to the next line. E.g., simi-lar, fif-ty,.

DIVIDING WORDS

Copy these words. They are divided as they would be if it were necessary to split them at the end of a line.

```
pa-per ex-pect be-fore Canada work-ing allow-ance
strength busi-ness world around con-tain run-ning
```

THINK AS YOU TYPE

Think of five words which have at least two syllables and which are not found in the above exercise. Type your words showing where each could be divided at the end of a line. Check with your dictionary if you are in doubt about the proper syllables or correct spelling.

Listening for the Bell

As the typewriter carriage moves towards the right margin, a bell rings to remind you that it is time to throw the carriage. Check your machine to see how many spaces there are between the sound of the bell and the point at which the right margin locks. *Note too*, that by pressing the margin release, you may type a few more strokes. When typing, you have to make a decision at the sound of the bell. One of the following will always apply:

1. Finish the word being typed, *if possible*. Do not lift your eyes, or you will lose your place and waste time.

2. If the word is one that cannot be divided, or is only one or two strokes too long, use your margin release. This will allow you to complete the word, without looking up.

3. If the word is a long one, and it lends itself to proper division, split it with a hyphen at the right margin. Throw the carriage and complete the word. Do not look up.

Job 2.   Prepare a Book Report on one of the books which you have read this year.

Lesson 133

WARMUP

Speed   From where he sits he can see the red jug but not the jars.

Numbers   trip 5480 tory 5946 type 5603 tier 5834 tyre 5643 tour 5974

Accuracy   Marvin quietly caught four wizards in six dozen big quilts.

Stencils   In Lesson 64 you learned how to prepare a master for a "spirit" duplicator. In this lesson you will learn how to prepare a stencil for a duplicating machine. If you have access to a stencil duplicator in your school, your teacher or a senior student will assist you in running off copies from your stencil.

Job 1.   On page 208 is an illustration of material typed on a stencil. Instructions and related information about the production of stencils are contained in the copy. Read it carefully before you begin to type a stencil.

Job 2.   Type the following Notice and Agenda on a stencil. You may find it helpful to set up your material on a sheet of standard size paper in advance of preparing your stencil.

OURTOWN SECONDARY SCHOOL
NOTICE AND AGENDA OF STAFF MEETING

Place: Team Teaching Room

Date: 19-- 04 16 at 15:15

Theme: Curriculum Innovations

Speaker: Dr. H. E. Knowzal
            Superintendent of Curriculum
            Education Centre
            Ourtown, Canada

Agenda: 1. Presentation by Dr. Knowzal
            2. Small group discussions
            3. Group reactions to Dr. Knowzal
            4. Refreshments in staff lounge
            5. Adjournment

PARAGRAPHS

The following paragraphs are set up with 60-stroke lines. Type each of them, using a 40-stroke line. You are to listen for the warning bell. In the first paragraph, if you listen and heed the bell properly, all lines will end so that the right margin is perfectly even.

In the second paragraph, however, you will find that some words have to be divided. While the right margin will be fairly even, it will not be perfectly aligned. This is what normally happens when you use a line length that is different from that of the copy.

Learning to listen for the ping of the typewriter bell and to act upon its warning sound is an important skill for you to master, just as you are striving to perfect your use of the keys. Learn to make the correct decision and to act upon it in the most suitable way. Then you will be well on the way to becoming a speed typist. It is a matter of real importance that you establish the habit of keeping your eye focused on the copy at all times.

From the beginning of the year you have found out that learning to type is a combination of many skills which must be perfected. It is difficult to concentrate on all of the rules at once. Your teacher, of course, will remind you as he watches you develop from a fumbling beginner to an even, speedy typist. Are you conscious of your posture? Are all strokes sharp and snappy? When you toss your carriage with a quick motion, are your eyes fixed on the copy beside you? Have you memorized the rules about dividing words so that a line may be even on the right margin? In all skills we try to save time.

TIMED WRITING

If any animal is responsible for the growth of our country, it is the   14
beaver. This large rodent has well and truly earned its position as a   28
symbol of Canada. It was the fur of the beaver which lured the French   42
and the British into opening the wilderness, and upon it was built the   56
great era of the fur traders.   62

The mass of a full-grown adult beaver may be 35 kg, and its body,   75
not including the tail, may be 60 cm or more in length. The beaver   89
has four strong cutting teeth, two in the upper jaw and two in the   102
lower. These teeth have sharp edges like chisels, and by patient gnaw-   116
ing the beaver can cut through the trunks of trees that are as much   129
as 60 cm thick. When a beaver senses danger, it will slap its flat   143
tail loudly on the water to warn other beavers. The beaver also uses   157
his tail as a rudder when he swims and to prop himself up while cut-   171
ting a tree trunk.   175

Lesson 132

WARMUP

Speed   We are sure that she can do this work in less than an hour.

Numbers   tire 5843 tore 5943 trip 5480 pity 0856 wipe 2803 pipe 0803

Accuracy   Twelve huge giraffes jumped quickly over two blazing boxes.

Job 1.   Review "Guide for Writing a Book Report" in Lesson 75. Type the following Book Report as instructed in "Typing Suggestions", Section B, Lesson 75. Set your left margin 15 strokes from the edge of your paper so that you can place your work in a notebook.

BOOK REPORT: BRAVE NEW WORLD

THE AUTHOR

The author of "Brave New World" is one of the famous novelists of Modern Classics. Aldous Huxley (1894-1963) belonged to a family of great talent. In addition to "Brave New World" he wrote many other novels, including "Limbo" and "Island." The son of Leonard Huxley, the editor of the Cornhill Magazine, he was educated at Eton and before devoting himself entirely to his own writing, he worked as a journalist and a dramatic critic.

STORY SUMMARY

In this unusual novel, the author is predicting the future. Babies are decanted from test tubes; they are not born. "Mother" and "father" are considered terrible words to use. Children are conditioned to be afraid of nature and books so they will not grow up to read and realize what an unsatisfactory life they are really having. Everyone in the novel is addicted to the drug "soma." They do not believe in God; instead, they worship Henry Ford, the creator of mass production.

The people are born into different "castes." These castes are Alpha, Beta, Gamma, Delta, and Epsilon — the latter being the lowest. People who have been born instead of being decanted are put on a "savage reservation."

The main characters are Lenina Crowne, her girlfriend Fanny, John the Savage, and the Director of the Hatchery. The novel tells the story of their lives. Complications arise when Lenina discovers she likes John the Savage, who hates her style of living. In the end, John is so upset with his life that he hangs himself.

COMMENTS

Although "Brave New World" is far-fetched, it really makes me wonder what the world will be like in the future. It is hard to believe that this kind of conditioning could ever exist. The characters seem to me to be unreal and unfeeling. This novel should serve as a warning to all of us.

Joanne Ricciardi

Lesson 30

WARMUP

Rhythm a;sldkfjghfjdksla;sldkfjghfjdksla;sldkfjghfjdksla

Shifting Zoe Peg Lex Quin Van Dick Myra Bud Fred Stan John

Numbers pop 090 poppy 09006 pit 085 pity 0856 pot 095 095

WORD FAMILIES

ter patter matter letter latter batter fatter ter

ther, mother father bother brother rather gather,

ion, action caution faction motion nation notion,

THINK AS YOU TYPE

Answer the following questions with a word or a phrase.

1. What is the title of this book?
2. What winter sport do you like best?
3. What summer sport do you like best?
4. What school subject do you like best?
5. What is your hobby?
6. In what town or city and province do you live?
7. Who is the Premier of your province?
8. What is today's date?

Rules for Using the Space Bar

A good typist knows the proper spacing to use at all times. Review the rules, and type the examples which follow.

Rules	Examples

DO NOT TAP THE SPACE BAR —

1. Before or after a hyphen
2. Before or after a dash
3. Between quotation marks and the words enclosed
4. Between parentheses and the words enclosed
5. Before or after a decimal
6. Between the # symbol and numbers
7. Before the % symbol
8. Before the symbols ' and " to mean minutes and seconds
9. When using a key fraction
10. Before the ¢ sign
11. Following a period within a group of small letters
12. Before and after a colon when expressing time

1. Our sister-in-law lives here.
2. I mean--you know what I mean.
3. "When can you come?" I said.
4. Ed Quin (the captain) scored.
5. The $20.00 hat sold at $4.88.
6. Get him some #1 grade apples.
7. The bond issue will yield 4%.
8. He ran the race in 3' and 5".
9. She won $8\frac{1}{2}$ points in $6\frac{1}{4}$ days.
10. Each of the pencils costs 7¢.
11. I saw animals; e.g. giraffes.
12. We are due to begin at 08:50.

a business firm or ~~who does business over~~ ~~the phone~~ must be able to project his personality into his voice, ~~or he will be~~ ~~unsuccessful.~~ A customer can be turned away by a poor telephone conversation ~~more~~ just as easily ~~as~~ ~~than~~ by a rude personal encounter.

There are ~~certain~~ qualities of voice which everyone ~~should~~ must develop in this day of ~~modern~~ "telephone business." What are these qualities?

Probably the most important quality of voice necessary is that of clear articulation. This is the ability to say words clearly and distinctly, so that no misunderstanding will occur during a conversation. Nothing is more annoying than a mumbler.

~~Three~~ further, necessary qualities of voice ~~that can~~ ~~be grouped together~~ are ~~voice~~ proper level, modulation, and tone. Level is a matter of keeping the voice loud enough, so that the listener does not have to strain ~~every~~ ~~nerve~~ to hear, but never so loud that it jars the listener or makes a private conversation sound like a broadcast. Modulation is the quality of speech that makes a voice distinctive and gives it personality. Flatness ~~can be taken out of~~ is avoided in speech by raising and lowering the pitch of the voice and by emphasizing words and phrases to bring out their meaning. Tone is the quality in a voice that makes it warm and friendly, rather than cold and impersonal.

Rules for Using the Space Bar

Rules	Examples

TAP THE SPACE BAR ONCE

1. After a comma
2. After a semicolon
3. After the period that indicates an abbreviation
4. Before a constructed fraction
5. Before and after the &
6. Before and after the @
7. Between the digits expressing year, month, and day
8. Between a number and the following metric symbol
9. Between groups of 3 digits to the left and right of the decimal

1. He came, gazed, and went off.
2. Do see the show; it is funny.
3. Dr. C. Fleming arrived early.
4. The fraction needed is 6 5/8.
5. She got them at Hart & Stone.
6. Get me 2 dozen @ 68¢ per doz.
7. Her birth date is 1977 07 16.

8. I plan to travel 98 km today.

9. Canada rated 3 000 000 units.

TAP THE SPACE BAR TWICE —

1. After the period ending a sentence
2. After the question mark
3. After the colon

1. They arrived. They departed.
2. Why is he here? To study it.
3. As follows: paper, ink, pen.

INITIALS

1. When typing people's initials, space once after the period.
OR, follow the modern trend, by omitting the space between initials.

1. Mr. J. R. MacKay

   Mr. J.R. MacKay

2. When typing a series of initials which stand for degrees or for names of well-known companies or organizations, omit the space after each period.
OR, follow the modern trend by omitting the period as well as the space.

2. I.G.A., C.P.A., B.A.

   IBM CNR YMCA

TIMED WRITING

Are you discouraged because of errors? Your teacher is always 14
reminding you to watch your posture. Do you heed him? One of the 27
most outstanding teachers of typewriting maintains that poor posture 40
is the one most common cause of typing errors. Perhaps, sitting too 54
close to your machine, you force your wrists to be bent outwards. This 68
results in all kinds of errors. Perhaps you sit too far away from the 83
machine. This means that you are straining to type and you get a 96
pain in your neck for your trouble. Then, because this makes you tired, 110
you make more mistakes than ever. Perhaps you sit "off centre" and 124
your reaches land in all the wrong places. Perhaps your hands are 137
placed too low or too high. Then, you cannot control your stroking. 151
It is so important that you check your posture every time you sit down 165
to type. 167

Job 1.

You are working in the Public Relations Department of the Telephone Company. Your superior has given you this list of points on how to use the telephone correctly in a business office. Type it, with corrections as marked.

CORRECT USE OF A BUSINESS TELEPHONE — *on line 8*

1. Answer Promptly--Never let a phone ring more than twice. The caller is entitled to courtesy, *and it is rude to keep him waiting.*

2. Identify Yourself--Always state your name, and *your* company, if necessary, on both incoming and outgoing calls.

3. Keep Pad and Pencil Handy--Much important information comes in by telephone. Write it down. Your memory can play tricks on you.

4. Transfer Calls Properly--If you cannot handle a call yourself, be sure that it is transferred to the proper department or office. Remember that it is your job to satisfy the customer.

5. Leave a Message When You Leave Your Telephone--If it is necessary for you to leave the office, let the operator or someone know where you can be reached and *when* you will be back.

6. Place and Receive your own Calls--This is a great time-saver that is overlooked in many offices. It is much more courteous to handle your own calls than to let someone else do it for you.

7. Keep a List of Frequently Called Numbers--An up-to-date list of the most used telephone numbers that is kept right at hand is a great time-saver.

8. Use a Courteous Manner and Voice--You represent *your* ~~the~~ company. The customer gets his impression from your manner and voice over the phone. Converse as if you were speaking to him in person.

9. End the Call Courteously--Make certain that both you and the customer understand all the details of the call. Be polite in closing the conversation. Allow the customer to hang up his receiver first.

Job 2.

Your superior has written this short article on voice in relation to the telephone. It is to be typed on one full page, using a 60-stroke line and double line-spacing. See if you can produce a fine piece of manuscript typing.

(Line 6)
Your Voice Represents Your Company

A person who answers the telephone for

Lesson 31

WARMUP

Horizontal Centring

Follow these steps to centre a line —

1. Bring the carriage to the centre point.

2. Using your *thumb* to operate the backspacer, press the backspace key *once for every two strokes* in the line to be centred. Say the letters and spaces to yourself (in pairs) accenting the second one as you backspace. For example: to centre Government of Canada — think of it in this way —

gOvErNmEnT (*space*) Of (*space*) cAnAdA

— the accented letters are capitalized.

3. If there is an odd stroke left at the end of the line, *always ignore it.*

4. Type the material to be centred.

5. To centre *a series* of lines, move your margin stops to the far left and right, clear all tab stops, and *set one tab at the centre point.* For each new line, throw the carriage, tab to centre, and follow the steps above. NOTE: There is never any punctuation after a centred line.

Job 1. Centre the following lines.

John Paul Jones

Robert Allan Alexander

922 Queen's Quay, Toronto

Government of Canada

Vancouver, British Columbia

Job 2. Centre the following lines one below the other.

```
            Teams
            Canadian Football League
            British Columbia Lions
            Edmonton Eskimos
            Calgary Stampeders
            Saskatchewan Roughriders
            Winnipeg Blue Bombers
            Hamilton Tiger Cats
            Montreal Alouettes
            Ottawa Roughriders
            Toronto Argonauts
```

Rate the following occupations in the order of your preference.

Pickle inspector
Wiper at a car wash
Toll collector

Explain why you rated the occupations in the order in which you did. Now pick an occupation that you would rate lower than any of the three.

What's in a name? Have you ever wondered who has the task of 13
thinking up thousands of names needed to designate streets, ave- 26
nues, crescents, and boulevards in Canada's cities? Have you ever 39
wondered why some street names become almost synonymous with 52
the name of the city itself? Portage and Main — the windiest corner 65
in all Canada — is known to Canadians as the heart of Winnipeg. 78
Barrington is a name filled with memories, good and bad, for any- 92
one who went overseas in Canada's armed forces by way of Halifax. 105
Sous le Cap is the narrowest street in Canada and is the spot that all 118
visitors in Quebec City must see, along with Grand Allee. Sherbrooke 131
and St. Catherine Streets, of course, mean Montreal. Sherbrooke Street 145
runs the full length of the Island of Montreal from east to west and 159
is over 29 km in length. Yonge and Bloor is the location of fashionable 173
Toronto shops. Bay Street in Toronto is the Wall Street of Canada. 186
Did you know that there is a Dundas Street in almost every town and 199
city along the shore of Lake Ontario? Simcoe and York are popular too. 213
These names spring from the early history of Upper Canada. Out on 226
the West Coast, Granville Street in Vancouver is also a name of histori- 241
cal significance. The desire to remind our folk of history, both local and 256
national, and the romance of many Indian words account for many 269
of the choices that are made when naming the streets of Canada's 282
towns and cities. 285

Lesson
131

WARMUP

Speed They must know that this firm will send him some cash soon.

Numbers peer 0334 poor 0994 peep 0330 weep 2330 pipe 0803 ripe 4803

Accuracy He lacquered the amazing boxes of jewellery a vivid bronze.

Lesson
32

Rhythm   a;sldkfjghfjdksla;sldkfjghfjdksla;sldkfjghfjdksla

Alphabet Jonke Myers Franz Quance Walsh Budge Potts Xavier

Numbers 10" 28' #37 4.6 $52 <u>673</u> 89% (73 64) 50½ 19¼ 1/356

Speed   To do that, would make it bad for men on the job.

Display Techniques

Use the following devices to make display typing more attractive:

1. Double Spacing and Triple Spacing.

2. Underscoring.

3. All capitals for a punch line, a title, or a heading
   — Press the shift-lock key which is just above the shift key

— Type the line of letters
— Release the shift lock

Stop! Remember This!

1. Release the shift-lock key for any character that cannot be typed in capitals, such as the numbers and the hyphen.

2. After a heading or title, always leave two blank lines — i.e., triple space.

Job 1.

Use the lines in Job 2, Lesson 31, on Canadian Football Teams. Set them up for display using the following means of making your typing attractive: use BLOCK CAPS for the heading, followed by two blank lines; *underscore* the second line; centre all lines, and double space.

Job 2.

Set up the following list of books, centring the heading and each title. Leave two blank lines after the heading (typed in BLOCK CAPS) and one blank line between the titles. Do not forget to omit punctuation.

OUR FAVOURITE BOOKS: Black Beauty; Robinson Crusoe; Treasure Island; Kon-Tiki; The Adventures of Sherlock Holmes; The Tale of Two Cities; Tom Sawyer; Mutiny on the Bounty; Around the World in Eighty Days; Men Against the Sea; The Wizard of Oz.

THINK AS YOU TYPE

What are your favourite television shows? Do you watch soap operas, comedies, tragedies, or once-in-a-lifetime specials? Rate your five favourite television shows, centring them horizontally on your paper.

Imagine that you could be transformed into something in each of the following categories. What four things would you choose and why?

Food   Colour   Furniture   Machine

Lesson 130

WARMUP

Rhythm is it if in we me be am at as do go so to by my on or of an

Top Row Ian's brother-in-law asked for 20% of Kenneth's $87.35 fee.

Attention Unscramble the following sentence.

roses blue in raises red He the white and old lilies house.

ACCURACY SENTENCES

Reservations for accommodation must be received immediately.
The banquet programme is organized by a competent committee.
A negative uncooperative attitude alienated his subordinate.

Job 1.

With the help of your dictionary, match each of the following terms with the proper definition. Set up in tabular form the terms and their corresponding definitions.

Terms	Definitions
perception	an exchange of thoughts, facts, opinions, emotions
attention	the process of understanding, interpreting, judging, deciding
comprehension	refers to consciousness or observation; a mental image; a concept; an insight
communication	the act of putting each of two things in the place of the other; exchange
interchange	the act of applying the mind to an object of sense or of thought

Job 2.

Compose complete sentences using each of the terms in Job 1.

It has been great fun learning to type, but we still need daily prac- 13
tice to master the skills we have learned. The sharp, snappy stroke, 26
good posture, keeping our eyes on the copy; these must become habits. 39
We must just vanquish bad habits with zest. 50

Now, we are going to apply our skills. The first step is to learn the 64
skills in Display Typing. Some of these are the use of double spacing, 79
centring, indenting, underscoring, and the use of all capital letters. 93
Each step in becoming an expert typist is more fun than the last. 107

Lesson 33

WARMUP

Rhythm to do so me ma la pa ha an am is it if or of us but

Numbers 92 or 83 or 74 or 65 or 56 or 47 or 38 or 29 or 10.

Speed We want all three to be in CLARK HALL by two today.

Vertical Centring

Count the lines required to type the given piece of work. In Job 1, for example there are five lines of typing, and since the material is to be double spaced, there is a blank line-space between each of the five lines. So a total of nine lines is required for the exercise.

Subtract this number from the number of lines available on the paper. After your subtraction, you have left the number of lines available for the spaces above and below your typing. Because these spaces are to be equal, divide the number by 2 (ignore any fractions). The result of your division is the number of line-spaces between the top of the sheet and the first line of typewriting.

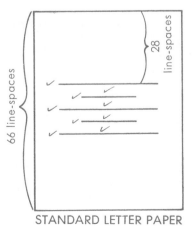

STANDARD LETTER PAPER

66 line-spaces
− 9 lines in exercise
2 / 57 line-spaces
28 line-spaces

Begin typing on line 29, leaving blank the 28 line-spaces

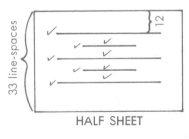

HALF SHEET

33 line-spaces
− 9 lines in exercise
2 / 24 line-spaces
12 line-spaces

Begin typing on line 13, leaving blank the 12 line-spaces.

Write a paragraph explaining what the situation would be like for you in each of the following instances:

(1) if you were 10 cm taller

(2) if you were 16 for the rest of your life

(3) if you were an animal (choose an animal you would prefer to be)

Lesson 129

WARMUP

Rhythm `a;sldkfjghfjdksla;sldkfjghfjdksla;sldkfjghfjdksla;sldkfjghf`

Top Row `Bills for $15.75, $8.20, $6.45, $9.61 and $7.30 are unpaid.`

Attention Complete the following words by adding "ie" or "ei".

s ze   w gh   forf t   rec ve   financ r   cash r   rec pt   w rd

WORD FAMILIES

```
eli elite elicit eligible eliminated eliminators elimination
ele elected election elements electric electricity elevators
hal hale half hall halo halves halibut halter hallmark halts
que antique clique critique opaque physique unique technique
```

Job 1.

On paper or cards 10 cm x 15 cm, list as much information as you can concerning yourself under each of the following headings.

Personal Data
Educational Record
Interests and Achievements
Work Experience Record
References

Job 2.

From the information you have listed in Job 1, type a full-page Data Sheet similar to the one in Lesson 128. Under each heading, type the most important facts first.

Job 1. Centre the following lines, double spaced, on a half sheet of paper.

```
MY MASTERPIECE - A CENTRING DISPLAY
    Typing Exercise Executed by
            Your Name
               for
        Your Teacher's Name
```

Job 2. Centre the following lines to make an attractive announcement. Use a half sheet of paper, and employ as many devices for display typing as you can. The / sign indicates individual lines.

```
Special Announcement/ to Business Education
Graduates/ 19.. / An Extensive Program of
Evening Session Graduate Study / in / Office
Management / at the / Ryerson Polytechnical
Institute / Toronto, Ontario
```

THINK AS YOU TYPE

Prepare and centre a menu for one of the following occasions:

A conference of Hallowe'en witches
A meal for a shipwrecked sailor
A dinner from another country

Lesson 34

WARMUP

Rhythm	and the for wit rut men sit six pen leg dog man fig
Alphabet	A B C D E F G H I J K L M N O P Q R S T U V W X Y Z
Numbers	147 268 #73 #45 $69 90% 678 (38 83) 50¢ 21½ 56¼ 1/5
Centring	DISPLAY TECHNIQUES

TIMED WRITING

Last week, six of us made a trip to a small lake that lies a long way 15
off the main paved road. The trip was not an easy one, but it was well 29
worth the effort of making it. We stayed in a small cabin owned by 43
one of our group, and, although we were crowded, we still remained 56
friends. The fishing was good, and the freshly caught fish supplemented 71
the canned food that we had taken with us. The work was shared by 84
all, and everyone enjoyed the simple life. It was refreshing to escape 98
from the noise and dirt of the city to the quiet beauty of the country. 113
We are determined to do it more often. 121

Applying for Employment

You are now developing skills which will enable you to accept part-time or possibly full-time employment. A letter of application for a job is similar to a sales letter. It is important that you know what you are selling (your services) and to whom. Your first step is to gather all the facts about yourself. Your second step is to learn all you can about the job and the firm where you wish to work.

Your summary of the facts about yourself is called a Data Sheet. It accompanies your letter of application. The Data Sheet is the technical part of your application and should be set up in an attractive form as in the example which follows.

Job 1.   Copy the following Data Sheet on a full sheet of paper.

DATA SHEET

for

Lorraine DesRosiers

A. Personal Data

    (1) Address: 2413 LaSalle Blvd., Cornwall, Ontario K3P 7D9
    (2) Date of Birth: 1960 07 17
    (3) Health: Excellent   Height: 158 cm   Mass: 50 kg
    (4) Social Insurance Number: 425 739 049

B. Educational Record

    (1) Will be completing second year Secondary School at Central Secondary in Cornwall on 19-- 06 14.
    (2) Attained above average marks in all subjects.
    (3) Studied the following business subjects:
          Consumer Education
          Introduction to Data Processing
          Typewriting — speed 45 words per minute
          Can operate duplicating equipment and electric typewriter

C. Interests and Achievements

    (1) Member of school Yearbook staff
    (2) Athletic representative on Student Council
    (3) Active member of YWCA
    (4) Volunteer worker at the General Hospital
    (5) Hobbies of skiing and music

D. Work Experience Record

    (1) Presently working part time as clerk at Brown's Bootery
    (2) Worked as YWCA Counsellor during the past summer

E. References (with permission)

    (1) Mr. Neville Brown, Manager   (2) Miss Muriel Stern
        Brown's Bootery   Business Education Department
        384 Canal Street   Central Secondary School
        Cornwall, Ontario K6J 2R9   Cornwall, Ontario K6H 2P5
        Phone No. 574-3847   Phone. No. 389-6730

EXTENDED   CENTRING

This is another display technique to make a centred line stand out. Each letter is capitalized and there is *one blank space* after each letter and *three blanks* between words. Follow these steps for extended centring.

1. Bring the carriage to the centre point.

2. Press the shift-lock key.

3. Press the backspacer (with your thumb) once for every letter and space in the line to be centred.

4. Type the material to be centred.

Job 1. Centre the following lines, using extended centring.

                    The Bank of Canada
                 The Government of Canada
                   An Outline of Art

Job 2. Type the following material on a half sheet, double spaced, following the instructions given in the copy.

              TO REPRODUCE TYPEWRITTEN MATERIAL

        You can set up any given piece of typed work by
    applying the rules for centring as you have been
    practising them.
        1.   For horizontal centring, find the longest
    line. Set your margin stops by centring this longest
    line.
        2.   For vertical centring, count the number of
    lines required, including both typed and blank lines.
    Subtract that number from the number of lines avail-
    able on the page. Divide by two to find your starting
    line.
        3.   Remember to follow the original copy exactly
    as to heading, spacing, and indenting for paragraphs.

Job 3. Type the following poem, following the instructions given in Job 2. Use a full sheet.

            A R O L L I N G   S T O N E

        THERE'S sunshine in the heart of me, *18*
          My blood sings in the breeze; *14*
        The mountains are a part of me, *15*
          I'm fellow to the trees. *12*
        My golden youth I'm squandering, *16*
          Sun-libertine am I; *9*
        A-wandering, a-wandering, *12*
          Until the day I die. *10*

                      --Robert Service

Use a complete sentence to answer each of the following questions:

1. What year will you be eligible to vote in the federal elections?
2. What answer do you get when you subtract 50 from the last Leap Year and divide that number by two?
3. What is the date of Canada's birthday?
4. What do you think is the cost of the typewriter you are now using?
5. What is your area code and telephone number?

TIMED WRITING

A lack of enthusiasm on the part of workers for the jobs they must   13
do is one of the vital problems facing modern industry. In former   26
times, this problem did not exist. All workers were artists who, with   39
their own hands, built the complete article. They always had the   52
reward of seeing the finished product.   60

Today's industry is based on the assembly line technique. The   73
workers reform only routine operations which they repeat many times   86
daily. Rarely do they see the finished product to which their labours   100
have contributed. Under these circumstances, it is difficult for workers   113
to be enthusiastic about their jobs.   122

Many industrial firms have found that it helps to take the new em-   135
ployees on periodic tours of the plant. In this way, they see the whole   148
process, and they understand and appreciate the part that their   161
labours play in that process. With this understanding, they perform   174
their tasks, however routine, with increased efficiency.   185

Another procedure that seems to help create and maintain interest   198
is to rotate people from job to job. There are no hard and fast guide-   213
lines as to the length of time that people can remain on a routine   227
assignment without getting so bored that their efficiency is impaired.   239

Lesson 128

WARMUP

Rhythm   a ; q p a ; s l w o s l d k e i d k f j r u f j g h t y g h

Top Row   **A 1964 bond yields 5%; it is 0.3% more than the 1958 issue.**

Attention   **?keew txen tnaw yeht sdoog eht meht dnes ot elba eb eh lliW**

DOUBLE LETTER WORDS

```
nn innocent dinner thinning tannery innovate winning minnows
oo look took tooth trooping booster bookkeeper foolproof too
pp tripped happy approval snapping stopped upper appreciates
rr arrange error sorrow arrive arrest errand borrow corrects
```

Lesson 35

Rhythm	a;sldkfjghfjdksla;sldkfjghfjdksla;sldkfjghfjdksla
Shifting	A B C D E F G H I J K L M N O P Q R S T U V W XYZ
Space-Bar	1. 2. 3. 4. 5. 6. 7. 8. 9. 10. 11. 12.
Extended Centring	T H E A R T O F T Y P E W R I T I N G

Job 1. Type the report below, NUMBERING OF POINTS IN A REPORT, following the instructions given in the copy itself. Do the work on a half sheet of paper.

NUMBERING OF POINTS IN A REPORT

Often you will wish to type a list of numbered items, a report, or notes with each point separate and distinct. Here are the points to remember:

1. Set margin stops so that material will be centred horizontally.

2. To keep numbers distinct from the rest of the material, indent all lines that do not begin with a number. Set the tab stop on the 4th space in from the left margin for this.

3. Space twice after the period following the number.

4. Letters (capitalized or lower case) or Roman Numerals may be used in place of numbers.

5. Usually, the material is single spaced with a blank line between numbered points.

Job 2. Set up and type the following report on the Planning of a Speech. Follow the instructions given in the preceding exercise.

STEPS IN PLANNING A SPEECH

double space

1. Select a topic in which you are interested.
2. Collect as much material as possible.
3. Organize your material into a rough outline.
4. Think out a good strong opening.
5. Write the speech.
6. Find an ending that will leave a lasting impression.
7. Edit and revise the speech.
8. Read and rehearse the speech.
9. Make a brief outline of your speech on a card to remind you of key points.

has chosen the purple violet, and Prince Edward Island is designated by the lady's slipper. Nova Scotia is represented by a dainty little pink mayflower. Newfoundland's choice is a more unusual flower, the pitcher plant, which is famous for its peculiarity of snaring insects.

Lesson 127

WARMUP

Rhythm `a;qpa;slwosldkeidkfjrufjghtygh fjrufjdkeidkslwosla;qpa;slwo`

Top Row `"75" #10 8 t $500 6½% 985 & 865 0.5 g (100) 1908 1369 1970.`

Attention Fill in the correct missing letter:

sep rate d scriptions indispens ble indefin te mainten nce.

WORD FAMILIES

```
ory story glory history rectory factory statutory directory
mas mass mast mask mash massage mastery massacre masquerade
exp expand expect expedition expert explain express explore
men menace menu mend menial mental mention mentor mendicant
```

WORD BUILDING

Look up in your dictionary the meaning of the word, "maxim."

Determine the correct maxim for the following maxi-maxims. Type both the maxi-maxim and the maxim. E.g. Maxi-maxim: Use the optical organs for the preparation of a short gain in altitude.

Maxim: Look before you leap.

(a) An equine quadruped may indubitably be induced to approach the well-known standard of specific gravity, but may not necessarily be impelled to imbibe thereof.

(b) That which casts off a spectrum of brilliance may not necessarily be a precious metallic chemical element of immense monetary value.

Job 3. Set up and type the following report in good form on a full sheet of paper.

CONDUCTING CLUB MEETINGS

1. Every meeting should be convened at 20:00 sharp with the singing of the national anthem.

2. The minutes of the previous meeting should be read by the Recording Secretary and should be approved by the members. This will require a properly seconded motion and a vote by the members.

3. Business arising out of the minutes should be discussed. Where decisions are necessary, they should be made by proper motions and votes.

4. The monthly financial report should be read by the Treasurer and approved by the members. Copies of the financial report should be given to the President and the Recording Secretary.

5. Reports of the various committee heads should be received. Opportunity should be given to the members for free and open discussion of each report.

6. Correspondence received since the last meeting should be read by the Corresponding Secretary. Members should be given an opportunity to discuss each letter and to make motions that are relevant.

7. New business should be introduced. Much of the new business will likely be introduced by the President, but the members should be given ample opportunity to introduce whatever business they deem desirable. It must be remembered that any motion to change the constitution cannot be entertained without a notice of motion that must be given in writing at least 60 days prior to the meeting.

TIMED WRITING

All typewriters make mistakes, don't they? Fingers have a way of hitting a wrong key once in a while, too. This is not too serious because you are gaining better control all the time. It is important, however, that you learn to detect any mistakes you have made. You must learn to be a careful proof-reader. Your future employer will be quite vexed if you allow any errors to be left in your work. On the other hand, you will know the joy of achievement when you can say with complete confidence, "There are no errors in this."

14
28
43
57
70
83
96
107

Lesson 126

WARMUP

Rhythm   abcdefghijklmnopqrstuvwxyz abcdefghijklmnopqrstuvwxyz abcde

Top Row   2830 3974 4279 5073 3965 2930 4072 5693 4082 3946 2075 3840

Attention   Use the necessary capitals:

we met miss hicks and miss joanis at the airport at malton.

SPEED SENTENCES

A sad melody brought a melancholy mood over the whole group.
His cousin from the country could bring the coupon with him.
The township council voted money towards getting a tow-line.
An autocrat authorized the use of automobiles in the parade.

Job 1.   Word Building

Type the root word for each of the following. Form a new word from the
same root. Arrange your material in three columns: given word, root, and
new word.

E.g.   freedom   free   freely

happiness, hopeful, attractive, taught, spoken, judgement, composition,
fought, precaution.

Job 2.   Meaning Clarification

Each of the following advertisements contains an unintended second meaning. Rewrite each advertisement to express clearly the proper meaning.

(a) The Piccadilly Shop has just received a shipment of large-size bathing
suits. Ladies, now you can buy a bathing suit for a ridiculous figure.

(b) Situation wanted: Young man, honest, will take anything.

(c) Deluxe Sedan, special job, just broken in, six new tires, won't last long.

ACCURACY PARAGRAPH

Can you name the ten flowers that symbolize the provinces of The
Dominion of Canada? British Columbia chose the dogwood which
recalls life in England to many residents. Alberta is represented by
the wild rose which grows in profusion during the early summer. Saskatchewan, in late August and in early September, is aflame with the
prairie lily, by which she is known. Manitoba has chosen the crocus
which blooms first in the spring, just as does Ontario's choice, the
trillium. Quebec's symbol is the wild blue flag or iris. New Brunswick

Lesson 36

Speed   The boy did the job, and yet he did not ask the man for pay.

Numbers   19-- 05 04 1 cm 10 mm 1 m 100 cm 1 km 1000 m 19-- 12:25 50 m

Alphabet   Five wizards quickly jumped over these fourteen green boxes.

Accuracy   Explain satisfactorily your involvement in this predicament.

TIMED WRITING

```
        By now you may have learned that there are two        9
sizes of type in common use on typewriters. The larger       20
size is named pica and the smaller one is named elite.       31
This timed writing is set up in pica type and if your        42
typewriting is the same size as this, you have a pica        52
machine. If your type is smaller than this and you are       63
able to get more strokes on a line of the same length,       74
you have an elite machine. Because it is important in        85
setting up a letter properly, you should know whether        96
your machine has pica type or elite type.                   104
```

TYPE SIZES

There are two main type sizes; namely, pica and elite. A 60-stroke line of elite type size occupies the same space as a 50-stroke line of pica type size. In other words, 10 pica spaces = 12 elite spaces.

Informal Personal Letter

It is quite acceptable today to typewrite a personal letter. You may choose to type your personal letter on paper smaller in size than the standard letter size.

When you begin to compose your personal letter, you are not likely to know how long it will be. A side margin of 6 spaces is generally acceptable. However, if your paper is quite narrow, you may use a side margin of 3 or 4 spaces.

The heading of a personal letter includes the sender's address and the current date. Start typing the first line of the heading on line 12, if you are using standard letter paper. If you are using smaller paper, you may start typing the first line of the heading on line 6. Each line of the heading and the complimentary closing usually begins at the centre of the page. The salutation and each line of the body of the letter begin at the left margin. This set-up is usually referred to as the blocked style.

The most modern way of typing the date is to express in numbers the year, month, and day in that order. Use 8 digits: 4 for the year, 2 for the month, and 2 for the day. Leave one space between each group of numbers.

Leave three line-spaces between the date and the salutation.

The most commonly used pattern of punctuation requires a colon after the salutation and a comma after the complimentary closing. All other display lines require no punctuation after them. This is referred to as Standard or Mixed Punctuation.

There are many variations for complimentary closings of a personal letter. The most commonly used closing for such a letter is "Sincerely". Be sure to WRITE your signature on a personal letter.

Job 4.

Suggested time: 20 minutes

Using the blocked style with open punctuation, complete as many form letters as possible in the time allotted.

19-- 04 01

Dear Mr.

This letter will remind you that your quarterly payment of $ for shares in the Canada Investment Fund, is due on   . Your remittance should be made payable to the Imperial Trust Company and should be mailed to the Imperial Trust Company, 184 St. James Street West, Montreal, Quebec H0B 1F3. The enclosed notice should accompany your remittance.

You will be pleased to learn that dividends amounting to $ were paid into your account on   . They will be used to purchase more shares of Canada Investment Fund for you.

Thank you for giving us this opportunity to help you share in the growth of the Canadian economy.

Very truly yours,

Thomas L. Henderson, Secretary-Treasurer

1. Mr. Thomas R. Rexton, 346 Quiller Blvd., Ottawa, Ontario K1K 7W3

quarterly payment, $125; due April 15; dividends, $42.60; dividends paid, March 31.

2. Mr. C. L. Christopher, 124 West Seventh Street, Calgary, Alberta T2S 2E5

quarterly payment, $200; due April 9; dividends, $75.80; dividends paid, March 15.

3. Mr. Frank Pickworth, 3412 University Drive, Saskatoon, Saskatchewan S7L 0T4

quarterly payment, $250; due April 7; dividends $106.30; dividends paid, March 31.

Job 5.

Suggested time: 15 minutes

Set up in good form the following invoices issued by Hillcrest Office Supplies, 2064 Main Street, Winnipeg, Manitoba R3E 1P6

Current Date; No. 1461; Cooper & Batten Ltd., 142 Euclid Ave., Winnipeg, Manitoba R2W 2X8 Order No. 113C; via Delivery; 8 doz. Ledger Sheets #4 @ 1.75—14.00; 3 doz. Hawk Stick Pens @ 2.50—7.50; 10 doz. File Folders #7 @ 1.75—17.50; Total 39.00.

Current Date; No. 1462; Crandall Brothers Ltd., 1206 Fourth Ave., Brandon, Manitoba R7B 2E4 Order No. 262; via C.P. Express; 48 Arrow Stencils #3 @ 0.20—9.60; 2 doz. Stenographers' Notebooks @ 1.80—3.60; 10 gross Paper Clips #4 @ 0.50—5.00; 5 Desk Blotters @ 3.50—17.50; Total 35.70.

Copy the letter below.

Heading (starts at centre)

191 Moss Street
North Bay, Ontario
P5K 3X4
19-- 12 06

Salutation

Dear Mike:

You will likely be surprised to get a letter
from me, and especially a TYPED letter. I am
taking a course in Personal Use Typing this
year and already I can type as fast as I can
write. We are all learning how to set up a
personal letter now, and after Christmas we
are going to learn how to set up our essays.
Think how much easier it will be for all my
teachers to read what I have to say. No one
could ever decipher my terrible handwriting.

We can double space our letters if we don't
have very much to say. As you know, I am
rarely at a loss for words so I am single
spacing mine. Next time I write, I may even
have to use a full sheet of typing paper.

Body of letter (4 space side margin)

My visit to your new cottage last summer was
really great. Is there any chance that you
might visit us over the Christmas holidays?
I am optimistic that Santa Claus will be so
pleased over my typing progress that he will
leave a typewriter under the tree this year.
Then you would be able to see for yourself
what a whiz I am!

Sincerely,

Gary

Complimentary closing (starts at centre)

Handwritten signature

Blocked style

Mixed punctuation

Job 2.

Suggested time: 10 minutes
Set up and type the following table of contents.

CONTENTS

Job 3.

Suggested time: 10 minutes
The following twenty words are spelled both correctly and incorrectly. Type the list using the correctly spelled version of each word.

fourty	forty
accommodate	accomodate
truly	truely
priviledge	privilege
cancelled	canceled
grammar	grammer
masacer	massacre
appearence	appearance
Fredericton	Frederickton
librarian	libraran
remitance	remittance
reciept	receipt
misspell	mispell
column	columne
excellant	excellent
proceedure	procedure
questionaire	questionnaire
precede	preceed
procede	proceed
restaurant	restaraunt

Lesson 37

WARMUP

Speed **Why did you say you and I are the ones who will do the work?**

Numbers **June 2, 1973; November 9, 1978; December 14, 1974; April 30**

Accuracy **dozen jugs squad zebra quit quick six rang lazy while frozen**

Letter Set Up

Job 1.   Type the following informal personal letter on a half sheet of regular Typing paper. Insert the shorter edge into the machine first. Follow the instructions in Lesson 36 for proper letter set up. Use the current date and your own address in the heading.

Dear George: Believe it or not, we actually arrived back safely after the hockey game Friday night. I thought the bus would never make it. The storm was so bad that many cars were off the road and stuck in snow banks. The first snow storm of the year always seems the worst. I hope the next one won't be quite as bad, especially if we are scheduled for another game out of town.

I want to thank you very much for inviting me to your home for dinner when I was in town. Your mother certainly is a good cook.

Thanks, too, for the book you lent me. I am enjoying reading about those hockey players I watch on television. I will return the book to you very soon. Sincerely,

Job 2.   Type the following informal personal letter on paper of your own choice. Use the current date and your own address in the heading.

Dear Pat: There is great excitement in our school these days. We are getting ready for the Christmas party which is being held next Tuesday morning, one week from today. The Student Council is organizing the activities. There will be some musical groups performing, a variety of skits, and some acrobatics. There is a rumour around that the teachers are going to do a skit which includes a chorus line. Can't you just see Mr. McDonald dressed up as a chorus girl!

We are allowed to invite a guest to our Chrismas party and I am hoping that you will be able to come with me. I can meet you at the bus station if you can arrive in town on Monday evening. It seems like ages since you were in town and I am sure you have lots to tell me about your new school and all your new friends. Aren't you lucky to have those ski slopes practically in your back yard!

I am really looking forward to seeing you so I hope you will let me know right away when you will be arriving. Sincerely,

Type the following cheques (Use today's date) :

#920 for $187.50 payable to John Ranton
#921 for $8.35 payable to Acme Cartage
#922 for $5000.00 payable to Receiver General of Canada
#923 for $36.40 payable to Mary Howard
#924 for $142.00 payable to Joan Findlay

THINK AS YOU TYPE

Using only the letters in the word RECUPERATION, type as many different words as you can. For each word containing three or fewer letters score one point; for each four-letter word score two points; for each five-letter word score three points; and for any word containing more than five letters score five points.

Lesson 125

Test

Job 1.

Suggested time : 15 minutes
Type two 5-minute writings. Score and hand in the better one.

Camping has become a favourite mode of vacationing for many	13
Canadians. What better way is there to see this vast and beautiful	26
land of ours than by driving in one's own car and stopping to set	39
up housekeeping for as long as desired before moving on to the	52
next camp?	54
A great deal of organization is required to get everything ready	67
and packed in or on the car, especially if you happen to drive one	81
of those small European cars. We have discovered that the trick, of	94
course, is to keep the inside of the car free for passengers, so that,	108
in our family, five people and a dog can have the maximum comfort	121
while driving. On the car-top carrier must be packed, covered, and	135
strapped, one tent, sleeping bags for the children, a cot, an air	148
mattress and blankets for Mother, and all the swimming equipment.	161
Behind the back seat, a food-cooler chest, a gasoline stove, at least	174
one water jug, dishes, cutlery, pots and pans, a pail, a dishpan, and	188
other miscellaneous articles must be arranged for easy accessibility	202
and re-packing. There are always dish towels, rope for clotheslines,	216
coat hangers, clothes pins, bug bombs, a first-aid kit, matches, an	229
axe, and a hammer.	233
Clothes must be provided for every conceivable type of weather	246
and for each member of the family. Since the weather will probably	259
include hot days, cool days, cold nights, and the rainy periods, this	273
is quite a chore.	277

Suggested procedure:

1. Type a draft of the body of the letter using double spacing. Your draft will include a short paragraph for each of the following points:

   (a) a thank you for the letter and invitation
   (b) time and date of arrival on the bus
   (c) a question about what clothing and sports equipment to bring with you.

2. Remove your paper from the typewriter. Using a pen or pencil, proofread your letter. Write in any changes you may wish to make in sentence structure and spelling.

3. Change to single spacing. On a half sheet of Typing paper, type your letter. Use the same set up as you used for Jobs 1 and 2.

Lesson 38

WARMUP

Speed **You can see many of the old cars at the far end of the road.**

Numbers **50 km/h 6630 km; 10 m; 0.8 g; 6 mm; 180 cm; 30 kg; 140 km/h.**

Accuracy **fever jump cedar waxed pink taste mop gaze waste lion freeze**

Personal-Business Letter

A popular form for a personal-business letter is illustrated on page 49. This kind of letter is typed on standard letter paper. Follow the suggestions given in Lesson 36 for the set up of an informal personal letter. In addition, note the following points:

1. Include the name and address of the person to whom the letter is being sent. This is called the Inside Address. Leave 6 line-spaces between the date and the inside address.

2. Double space before and after the salutation.

3. Use a business complimentary closing, such as Yours very truly, or Very sincerely yours.

4. Type the sender's name 6 line-spaces after the complimentary closing.

The personal-business letter on page 50 is typed on school letterhead paper. When the heading is printed on the paper, there is no need for the sender to type his return address. On occasion, you may be required to type a letter for a club for which you are the secretary, or to write on behalf of your school or class to thank a speaker. It will then be in order for you to use the appropriate letterhead paper.

When typing on letterhead paper, start the date on line 14, or two line-spaces below the printed heading.

Job 3.

Address large envelopes for each of the letters in Jobs 1 and 2. Prepare self-addressed envelopes which are to be enclosed in each of the letters.

THINK AS
YOU TYPE

Write a letter to a well-known personality in your community asking for his/her views on the importance of spelling. Request that he/she list ten words which, from his/her observation, are frequently misspelled. Explain that several letters are being sent out from students of your class to members of the community. From the replies to your letters, your class plans to prepare a list of frequently misspelled words which each of you hopes to master.

Lesson 124

WARMUP

Speed   If they plan to come, all your new work should be done soon.

Accuracy   Design the corporation's headquarters in contemporary style.

Numbers   Type by 5's from 0 to 100.

Job 1.

Review the invoice form on page 183, and then type up invoices for the following orders (Use today's date):

(a) Order #67541
    From: Western Book Store 167 Portage Ave
          Winnipeg, Manitoba   R2L 2X2
    To be shipped to: same
    Via: CN freight
    Items:

50 Leonard — Canadian Accounting	6.00	300.00
40 Shaffer — Canadian Retailing	7.00	280.00
10 Price — Auditing Practice	7.50	75.00
Total		655.00

(b) Order #235
    From: Students' Book Cooperative 126 Graham Avenue
          Brandon, Manitoba   R7B 5J2
    Ship to: same
    Via: Hoyt's Transport
    Items:

100 Lavers — Junior Mathematics	3.75	375.00
250 Eston — World Geography	4.25	1062.50
75 Roth — Organic Chemistry	5.10	382.50
Total		1820.00

Job 1. Copy the letter below.

5 Fellbrigg Avenue
Toronto, Ontario
M8N 2E4
19-- 11 21

Miss Joan Stevens
2742 Cypress Street
Vancouver, British Columbia
V6S 8B3

Dear Miss Stevens:

This letter shows you how you use the blocked style
to type your own personal-business letters on plain
paper.

This type of letter differs from an informal personal
letter in that the inside address is included. The
appropriate title, Miss, Mrs., Ms., or Mr., is typed
before the name in the inside address. If the letter
is short, the space between the date and the inside
address may be extended to 9 lines.

At the bottom of the letter, type your name below the
space where you will sign the letter. Always be sure
to include your handwritten signature.

Yours very truly,

John P. Wilkinson

John P. Wilkinson

Lesson 123

WARMUP

Speed If I send the goods next week, will you be able to use them?

Alphabet To adjust quickly even the best tax programme was hazardous.

Numbers we 23 up 70 yet 635 tip 580 ripe 4803 tore 5943 puppy 07006

TIMED WRITING
1 AND 3 MINUTES

All around us there seem to be unhappy people who cannot arouse 14
any enthusiasm for their daily work. When I view their sad plight, 27
I am reminded of the story of the two men who were laying bricks on 40
a big construction job. A visitor, who had stopped to look, asked the 54
first man what he was doing. "I'm laying bricks. Can't you see?" was 69
his short and surly answer. The visitor then asked the second man 82
what he was doing. He replied, "Sir, I am building a cathedral." In 95
that little story lies the secret of being happy in the work you do. 109

If you can see that your job, however junior it may be, contributes 123
something essential to the total effort of your organization, then 135
there will be kindled in you an enthusiasm that will make each day a 149
new and happy experience. But if you never see beyond the routines 162
of your own little job, if you never look at your work in terms of a 176
contribution to a greater whole, then you will feel that your daily 189
stint is only a drudgery to be endured. 197

Job 1.

Set up the following letter using blocked style and open punctuation.

19-- 03 22

Fort Garry Hotel, 590 Maitland Avenue, Winnipeg, Manitoba R3E 1V5
Attention: Reservation Clerk, Gentlemen:

Will you please reserve a single room with bath for Mr. Antonio
Giacomelli, commencing April 4. Mr. Giacomelli will be travelling Air
Canada and his flight is scheduled to arrive in Winnipeg at 18:45.

Mr. Giacomelli expects to remain in Winnipeg for one week and
would like to have a fairly large room in which he can entertain guests.

A confirmation of the reservation would be appreciated. Enclosed
is a self-addressed envelope for your convenience. Very truly yours,
Louanna Rawana, Sales Secretary.

Job 2.

Send the same letter as in Job 1 to the Bessborough Hotel, 496 River Road,
Saskatoon, Saskatchewan S7M 0H4. Mr. Giacomelli will be arriving there
on April 11 at 20:15 via Air Canada.

Student Council

CENTRAL SECONDARY SCHOOL

P.O. Box 430   Milk River, Alberta

TOK 1M0

January 7, 19..

Mr. M. Caliri, Manager
Transway Bus Company
4750 Fairway Road
Lethbridge, Alberta
T3M 4S1

Dear Mr. Caliri:

As Secretary of the Student Council at Central
Secondary School, I wish to enquire about the
facilities your company has for bus tours.

There are 23 students in our Council, and we
are planning to visit the new Urban Centre in
Calgary. Will you please let me know if you
can accommodate our group, what the rates would
be, and how much time would be required for the
trip there and back. We would like to visit
Calgary on the first Saturday of February.

Please let me have this information as soon
as possible as we are anxious to get our plans
under way.

Very truly yours,

Gloria Hunter

Gloria Hunter, Secretary
Student Council

Job 3.   Type the following on a single sheet.

PREPARE FOR JOB APPLICATION

Here are some tips that will help to put you at ease and to make the best possible impression when you go to apply for a position:

1. Be immaculately clean. Hair should be shining and simply arranged. Hands should be clean and well cared-for. Fingernails must be short for efficient office work. Use make-up carefully and sparingly.

2. Clothes should be neat and suitable for business. A suit or simple tailored outfit is best. Leave elaborate jewellery for party wear. Wear smart shoes which suggest neither a sports event nor a dance.

3. In your handbag, carry a couple of well-sharpened pencils, a pen, a pocket dictionary, and a good, clean eraser. A piece of chalk helps to hide an erasure.

4. Make a list of the questions you are likely to be asked. Have someone ask you these questions and practise expressing your answers in a clear, concise manner.

5. If you have any certificates for skills achieved, take these along to show if they are asked for.

6. Do some research on your prospective employer. Find out as much as you can about the company and its activities. If there are products involved, learn what they are and how they are used.

7. Determine how much time will be needed to arrive at the interview punctually and without rushing. Include some time for unforeseen delays.

Job 4.   Type the following Bibliography on a single sheet of paper.

BIBLIOGRAPHY

DeVaughn, A. G., "Why Good Beginners Fail in the Office," BALANCE SHEET, Vol. 36: 103-105, 107.

Haskell, Francis L., "What to Expect of Office Beginners," OFFICE FORUM, Vol. 25: 3-6.

Liles, Parker, "An Appraisal of the Beginning Office Worker," MODERN BUSINESS EDUCATION, May, 1972.

Scheer, Wilbert E.: "Why Are So Many Job Applicants Rejected?" BUSINESS EDUCATION WORLD, Vol. 37: 19.

Seeley, Horace I., "Personal Standards for Office Workers," CANADIAN BUSINESS, Vol. 36: 345-47.

Whale, Leslie J., "Standards for Beginning Office Workers," BUSINESS EDUCATION FORUM, Vol. 5: 14-15.

Job 5.   Type a Cover Sheet for this Report. Refer to Lesson 110. Use the heading, "A Report on Job Application for the Beginning Office Worker."

Lesson 39

WARMUP

Rhythm be on to he in so if at by go as is or do an my am me it we

Alphabet abc def ghi jkl mno pqr stu vwx yza bcd efg hij klm nop qrs

Numbers 123 456 789 012 345 678 901 234 567 890 123 456 789 012 345

Letter Set Up

Job 1. Type the following personal-business letter in blocked style, using mixed punctuation.

```
                                        Your address
                                        Today's date

        Mr. John R. Grover
        10694 Jasper Avenue
        Edmonton, Alberta
        T5J 2A5
        Dear Mr. Grover:
        The executive and members of the Strathcona Young Peoples'
        Club have asked me to express to you their thanks for the
        splendid talk you gave at the October meeting.
        Your remarks were timely, interesting, and inspiring and
        aroused much favourable comment among the members. Two of
        our study groups plan to use the topics suggested in your
        talk.
        We hope that we may have the pleasure of listening to you
        again soon.                     Very truly yours,
                                        Eric Anderson
```

Job 2. Type the following personal-business letter in blocked style, using mixed punctuation. Use letterhead paper if possible.

```
        Mr. R. Jackson
        Central Secondary School
        155 Oneway Street
        Ottawa, Ontario
        K1S 2E5
        Dear Mr. Jackson: On behalf of the Boys' Athletic Council
        at West Park Secondary School, I would like to thank you for
        taking part in our special auditorium program of January 10.
        It is not often that we are privileged to have anyone as
        well known in the sports world as yourself come to speak to
        us. The message which you brought on opportunities in sports
        will be remembered by all for many years to come.
        We appreciate your taking the time to spend the morning with
        us. Very sincerely yours, Brian Morrison
```

Lesson 122

Rhythm a b c d e f g h i j k l m n o p q r s t u v w x y z a b c d

Shifting Halifax Moncton Hamilton Quebec Windsor Saskatoon Vancouver

Numbers tier 5834 tire 5843 try 546 tree 5433 trip 5480 tripe 54803

Job 1.

The following jobs go together to make up a brief report, similar to the one you typed in Lessons 106-110. Type each job on a separate sheet of paper, assemble them, and staple them together. You will type a Table of Contents, the first two parts of the report (Jobs 2 and 3), the Bibliography, and a Cover Sheet.

TABLE OF CONTENTS

Job 2.

Type the following on a single sheet. Use a 60-stroke line and double line-spacing, except for the tabulated list.

THE COMMERCIAL GRADUATE AND THE WORLD OF BUSINESS

Before you think of looking for employment, you should take a long look at yourself to see where you would fit into an employer's estimate of the qualities needed by beginning office workers. The following is a list of factors which are taken into consideration by personnel officers when they are hiring office workers:

Attitude	Personality
Potential	Education
Intelligence	Energy
Common Sense	Health
Skill Developed	Appearance
Accuracy	Age and Maturity
Experience	Enthusiasm

Now is the time to do something about any of the points about which you feel inadequate. Your teachers will be glad to help you. Be prepared! Nothing will give you more confidence and self-assurance.

Type a personal-business letter to a Steel Company near you. Your class is working on a project dealing with the manufacture of steel. You are writing on behalf of your class requesting information which could be used in the project. Your class project is due three weeks from today. Type a draft of your letter, make changes and corrections in pen, and retype your letter in proper form.

Lesson 40

WARMUP

Rhythm Go to the end of the road to see what you can see.

Alphabet The quick brown fox soon jumped over the lazy dog.

Numbers 500 coats, order #6780, dated September 8, $169.75

Addressing Envelopes

1. The writer's complete address should be single spaced in the upper left hand corner of the envelope. It should begin on line 3, three spaces from the left edge of the envelope.

2. On small envelopes, the address block should usually begin on line 12, ten spaces to the left of the centre of the envelope. Make sure, however, that the address starts high enough so that the Postal Code appears between 5-8 line-spaces above the bottom of the envelope. The Postal Code must be on the last line of the address.

3. The first line of the address gives the individu-

al's name, complete with title (Mr., Mrs. Miss, Ms., Dr., etc.).

The second line gives the name of the company, school, or other organization with which the individual is connected.

The third line gives the street address (or rural route number) and the apartment number, if any.

The fourth line gives the city or town and the province. The province may be typed in full, or one of the accepted abbreviations may be used. See list on the next page.

The last line of the address gives the Postal Code.

The day the threshers arrived was the most wonderful day of the 14
year to farm youngsters a half century ago. The children had been 27
looking forward to it ever since the hum of the binders had been 40
heard from the fields. Now the grain had all been cut and heaped 53
in beautiful stacks of sheaves. The stacks stood four to a group, far 67
enough apart each way so that the separator could be spotted to take 80
advantage of the wind at the time. The youngsters kept a sharp eye 94
on the weather and on the road. Presently the cry, "Here they come," 107
was heard from the scouts at the gate, and everybody rushed into 120
the field to watch the machines being spotted for the first setting. 134

Down the road came the big separator, drawn by two teams of 147
beautiful horses hitched tandem. They swung into the field and, 161
directed by the man in charge, drew up between the first two stacks 175
in such a way that dust and straw would be blown to the rear of the 188
machine and the wind would aid the pitchers, whose task it would 201
be to pitch the sheaves from the stacks to the feeder of the separator. 215

Then followed the huge steam engine, also drawn by two teams. 228
It made a wide swing around the stacks and stopped facing the 241
separator at a spot marking the end of the great drive-belt that had 254
been run out by the separator man. Holes were quickly dug behind 267
the big hind wheels of the engine, the belt was put on the fly-wheel, 281
and the engine pushed back by the pole team until the wheels settled 295
in the prepared holes, thus tightening the long belt to the desired 308
tension. The water tank pulled up beside the engine, the pitchers took 322
their places on the stacks, the grain wagons backed up to the bagger, 336
and all was ready to start the yearly threshing chore. 347

Job 1.

Write sentences using each of the following words correctly:
affect, effect, weather, whether, then, than, access, excess, raises, rises.

Job 2.

Type each of the following sentences replacing the word "fantastic" with a
more suitable alternative.

1. The ride through the Rocky Mountains was fantastic.
2. My sister has a fantastic job.
3. Our school band gave a fantastic performance.
4. Many fantastic people will attend our Athletic Banquet.
5. We notice a fantastic drop in the stock market today.

THINK AS
YOU TYPE

Form nouns ending in "ance" or "ence" from the following words:
depend, resist, accept, persevere, insure, excellent.

Check with your dictionary for the correct spelling and meaning of each
word. Compose six complete sentences using each of your nouns.

CANADIAN PROVINCES
AND TERRITORIES

Usual Abbreviation		Official Abbreviation		Usual Abbreviation		Official Abbreviation
Alta.	Alberta	AB		N.S.	Nova Scotia	NS
B.C.	British Columbia	BC		Ont.	Ontario	ON
Lab.	Labrador	LB		P.E.I.	Prince Edward Island	PE
Man.	Manitoba	MB		P.Q.	Quebec	PQ
N.B.	New Brunswick	NB		Sask.	Saskatchewan	SK
Nfld.	Newfoundland	NF		Y.T.	Yukon Territory	YT
N.W.T.	Northwest Territories	NT				

The Canadian Postal Code

The Canadian Postal Code was introduced April 1, 1971, in the city of Ottawa. Now all addresses in Canada have a Postal Code. Each Code uses this pattern of letters and numbers:

LetterNumberLetter one space NumberLetterNumber

For example, an address in Winnipeg might have the following code:

R2H 1H8

The first group of three characters indicates a postal area; the second group indicates a local delivery unit such as a large apartment building, or one side of a city block, or a single rural route.

A Postal Code should appear on a line by itself below the last line of the address, within the last 5-8 line-spaces above the bottom edge of the envelope. At the post office, Optical Character Recognition Equipment reads typewritten Postal Codes and sorts the mail mechanically, with great speed and accuracy. (Mail that does not bear a Postal Code must be sorted, much more slowly, by hand.)

It is expected that in the near future OCR Equipment will be capable of reading handwritten Postal Codes also.

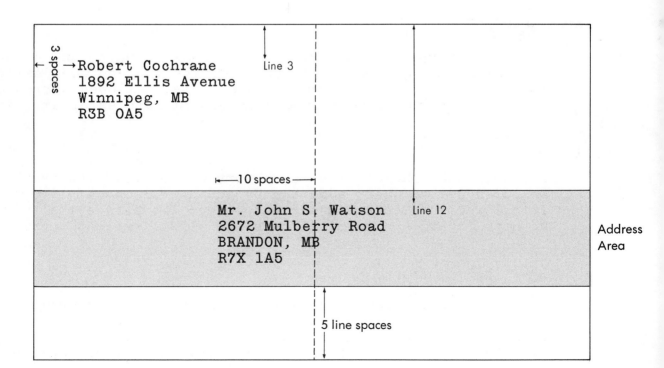

You are the head of the Fund Drive for St. Andrews College Alumni, Ottawa Branch. Write a letter to Miss Elva Roberts thanking her for her contribution of $25 to your Memorial Building Fund. Enclose a receipt for this amount. Supply all necessary letter parts. Prepare an envelope for your letter. Place the receipt on top of the letter when folding for insertion in the envelope.

Lesson 121

WARMUP

Rhythm abcdefghijklmnopqrstuvwxyz abcdefghijklmnopqrstuvwxyz abcdef

Top Row #89 "65" 9 g $12 10% 678 & 890 (142) 8 mL 785* 9 cm 1 890.00

Attention Type the following line according to the instructions contained in it.

Type in all capitals every word that has a T anywhere in it.

WORD FAMILIES

unk chunk flunk chipmunk junk skunk spunk trunk shrunk plunk
add added adding addicts addition address adduced addressing
wed sewed sawed vowed viewed slowed glowed followed borrowed
ext extra extinct extend extension exterminate extol extract

SPEED SENTENCES

The chipmunks showed great spunk trying to avoid the skunks.
Children polish their addition by adding columns of figures.
I followed in a borrowed car and viewed the parade that way.
We hope to avoid extermination of an almost extinct species.

ACCURACY SENTENCES

The deficiencies cannot be attributed to small expenditures.
Technicians are puzzled and bewildered by the peculiarities.
Major discrepancies in the inventories agitated accountants.
Absenteeism and lack of punctuality irritated your employer.

Job 1.   Using actual envelopes or slips of paper cut to envelope size, address the envelopes that you would send to the following persons.

```
Miss Margaret Conroy          Mr. P. T. Esposito
274 Lawrence Avenue West      1625 Wellington Street
Toronto, Ontario              Arnprior, Ontario
M3H 2A5                       K8N 2E7


Mr. Victor Pieczonka, Manager Mr. Robert Wexford
Regal Publishing Company      19 Linden Lane, Apt. 504
1836 Monroe Avenue            Prince Albert, Saskatchewan
Victoria, British Columbia    S6V 2P5
V5R 1S4
```

Job 2.   Type the following personal-business letter using today's date. For your address, use 68 Glenridge Road, St. Catharines, Ontario, N6T 9K5. Address an envelope for your letter.

```
Booth's Hobby Shop
173 Concession Street
Hamilton, Ontario
N3P 4S4
Gentlemen:  On a recent visit to your city, I purchased an
H. O. Lionel model railroad set from your store.  I
assembled the model exactly according to instructions, but
the transformer overheats.
I would like to exchange this transformer for one that will
work.  However, as I will not be able to get to your store
until next month, will you please send a new transformer
to me at the above address. I will bring in the one I now
have next month when I go to Hamilton. Sincerely yours,
```

Lesson 41

WARMUP

Rhythm **the and but for was you are she her yet not out it**
Alphabet **Fox Zebra Beaver Lion Tiger Monkey Elephant Walrus**
Numbers **On August 4, 3795 members from 68 clubs will meet.**

Lesson
120

Speed   He plans all his work so that it will be done when you come.

Accuracy   Maximum consequences from minimum initiative are attainable.

Numbers   Beginning with 4, type every fourth number up to 92.

Business Forms: The Receipt

Another form that requires typing on ruled lines is the receipt. A carbon copy is usually required.

```
                                        19-- 02 14
                                       _____

Received from  The Board of Education, Borough of West York
              _____
The sum of     One Hundred and Nine - - - - - - - -50 DOLLARS
              _____ 100 _____
For                    On account
              _____
                                   The Regent Publishing Company

No. 65        _____
```

Job 1.   Make a copy of the receipt illustrated above.

Job 2.   Prepare receipt #66, dated August 15, for $85.60, received from John Graham for August payment.

Job 3.   Prepare receipt #67, dated August 15, for $106.70, received from Michael Loring, payment for invoice #679-B.

Job 4.   Prepare receipt #68, dated August 16, for $8.45 received from Joan Cartwright on account.

Job 5.   Prepare receipt #69, dated August 17, for $15.65, received from Gordon Matheson on account.

When the first settlers arrived in Canada, they found it to be a 14
land of forests. Since that time, large areas have been cleared, but 28
much of the country is still under forest cover. It is estimated that 42
almost half the land surface of Canada is wooded, and that three-fifths 56
of this area is capable of producing marketable timber. 68

A large part of the forest wealth lies in remote regions which are 82
hard to reach. However, with greater demands for forest products 95
and with the development of new ways of transporting the logs, much 108
of the timber not now available will be used. 117

Centring a Single Column

1. Set the machine for single spacing.

2. Clear the machine: move the margin stops to the ends of the line and clear out any tab stops that may already be set.

3. Find on what line typing should begin in order to centre the material vertically. (see Lesson 33)

4. Insert paper, straighten it, and space down to the line on which typing is to begin.

5. Centre and type the title.

6. Space down three lines to the body of the table (this will leave two blank lines between the title and the body). Centre the carriage.

7. Select the *longest* item in the column. This is your **column key.**

8. Backspace so as to centre the column key.

9. Set the left margin at the point to which you have backspaced.

10. Type the column beginning each item at the margin stop.

Job 1.

```
Ash
Robin
Elm
Lark
Oak
Canary          Column Key
Pine
Crow
Spruce
Duck
Maple
Gull
```

Centring Two Columns

1. Clear the machine.

2. Find on what line typing should begin to centre the material vertically.

3. Insert the paper. Space down to the starting line.

4. Centre and type the title.

5. Space down three lines to the body of the table. Centre the carriage.

6. Select the column key (the longest item) in *each* column.

7. Backspace so as to centre the column keys six spaces apart.

E.g.   SprucexxxxxxCanary
            sPrUcExXxXxXcAnArY

8. Set the left margin at the point to which you have backspaced.

9. Tap the space bar once for each stroke in the column key of column 1 (Spruce) and for each of the six spaces between the columns. Set a tab stop at this point.

10. Pull the carriage back to the margin. Type the first item in column 1. Tabulate to the stop and type the first item in column 2.

11. Return the carriage and begin the second line.

Business Forms: The Cheque

Many of today's business forms require typing on ruled or dotted lines. When this is necessary, adjust the paper so that the line on which you must type is in the same position as the *underscores* would be. Use the variable spacer in the left cylinder knob to adjust your paper.

The Board of Education
Borough of West York
8000 King Street
Dixon, Ontario
N8K 6Z9

No. 84   February 6   19—

Pay to the order of The Regent Publishing Company $ 109.50

One Hundred and Nine – – – – – – – – – – – – 50 DOLLARS
                                                100
                                        The Board of Education
                                        Borough of West York

Commercial Bank of Canada
Maple Branch
Dixon, Ontario
N9P 3V4

Job 1.   Copy the cheque illustrated above.

Job 2.   Prepare: Cheque #85, dated June 6, payable to Mr. John Fortin for $275.40.

Job 3.   Prepare: Cheque #86, dated June 7, payable to Eileen Forbes for $87.75.

Job 4.   Prepare: Cheque #87, dated June 10, payable to Dr. E. C. Scott for $7.50.

Job 5.   Prepare: Cheque #88, dated June 10, payable to The Courtland Ink Co. for $111.

THINK AS
YOU TYPE

Type a paragraph, discussing what you think are the three qualities most necessary in an office worker, e.g., honesty, a pleasant personality, good manners, good character, punctuality, skill at typewriting, ability to spell, ability to do arithmetic.

Job 2.

NATURE NAMES

	Ash	Robin	
	Elm	Lark	
	Oak	Canary	**Column Key**
	Pine	Crow	
Column Key	Spruce	Duck	
	Maple	Gull	

Lesson 42

WARMUP

Rhythm the not for was are you top but and cut out now new car use.

Alphabet Even the expert's query emphasized the growing lack of jobs.

Numbers $47 $28 $39 $10 $56 $47 $28 $39 $10 $56 $47 $28 $39 $10 $564

Centring Tables with Several Columns

The procedure is exactly the same as that for a 2-column table. The column key must be selected from each column and allowance must be made for a 6-space blank area between columns. In Job 1, for example, the column keys which determine the tab stops are:

SprucexxxxxxCanaryxxxxxxCrocus
  ↑   ↑   ↑
Left Margin   Tab 1   Tab 2

RULE: ALWAYS PUT 6 SPACES BETWEEN COLUMNS UNLESS YOU ARE INSTRUCTED TO DO OTHERWISE.

Job 1. Use a half-sheet of paper.

NATURE NAMES

Ash	Robin	Rose
Elm	Lark	Crocus
Oak	Canary	Tulip
Pine	Crow	Peony
Spruce	Duck	Daisy
Maple	Gull	Pansy

Job 1.   Copy the statement of account illustrated on page 184.

Job 2.   Prepare a similar statement to be mailed out on 19-- 06 30 for:

Mr. T. M. Kennedy, 374 Harrington Road, Guelph, Ontario N2T 4X9

	Purchases	Credits	Balance
Previous Balance			14.75
June 4	15.00		29.75
7	12.00		41.75
14		15.00	26.75
22	10.40		37.15

TIMED WRITING
1 AND 3 MINUTES

Canada is still one of the most sparsely settled regions of the world. 15
In area, ours is the second largest country in the world, being exceeded 29
in size by only the Soviet Union. But our millions of acres are popu- 43
lated by only twenty-two million people. 52

Moreover, our population is not spread evenly over our vast area. 66
Most Canadians live within a distance of 320 km of the Canada-United 79
States border, and more than one-quarter of them inhabit our five 92
largest metropolitan areas. This means that vast stretches of our 105
country, particularly in the North, contain very few people or even 118
none at all. 121

There are many reasons for the uneven distribution of Canada's 134
population. Severe climatic conditions, rugged terrain, and lack of 148
transportation facilities have discouraged settlement of many parts 163
of our country. However, as transportation methods improve, as we 176
learn to overcome climatic hazards, and as Canadians have need of 190
more mineral resources, the empty spaces of Canada will be filled. 203

Lesson 119

WARMUP

Speed Try to plan your new work so that it is done when she comes.

Accuracy Standardization of our manufacturing processes is necessary.

Numbers Beginning with 3, type every third number up to 75.

Job 2. Use a half-sheet of paper.

EASY WORDS

the	not	for
was	are	you
top	but	and
cut	out	now
new	car	use
men	job	saw
his	pay	one
her	old	all

Job 3. Use a half-sheet of paper.

STUDENTS' NAMES

Arnold	Phyllis	Helen
Mary	Ian	Jessie
Charles	James	Orville
Frank	Valerie	Phillip
Sharon	Florence	Rupert

Lesson 43

WARMUP

Rhythm from the, from them, from this, from these, from it

Accuracy a b C d e F g h I j k L m n O p q R s t U v w X y Z

Numbers we 23 you 697 top 590 yet 635 owe 923 toy 596 to 59

TIMED WRITING

One of the jobs that you will be called upon to do most often is to 14
arrange information in columnar form. If you follow the few simple 28
rules listed here, you will find the task is easy and pleasant. Information 44
so arranged not only looks neater but is also much more easily read. 58
In your own personal typing and in office typing, look for opportunities 73
to use this attractive, convenient arrangement. The reader will appre- 87
ciate your thoughtfulness in conveying the information in such an 100
effective form. 103

Lesson 118

WARMUP

Speed   I shall try to plan the work so that it is done when I come.

Accuracy   His reservations for temporary accommodation were cancelled.

Numbers   1904 was a leap year. Type all the leap years since then.

Business Forms: The Statement of Account

Another business form whose preparation can be speeded up by the use of the tabulator is the Statement of Account. Frequently, this form is prepared on the bookkeeping machine, but in smaller offices and in service businesses, you may be called upon to prepare it on the typewriter. The Statement of Account lists the purchases and payments which have been made during the previous month.

STATEMENT

The Regent Publishing Company
68 Maple Avenue
Toronto, Ontario
M1P 4B3

The Board of Education
for the Borough of West York
8000 King Street,
Dixon, Ontario
N8K 6Z9

Amount Paid

$ _____

Billing Date 19-- 01 31

Please detach and return this top portion with your payment

- -

Date	Purchases	Credits	Balance
			40.75
Jan. 4	25.00		65.75
7		25.00	40.75
18	39.90		80.65
24		10.00	70.65
27	38.85		109.50

The last amount in the balance column is now due
THE REGENT PUBLISHING COMPANY

Job 1. Set up on a half-sheet of paper.

COMMON WORDS

will	able	that	this
this	well	cash	over
give	from	sale	near
call	were	cost	gave
time	into	ever	take
come	gone	quit	them

Job 2. Set up on a half-sheet of paper.

TIMES IN THE DAY

Customary Method	24-hour Clock
2:30 a.m.	02:30
6:15 a.m.	06:15
10:23 a.m.	10:23
12:00 a.m. (noon)	12:00
1:30 p.m.	13:30
4:00 p.m.	16:00
4:08 p.m.	16:08
11:30 p.m.	23:30
12:00 p.m. (midnight)	00:00 or 24:00

THINK AS
YOU TYPE

Do you know Canada?

Set the left margin of your typewriter at 20. Set a tabulator stop at 52. Beginning at the left margin arrange the provinces of Canada in either alphabetic or geographic order. Tab over and beside each province type the name of its capital city as in the example below.

Alberta   Edmonton

Lesson 44

WARMUP

Rhythm   a ; s l d k f j g h f j d k s l a ; s l d k f j g h f j d k

Speed   You must know that this firm will send them some cash soon.

Numbers   the 4 the 7 the 2 the 9 the 3 the 8 the 5 the 6 the 9 the 6

Business Forms: The Invoice

An invoice is a bill which is sent by the supplier to the purchaser for goods received. In our example, The Regent Publishing Company is billing the Board of Education for the Borough of West York for books ordered on Purchase Order No. T4168.

INVOICE No. **6741**

The Regent Publishing Company
68 Maple Avenue
Toronto, Ontario
M1P 4B3

Sold To

The Board of Education
Borough of West York
8000 King Street
Dixon, Ontario
N8K 6Z9

Ship To

Winston Churchill C.I.
803 Queen St.
Clarkville, Ontario

Date 19-- 01 04   Via Truck   Order No. T 4168

Quantity	Author	Title	Price	Amount
3	Bigelow	Science Magic	2.25	6.75
5	Chantrell	Canadian Scene	1.50	7.50
2	Zsep	Working with Wood	3.15	6.30
1	Westbury	Economic Future of Canada	4.45	4.45
				$25.00

Job 1.   Copy the invoice above.

Job 2.   Type a similar invoice for goods ordered on Purchase Order No. T4169 in Lesson 116. Use surnames of your classmates under the column heading "Author."

Job 3.   Type a similar invoice for goods ordered on Purchase Order No. T4170 in Lesson 116. Use surnames of your classmates under the column heading "Author."

I Centring a Column Heading Which is Shorter than the Longest Item in the Column

1. Set Margin and tab stops as usual, disregarding the heading.

2. Find the difference between the length of the heading and the length of the longest item in its column,

E.g., *Girls* – 5 spaces

Catherine – 9 spaces
difference – 4 spaces

3. Divide the difference by 2 (ignore any resulting fractions); the answer is the number of spaces to indent the heading from the left edge of the column.

E.g., in Job 1.
```
        Girls
      Catherine
```

Rules for Displaying a Column Heading

1. Separate it from the title by 2 blank lines.

2. Separate it from the column by 1 blank line.

3. Underscore it. If it consists of two or more words, underscore them solidly.

4. Centre it above its column (see procedure above).

5. Capitalize each important word.

II Blocked Column Headings

If the column heading is the same length as or shorter than the longest item in the column, it is quite acceptable to start each column heading at the point at which its column begins.

Job 1. Set up on a half-sheet of paper.

OUR CLASS

Girls	Boys
Margaret	Kenneth
Jean	Graham
Dorothy	John
Catherine	George
Grace	Peter
Rose	Richard

Job 2. Set your left margin at 30 and set a tabular stop at 45. Use the words "singular" and "plural" for your column headings. Complete the following exercise.

Singular	Plural
lady	ladies
man	
banquet	
monkey	
deer	
mouse	
moose	
boundary	
niece	

Job 2.   Type a similar purchase order for books to be shipped to: Sir John A. Macdonald C.I., Quincy Crescent, Appleby, Ontario. Purchase Order No. T4169

6	Famous Pirate Stories	3.25	19.50
2	Hockey Heroes	2.75	5.50
1	Building the C.P.R.	4.10	4.10
3	Bush Pilots	3.60	10.80
		Total	39.90

Job 3.   Type a similar purchase order for books to be shipped to: Strathcona C.I., 201 Aylmer Ave., Holton, Ontario. Purchase Order No. T4170

4	Express to the Stars	5.75	23.00
3	The Young Islanders	2.95	8.85
2	Exploring the River	3.50	7.00
		Total	38.85

Job 4.   Set up in good form on a half-sheet of paper.

CANADIAN FACTS

Province	Capital	Largest City
British Columbia	Victoria	Vancouver
Alberta	Edmonton	Edmonton
Saskatchewan	Regina	Regina
Manitoba	Winnipeg	Winnipeg
Ontario	Toronto	Toronto
Quebec	Quebec	Montreal
New Brunswick	Fredericton	Saint John
Prince Edward Island	Charlottetown	Charlottetown
Nova Scotia	Halifax	Halifax
Newfoundland	St. John's	St. John's

Lesson 117

WARMUP

Speed   We must not make any plans to do the new work until he comes.

Accuracy   The elementary curriculum was determined by expert educators.

Numbers   Type the even numbers between 1 and 49.

Set up the following information in tabular form. Your first column will contain these words which are masculine: boy, man, drum major, count, bull, duke, ram, peacock, prince. Your second column will contain the feminine form of each of these words. Choose suitable column headings.

Lesson 45

WARMUP

Rhythm for the and wit aid die sow man sit pay six leg did nap pen

Speed She saw the old man hit the boy and cut his arm and his leg

Numbers we 23 up 70 to 59 it 85 or 94 pi 08 top 590 toe 593 you 697

Centring a Column Heading Which is Longer
Than the Longest Item in the Column

1. The heading itself is the "column key" for the column and is used in setting margin and tab stops as usual.

2. Type the headings.

3. Find the difference between the length of the heading and the length of the longest item.
E.g. in Job 1   Name of student – 15 spaces
Allan, Fred – 11 spaces
difference – 4 spaces

4. Divide the difference by 2 (ignoring any resulting fractions); the answer is the number of spaces to indent the column.

5. Reset the margin and tab stops to indent the column.

E.g. in Job 1.

Name of Student
Allan, Fred

Job 1.

DEBATING CLUB

Name of Student	Mark
Allan, Fred	68
Brown, Joan	72
Cowan, Eva	86
Gore, John	57
Harris, Rita	65
Jones, Roy	83
Moore, Jean	73
Rowe, Bill	79
Tait, Bill	69

Lesson 116

Speed   He came only to see what plans we had made for the new work.

Accuracy   His pugnacity jeopardized your usual amicable relationships.

Numbers   Type the odd numbers between 2 and 50.

Business Forms: The Purchase Order

A well-designed business form is so arranged that the typist can use the tabulator to type each column of information quickly. The *Purchase Order* below can be typed quickly using three tabulator settings.

A Purchase Order is a request to a manufacturer or wholesaler for supplies. In our example, the Board of Education for the Borough of West York wishes to purchase books from the Regent Publishing Company for use in Winston Churchill Collegiate Institute.

PURCHASE ORDER

The Board of Education
Borough of West York
8000 King Street, Dixon, Ontario
N8K 6Z9

To

The Regent Publishing Company
68 Maple Avenue
Toronto, Ontario
M1P 4B3

Date December 7, 19--

Order No. T 4168
Via: Truck

Ship To:

Winston Churchill C.I.
803 Queen Street,
Clarkville, Ontario

Quantity	Title	Price	Amount
3	Science Magic	2.25	6.75
5	Canadian Scene	1.50	7.50
2	Working with Wood	3.15	6.30
1	Economic Future of Canada	4.45	4.45
		Total	$25.00

Job 1.   Copy the purchase order above.

Erasing

Even if you are a fairly accurate typist, you may need to use a typewriting eraser. You can still be proud of your typewritten page even if it contains one or two skillfully made corrections. Follow this procedure when erasing on a single copy:

1. Lift the paper bail and turn the paper up so the error is on top of the cylinder. If the error is near the bottom of the page, turn the cylinder backwards.

2. Use the margin release to move your carriage to the extreme left or right.

3. Use your fingertips to hold the paper from slipping as you erase lightly, moving the eraser in a circular motion.

4. Brush away the eraser particles before returning the paper to the original printing point.

5. Type the correction lightly so your copy will have even shading.

Corrections on a single sheet are often made by using correction fluid or other cover-up materials which are on the market. Typewriting paper is now available on which you can make erasures with a regular pencil eraser.

Technique Pointers – Squeezing Words

Occasionally, in typing, it is necessary to erase and then squeeze extra letters into a space intended for fewer letters. This takes practice and is a skill all in itself. It has to be done well, or the whole piece of work will have to be repeated. Examine the examples:

```
I cannot do this.  It will cost 78.50.  Stand up straight.
I may not do this.  It will cost $78.50.  Stand up straighter.
```

To crowd letters together and to leave less than a full space between words, "hold" the carriage by slightly depressing the backspace key to keep the carriage from spacing normally. Practise the above two lines. See if you can get each of them in the same amount of space. The underlined parts of the second line are where the "squeezing" is required.

Technique Pointers – Spreading Words

Sometimes it is necessary to reverse the squeezing technique. You may need to spread a word to fill more spaces than are normally used by the word. To "spread" a word, you must hold the carriage to control the spacing, much as you did for squeezing. This takes practice. To gain practice, type the following lines, spreading the words that are underlined.

```
Everyone should belong. He must stay. I said it was not so.
Everyone must belong. He may stay. I say  it is not so.
```

Job 2.   Set up in semi-blocked style, using mixed punctuation.

June 23, 19 — —, Mr. T. R. Marling, 846 South Street, Saskatoon, Saskatchewan S8K 7S8 Dear Mr. Marling, subject: your policy #68421.

The policy which, for the past three years, has protected you against loss by theft or burglary, expires on July 1. To maintain the peace of mind and security that your insurance provides, you should renew your policy now.

All that you need to do to continue this fine protection is to sign the enclosed renewal form and return it to us before the end of the month. You will be billed for the premium later.

You will be pleased to know that the cost of your protection is the same as it was three years ago. The efficiency of the law-enforcement agencies in your community enables us to offer our insurance at the same low price.

Protect your valuable possessions by returning your signed renewal form today.

Very truly yours, The Royal Insurance Company Limited, F. R. Fraser, Regional Manager, Encl.-1.

Job 3.   Address small envelopes for each of the letters in Jobs 1 and 2.

THINK AS
YOU TYPE

You are the Credit Manager of ABC Rug Company. Compose a letter to Mr. Melvyn Schmidt requesting that he pay the $372.45 still due on the wall-to-wall broadloom that was installed in his house a year ago. Mr. Schmidt has paid $75 on his account. He has not made a payment during the last six months although you have written to him three times. Your company is impatient and is ready to place the account in the lawyer's hands.

Use the current date and supply the necessary addresses. Use a letter style of your choice. Address an envelope for your letter.

Lesson 46

Special Characters on the Typewriter

Most of the "Special Characters" on the typewriter have a standard position, just as the letters of the alphabet do. However, for a few of these special characters, there is a variety in the placement of the keys. Some of them do not even occur on the keyboard at all. For instance: (i) You may have @/¢ together to the right of the ";" key; or you may have ¢/6 and @/2; (ii) You may have */- or */8; (iii) Perhaps you have !/1 controlled by the "a" finger; or !/¾ controlled by the ";"

finger; or you may not have a ! at all. There are at least four other variations. Study your keyboard for the position of these special characters. If any are present on your keyboard, practise the correct reaches – from the home row key to the key desired. If a character is required that is not present, consult the chart below for the method of constructing the character. Where keys are used to intersect each other, use the backspacer Where the alignment is changed, use the variable line spacing mechanism, operated by hand.

Special Character	Use	Method of Construction
Addition (Plus)	$76 + 27 = 103.$	Hyphen intersected by apostrophe.
Subtraction (Minus)	$103 - 27 = 76.$	A single hyphen.
Multiplication	What is 3 x 3?	Use small letter x.
Division	$121 \div 11 = 11.$	Hyphen intersected by the colon.
Equality	$11 \times 11 = 121.$	Two hyphens, one below the other.
Degrees	Freeze at 0°C.	Small "o" raised above the line.
Superiors	$a^2 - b^2 = 285.$	Type number or letter above line.
Inferiors	H_2SO_4 and $H_2O.$	Type number below the line.
English Pound	The price, £5.	Capital L typed over small f.
Caret	He ran/slowly. very	Underscore, diagonal; centre word above.
Exclamation Point	Hurrah Hurrah!	Apostrophe over the period.
Solidus	120 km/h.	Use / meaning "per" with metric symbols.

Job 3. Set up in blocked style, using open punctuation.

19-- 01 17, Mrs. Paul Wallington, 714 Elm Crescent, Owen Sound, Ontario N7D 4H9 Dear Mrs. Wallington:

We are sending you by express today a new Ace floor polisher, model 66, to replace the defective one that you told us about in your letter of January 10.

In spite of the rigid inspection given to each polisher before it leaves our factory, an occasional machine fails to perform satisfactorily and to give the high standard of service that our customers have learned to expect from our product. We are always anxious to learn about these failures and to see that the machines are replaced immediately. Please return the defective polisher to us at our expense.

Very truly yours, T. S. Galbraith, Claims Manager.

Job 4. Address "small" envelopes for each of the letters in Jobs 1, 2, and 3.

Lesson 115

WARMUP

Speed We shall adjourn the meeting now and return again next week.

Accuracy The interior of an old building provides interesting relics.

Numbers E6J 3K6 S8K 7S8 H2N 9H6 N4G 5T7 E6J 3K9 P2R 4A3 1 000.

Job 1. Set up in blocked style, using open punctuation and the current date.

The National Nickel Company Ltd., 118 St. Clair Avenue West, Toronto, Ontario M3D T4P Attention: Publicity Department, Gentlemen:

We are preparing a geography textbook for use in Ontario high schools at the senior level. In the book, we are including a description of Canada's mining industry and the important role played by nickel.

To supplement the descriptive material, we want to obtain three or four black and white photographs. Ideally, these photographs should portray the mining of the ore and some of the refining processes.

We shall be grateful for any material that you can provide or for any suggestions that you would care to make.

Very truly yours, E. L. Henderson, Editor-in-Chief.

SENTENCES

Please deliver 10 @ 25¢ and 15 @ 50¢ early today.

The temperature varied from 0 °C to 9 °C yesterday.

"Come on!" yelled Phil, "Three cheers for Eliza!"

Solve the problem: (89 - 36) - (10)^2 = (14 x 4).

The chemical formula for Sulphuric Acid is H_2SO_4.

When in England, we had to pay £3 for a souvenir.

THINK AS YOU TYPE

A bulletin board tells who, what, whom, where, why, and how. Type a notice for the bulletin board concerning any activity which is to take place in your school or community in the near future. Make use of some of the special characters which you have learned in this lesson to give your bulletin board notice an attractive appearance. You may wish to design a border by combining several characters.

TIMED WRITING

What could be more fun than a parade? Here comes the first band,	14
drums rolling, and the brass section booming. Then march the men of	28
the Forces, each group showing pride in its uniform, each man erect	42
and straight as he strides smartly in step with his comrades. A thrill	56
passes through the cheering crowd at the sight. To add gaiety to the	70
day, the clowns trip along, pulling stunts to amuse the children. The	84
first float is very beautiful. The next one has a crazy clown doing a	98
dance. The very last one bears the Queen of the show. The noisy crowd	112
becomes hushed and quiet, and then it breaks once more into a loud	126
cheer. The strange part of it all is that the people who are watching	140
the parade are just as much fun to watch as the show itself.	152

Lesson 47

WARMUP

Rhythm   a; sl dk fj gh fj dk sl a; a;sldkfjghfjdksla;sldkfj

Shifting   A B C D E F G H I J K L M N O P Q R S T U V W X Y Z

Centring   TYPEWRITING TECHNIQUES

Extended Centring   T Y P E W R I T I N G   T E C H N I Q U E S

Job 1. Set up in semi-blocked style, using mixed punctuation.

19-- 02 15, Barry Bros. Ltd., 1836 Main Street, Winnipeg, Manitoba R3C 6D5 Attention: Mr. T. R. Hunter, Gentlemen:

Thank you for your letter of February 12 inquiring about our new filing equipment.

Mr. John Anderson, our sales representative, will be in Winnipeg on February 23 and I have asked him to call on you. Mr. Anderson is well qualified to advise you about filing equipment. He is prepared to survey your present equipment and to recommend new equipment that will improve the efficiency of your filing department.

A copy of a new brochure, "Filing in the Modern Office," is enclosed. It contains new and useful information about filing equipment and methods.

Very truly yours, W. L. Davidson, Sales Manager

Job 2. Set up in blocked style, using open punctuation.

19-- 04 24, Mr. Frank Carson, Crescent Heights Electric Co., 276 Union Street, Saint John, New Brunswick B6J 3K6 Dear Frank:

Our sales manager, Mr. George Fraser, will be in Saint John from May 3 to May 6. The purpose of his visit is to study sales methods in the electrical appliance field.

I have told Mr. Fraser about the success of your enterprises and have suggested that he contact you after his arrival in Saint John. Anything you can do to make his visit profitable and enjoyable will be very much appreciated.

Best personal regards to you and your family.

Sincerely yours, F. W. Manton, Managing Director.

Jack Vizen oft quit bridge to watch Miss Lex pay.

Six queer lazy black dogs jump over no waterfall.

Vonda exited quickly when Ferg jumped this zebra.

Job 1.   Make an exact copy of the following, "Typing Department — Bulletin No. 1." Use a full sheet of paper.

TYPING DEPARTMENT--BULLETIN NO. 1

September 10, 19--

C A R E   O F   T H E   T Y P I N G   R O O M

The routine jobs involved in the care of the typing room will help you to learn to keep your office in efficient working order. Develop habits of neatness and learn to care for all equipment that you use. Note the following:

1. All waste paper must be deposited in the waste receptacle.

2. Each typewriter carriage must be centred when the machine is not in use.

3. The typewriter cover is to be folded and put out of sight when the machine is in use. The cover must be placed on the machine for the over-night period.

4. All chairs should be pushed into the kneeholes of the typewriter desks when not occupied.

5. All the books should be stacked in a neat and orderly fashion on their assigned desks. Any other equipment should be stored away in the drawers and cupboards.

A TIDY ROOM PROMOTES EFFICIENT WORK

Job 2.   Type the same letter in the blocked style. This time begin the subject
line at the left margin and underline it. Address the letter to:

Mr. F. N. Chester, 722 Oxford Street, London, Ontario   N8G 7A3
mortgage #9247; due, April 12; principal $300.00; interest, $15.96.

Job 3.   Type the same letter in the blocked style. This time begin the subject
line at the left margin and put it in caps. Address the letter to:

Mr. Kenneth Conway, 630 Talbot Street, St. Thomas, Ontario   N5C 9E2
mortgage #7483; due, April 15; principal, $250.00; interest, $164.75.

Job 4.   Address "small" envelopes for each of the letters in Jobs 1, 2, and 3.

THINK AS
YOU TYPE

Type a paragraph entitled "Be on Time." Develop three reasons why you
think punctuality is a desirable characteristic.

Lesson 114

WARMUP

Speed   You can do the job now or you can do it as she does her job.

Accuracy   Reservations for accommodation must be received immediately.

Numbers   V3N 2B3   T4P 5L4   C5R 6D5   R3C 0A3   N7D 8E7   N9G 4H9   May 9.

Job 2. Set up on a full sheet of paper.

TYPING METRIC SYMBOLS AND NUMBERS

1. When associated with numbers, symbols for metric terms are used, e.g., 5 kg (not 5 kilograms).

2. Symbols have the same form in the plural as in the singular, e.g., 5 km (not 5 kms).

3. Do not put a period after a symbol except when it occurs at the end of a sentence.

4. Leave one space between the digit and the metric symbol, e.g., 10 cm, except when expressing temperature, e.g., 12°C.

5. In numbers of less than one, a zero is placed to the left of the decimal marker, e.g., 0.85.

6. Spaces (instead of commas) are used to separate numbers into groups of three, e.g., 22 629.423 236. The space is optional in 4-digit numbers, e.g., either 1 048 or 1048 is acceptable.

Job 3. Set up the following Menu on a half-sheet of paper, inserting the short side of the paper into the machine. Triple space.

Set the margin stops for 44 strokes. For the first line, type Sweet Mixed Pickles at the left margin. Move the carriage to the right margin stop. Backspace once for each stroke and space in Celery Hearts, then type. It will end at the margin. For the last line, begin Tea at left margin, centre Coffee, and backspace from right margin for the word Milk.

M E N U

Sweet Mixed Pickles   Celery Hearts

Tomato Juice

Roast Sirloin of Beef

Brown Gravy and Horseradish

Creamy Whipped Potatoes

Fresh Frozen Green Peas

Rolls and Butter

Strawberry Shortcake

Tea   Coffee   Milk

Job 4.   Address a large envelope for each of the letters in Jobs 1, 2 and 3.

THINK AS
YOU TYPE   Type a paragraph entitled, "How I Could Earn a Living if I Left School Now." What are you trained to do? Are you old enough to be employed? What sort of jobs could you do well enough to be paid for them? What kind of a future is there in these jobs?

Lesson 113

WARMUP

Speed If he will go now, he will be able to go as far as she did.

Alphabet zero quit just next from gave back hard your when pull will

Numbers August 18, September 27, October 25, November 4, December 6

Job 1.   Type the following letter in the semi-blocked style. Centre the subject line.

April 4, 19 — —, Mr. T. S. Terman, P.O. Box 657, Paris, Ontario N4D 6L2 Dear Mr. Terman: MORTGAGE #8167

You are reminded that the quarterly payment on the above mortgage will fall due on April 16. The payment amounts to $236.75, made up of principal, $200.00, and interest, $36.75.

For your convenience in making this payment, a cheque form and an addressed envelope are enclosed. Complete the cheque by filling in the name and address of your bank, sign it, and return it to us in the envelope.

If your quarterly payment is not received by the due date, a penalty payment must be levied against you. Don't delay — send your cheque today.

Yours truly, CROWN LOAN AND MORTGAGE COMPANY, R. Henning, Treasurer.

Lesson 48

Rhythm   with work wish they them such hand duty paid maid
Accuracy Montreal, Toronto, Vancouver, Winnipeg, Hamilton.
Numbers   1960 1961 1962 1963 1964 1965 1966 1967 1968 1969

TIMED WRITING

The next time that you hear someone say that he likes your city, 14
ask him why. His answer may surprise you. Most of us like a place 28
not because of its beauty, nor its graceful buildings, nor its fine shops, 42
but because of the people who live there. If the people are cheerful 56
and friendly, we like the place; if they are cold and aloof, we dislike 71
them and the place in which they live. Your town or city will be as 85
popular as the people who live in it – no more, no less. 96

Job 1.

You are Secretary of the Creative Typing Club in your school. Write a personal-business letter to the Editor of your school newspaper. Supply suitable heading, inside address, salutation, complimentary closing, and signature. The body of the letter is as follows:

The three winners of the recent contest for the "Creative Typing" award are members of the first-year typewriting class. The students' names and their topics are as follows:

Jim Peterson   The Sixteenth Round
Karen Timberly   Bronze Boots
Greg Webb   The Pearly Gates

These students are happy to give you permission to print any or all of their material in our school newspaper.

We think our school newspaper is the best ever printed. Thank you for the encouragement you are giving to all of us to contribute material for publication.

Job 2.

Address an envelope for the letter in Job 1.

THINK AS YOU TYPE

Type an informal personal letter to each of the winners of the "Creative Typing" award mentioned in Job 1. Congratulate them, and thank them for offering their compositions for publication in the school newspaper. Invite them to submit material for the next competition, which will be announced soon.

Lesson 112

WARMUP

Balanced hand land paid wish torn pale hang their blame towns title shape.

Alphabet Jackson was puzzled by the five or six queer green plywoods.

Numbers January 30, February 28, March 17, April 26, May 15, June 24

Job 1. Type the following letter in the semi-blocked style. Remember to indicate enclosures.

> The Jarvis Manufacturing Company, 786 Wellington Street, Ottawa, ON K7B 2T8 Attention: Mr. R. Raymond, Gentlemen:
>
> Our organization is making a survey of the accounting procedures used in this community. It is our hope that the results of this survey will be useful to the business schools in planning their courses and in teaching their students to be competent and efficient employees.
>
> You can help us to make this survey by answering the enclosed questionnaire and returning it to us before December 1. This question-naire has been carefully compiled by a committee of teachers so that you can provide the required information in the least possible time.
>
> When the results of the survey have been tabulated, a copy of the report will be mailed to you.
>
> Thank you for your co-operation and assistance.
>
> Very truly yours, OTTAWA BUSINESS EDUCATION ASSOCIATION, T. R. Phelps, Secretary.

Job 2. Type the same letter in the blocked style beginning the attention line at the left margin. Address it to:

> Ottawa Fuels Limited, 892 Carling Avenue, Ottawa, ON K4D 9Y6 Attention: Mr. R. Fraser.

Job 3. Using the blocked style and beginning the attention line at the left margin, type the same letter but address it to:

> Capital Business Equipment Limited, 618 Bank Street, Ottawa, Ontario K8T 9Y4 Attention: Chief Accountant.

Lesson 49

Rhythm if it is to be who and all for the men they will have this.

Speed Send the order now, and you may pay when you have the cash.

Upper
Reaches We thought that $751 was too much for only 34% of the time.

TIMED WRITING

It was a bright fall day, and the woods stretched invitingly beyond   15
the house. After lunch John took his gun from the rack and started   28
up the west trail. The warm sun soon caused him to shed his coat, and   43
he hung it on an old stump that had stood for years at a bend in the trail.   58
When he reached the brow of Lookout Hill, John remembered that   70
the shells for his gun were still in the pocket of his coat, but he decided   86
to go on without them. It was a decision that he was to regret for the   100
rest of his life.   104

Job 1.

Use a half-sheet of paper.

COMMON WORDS

if	and	will	first
is	all	more	large
it	for	have	order
to	the	like	small
be	men	this	could
by	who	they	bring

Job 2.

Use a half-sheet of paper.

CANADIAN PLACE NAMES

Sydney	Halifax	Yarmouth
Quebec	Moncton	Montreal
Ottawa	Toronto	Hamilton
Sarnia	Windsor	Kingston
London	Sudbury	Winnipeg
Barrie	Brandon	Edmonton
Oshawa	Yorkton	Red Deer
Regina	Calgary	Victoria

Commonwealth Products

KNOWN THROUGHOUT THE NATION

Executive Offices ....   220 Berkeley Street, OTTAWA, ONTARIO K2L 8D4

19-- 09 17

Miss Florence Greenley
Secretarial Department
Bruce District High School
Lynton, ON
N6D 9P3

Dear Miss Greenley:

10sp   SUBJECT: LETTER STYLES

In response to your enquiry of August 7, we are enclosing
a brochure entitled "Letters in Business" and a leaflet illustrating letter forms. These will answer your questions about
the various letter styles used in Canadian offices.

You enquired particularly about the display line known as
the "subject line." We have illustrated it for you in this
letter. You will notice that it is typed between the salutation and body and that one blank line is left above and below
it. Like the attention line, it can be either underscored or
typed all in capitals. It is commonly centred, but may start
at the left margin.

When something is to be mailed with a letter, the word
"Enclosure" is typed beneath the initials. This reminds the
typist to make the enclosure when the letter is folded and
inserted in the envelope. If more than one item is to be enclosed with the letter, a numeral indicating the number of
such items is typed after the word "Enclosures."

Yours very truly,

COMMONWEALTH PRODUCTS

Thomas D Inman

Thomas D. Inman
Correspondence Supervisor

10 →
Tab 20.
Tab 50

TDI:urs
Enclosures -- 2

Use a half-sheet of paper.

METRIC UNITS

Length Unit	Symbol	Mass Unit	Symbol
kilometre	km	tonne	t
metre	m	kilogram	kg
centimetre	cm	gram	g
millimetre	mm	milligram	mg

THINK AS
YOU TYPE

How athletically minded are you? Each of the following terms is used in a sport. Match each of these terms to the sport in which the word is used. Tabulate your two columns on a full sheet of paper. The first column will contain the terms used in a sport, and the second column will contain the names of the sports. Double space between each line and be sure to vertically centre the material. Use extended centring for a title for your exercise.

Snow Plow, Catcher, Foul Line, Infielder, Eight Ball, Butterfly, Guard, Spike, Gutter, Puck, Shortstop.

Lesson 50
Test

Job 1.

Suggested time: 15 minutes

Type two 2-minute writings. Score and hand in the better one.

Winter sports in Canada speak for the vigour	10
of our way of life. Most children learn to skate	20
before they start to school. Before long, we may	30
expect to observe them whizzing and twirling with	40
their sharp blades on the keen ice. Little girls	50
tend to favour figure skating while the boys just	60
love to play hockey. The young people of Eastern	70
Canada are fond of skiing, while on the prairies,	80
snowshoeing is quite popular. Next comes curling	90
which is a game that more people enjoy each year.	100
In a quest for thrills, the toboggan and the sled	110
provide fast rides over our snowy land.	118

Commonwealth Products

KNOWN THROUGHOUT THE NATION

Executive Offices . . . .   220 Berkeley Street, OTTAWA, ONTARIO   K2L 8D4

19-- 02 16

The Royal Publishing Company, Limited
1872 King Boulevard
Hamilton, ON
N6T 5L7

                    Attention: Miss L. Raymond

Gentlemen:

This letter contains a common display line known
as the "attention line." Although this letter is
addressed to a company, the attention line directs
it to the attention of a particular individual in
the company.

The attention line is typed between the address and
the salutation. A blank line is always left above
and below it. This display line is either centred
or begins at the left margin.

To make it stand out, the attention line is either
underscored or is typed all in capitals.

Sometimes it is considered desirable to include the
name of the company in the closing lines. Such company names are normally typed in capitals a double
space below the start of the complimentary closing.

                    Yours very truly,

                    COMMONWEALTH PRODUCTS

                    T. R. Ringwood

                    T. R. Ringwood, Manager

TRK:urs

Job 2.

Suggested time: 15 minutes

Type the following personal-business letter in blocked style, using mixed punctuation. Use today's date, and if possible, your school letterhead. Address an envelope for the letter.

Dr. Hugh Gagnon
Dean of Political Science
Mount Allison University
Sackville, New Brunswick
G2R 6A3
Dear Dr. Gagnon: The United Nations Club of our school is holding a special United Nations Assembly on the morning of March 10, 19--, commencing at 09:00. We wish to invite you to speak to us at that time.

The topic for our special assembly is "People of Other Lands". We have read many of your interesting articles on the work which you have done in other parts of the world. We hope you will share with us some of your experiences.

We hope that you will let us know that you will be able to accept our invitation to speak to the students of our school.

Sincerely yours, Marie Richard, Secretary

Job 3.

Suggested time: 15 minutes

Compose and type a personal-business letter in which you thank Dr. Gagnon for having spoken at the special United Nations Assembly on March 10.

Job 4.

Suggested time: 15 minutes

Type the following table in good form on a half-sheet of paper.

NEW LIBRARY BOOKS

Author	Title	Publisher	Pages
Browne, Ernest	Western Trails	Evergreen	320
Durand, Lois	Christmas Belles	Regal	352
Galland, John	Tommy Tucker	Empire	88
Martin, Helen	Lady at Court	Regal	369
Palmer, Francis	Gallant Pilot	Jupiter	480
Regan, George	Endless Frontiers	Evergreen	272
Stanton, Brian	Reckless Riders	Maple	336
Trevor, Cora	Seaside Saga	Styron	176
Walker, Hugh	Indian Days	Empire	354

Lesson 111

Speed   If you can type well, then you will like to do the job here.

Numbers   Anthony's speed increased from 100 km/h to 140 km/h in 10 s.

Accuracy   He emphasizes the extreme importance of productive capacity.

TIMED WRITING

1 AND 2 MINUTES

You are learning to type for one of two reasons. Either you want   14
to use the skill to help you earn a living, or you want to use it for   28
your own personal pleasure and satisfaction. In either case, the most   42
frequent use to be made of your skill will be in the typing of letters.   56
Because letters form a major part of the typewriting done in the   69
office and in the home, much of your practice time should be devoted   82
to this kind of material. It is not enough to set up a letter attractively;   97
it must be typed quickly and efficiently.   106

Display Lines in Letters

In this and succeeding lessons, lines that are added to the ordinary letter setup are illustrated. Some of the more common display lines are:

the Attention Line — this line directs the letter to the attention of one particular individual. It is inserted between the inside address and the salutation and is either underscored or typed all in capitals. It may be centred or start at the left margin. *This line has no effect upon the salutation, whose form is determined solely by the inside address.*

the Company Name as Part of the Signature — sometimes the name of the writer's company is inserted as part of the signature. It is usually typed in capitals a double space below the start of the complimentary closing. However, if the company name is a long one, it should be centred under the complimentary closing, so that it will not project too far into the right margin.

the Subject Line — the subject line is used to indicate what the letter is about. It is typed between the salutation and the body of the letter with a blank line above and below it. It may be underscored or typed all in capitals. It may begin at the left margin, but more commonly it is centred.

the Enclosure Line — to indicate that something is being enclosed with the letter, the word "Enclosure" is typed on the line immediately below the reference initials. If more than one item is to be enclosed, the word "Enclosures" followed by a numeral indicating the number of such items is used. The purpose of this line is to remind the typist to make the enclosures when the letter is folded and inserted in the envelope.

Job 1.   Copy the sample letter on page 173.

Job 2.   Copy the sample letter on page 174.

Job 3.   Address "small" envelopes for each of the letters in Jobs 1 and 2. Type the Attention Line below the return address as instructed in Lesson 62.

Job 5.   Manuscript Typing

Suggested time: 15 minutes

Set up the following program on a half-sheet of paper. Use a 50-stroke line. Remember to backspace so that each name ends at the right margin.

CONGREGATIONAL DINNER

CENTRAL UNITED CHURCH

Tuesday, 6:30 p.m.   October 10, 19--

Grace   Bill Jones
Dinner   Courtesy of W. A.
Scripture and Prayer   Rev. J. T. Spence
Proposals for next year   Ann Thomson
Supporting our Proposals   John Smith
The Annual Canvass   Keith Brown
Hymn Sing   Bob Black
Guest Speaker   Rev. K. T. White
Appreciation   Rev. J. T. Spence
Question Period   Rachel Williams
Closing Prayer   Rev. J. T. Spence

Job 6.   Suggested time: 10 minutes

Type the following sentences twice. Check and hand in the better copy.

1 The chemical equation was $2NaOH + H_2SO_4 = Na_2SO_4 + 2H_2O$.
2 They bought 250 shares @ $15.65 and 500 @ $16.37.
3 He got £500 from his aunt and £100 from his uncle.
4 Prove: $(250 - 100) \div (35 - 30) = (900 \div 10) - (600 \div 10)$.
5 As he fell into the hole, Fred cried, "Help! Help!"
6 He should interview Smith & Jones and/or Black & White before Friday.

Job 1.

A "Title Page" or "Cover Sheet" is often required for typewritten material. You have been saving exercises done in this section of manuscript typing. Make your own cover sheet for this group of exercises. Use the information given below.

T Y P I S T ' S   M A N U A L

A set of rules to be used
in the typewriting classes
at
(YOUR SCHOOL)

Prepared by
(Your name and class)
for
(Your teacher's name)
(date)

Job 2.

Collect in proper sequence your typewritten jobs from the last four lessons. Take each page in turn, insert in your typewriter, turn down to line 5, and type on it the page number as follows:

Typist's Manual   Page 1

Job 3.

Set up and type a "Table of Contents" page for your manual. Centre it both vertically and horizontally, and double space the items. Now with the Title Page on top, followed by the Table of Contents and the pages in correct sequence, staple the sheets in the upper left-hand corner. Your Manual is complete.

THINK AS YOU TYPE

Type as many words as you can make using only the letters in the word ENCOUNTERS. For each word containing three (or fewer) letters score one point; for each four-letter word score 2 points; for each five-letter word score three points; and for any word containing more than five letters score five points. A score of 75 is good; a score of 100 is excellent; a score of 150 is outstanding!

Lesson 51

Rhythm   a;qpa; slwosl dkeidk fjrufj ghtygh fjrufj dkeidk slwosl a;q

Alphabet   axe size quite jam bad fat can was ago van cry pal keg hello

Speed   dad mum tot sis bob non pop pip eye did pup wow tut gig bib

Numbers   1 and 2 and 3 and 4 and 5 and 6 and 7 and 8 and 9 and 0 and

Punctuation

The proper use of punctuation marks makes the material which you compose at the typewriter easier to read and understand. You will be able to communicate your thoughts to your reader more clearly if you use appropriate punctuation marks and correctly spelled words.

Apostrophe Guides

1. If you wish to make a singular noun possessive, add 's to show ownership. E.g., the boy's bike.

2. If you wish to make a plural noun possessive,
(a) add ' if the plural noun ends in s
(b) add 's if the plural noun does not end in s.

E.g., the boys' bikes, the men's cars

3. If you wish to form the plural of signs, numbers, or letters, add 's. E.g., #'s, 10's, A's, and B's.

4. If you wish to show the omission of letters or figures, indicate the omission by inserting an apostrophe. E.g., don't, class of '72.

APOSTROPHES ILLUSTRATED

Copy each sentence, noting the use of the apostrophe.

1 Jim's book was in his brother's room near his friend's coat.
2 The women's screams echoed among the woods' towering timber.
3 I.Q.'s are not rated by the number of A's, B's, C's and D's.
4 We're unable to attend the next reunion of the class of '68.

THINK AS YOU TYPE

A Retype the following sentences, inserting apostrophes where necessary.

5 When a skunk lifts its tail, thats a sign its frightened.
6 The childrens aunt spent the last half of the 1970s in Asia.
7 Electricians helpers dont help carpenters.
8 Its Jacks car, isnt it?
9 Both boys boots were too small for Petes big feet.

B Use each of the following verb forms in a separate sentence. As you compose each sentence, remember that the subject must agree with the verb.

type, was crying, went, drive, will eat
goes, have been walking, erases, swim

III. Books of Facts
1. _The World Almanac_, New York, The New York World - Telegram and The Sun.
2. _Columbia Encyclopedia_, New York, Columbia University.

IV. Directories
1. Local city directory.
2. Local telephone directories

V. Geographic and Travel Information
1. _Rand McNally Commercial Atlas_, New York, Rand McNally and Company.
2. _Canada Postal Guide_, Ottawa, The Queen's Printer.
3. Road maps and travel-information service companies.

VI. English Grammar and Style Books
1. Smith, Reed: _Learning to Write_, Revised Edition, Toronto, The Macmillan Company of Canada Ltd.
2. Stewart, Lanham and Zimmer: _Business English and Communication_, Canadian Edition, Toronto, McGraw-Hill Ryerson Limited.

Lesson 110

WARMUP

Rhythm — a;qpa; slwosl dkeidk fjrufj ghtygh fjrufj dkeidk slwosl a;q

Shifting — Canada United States Newfoundland New Brunswick Nova Scotia

Numbers — It has 14.1 mg iron and 20.4 g protein per 100 g of cereal.

Henry led a very dull life. Each day he drove in his car to an office 14
which was located in an old and dreary building. There he checked 27
invoices to see that they had been made out properly and added up 40
correctly. If he found an error, he sent the offending invoice back to 54
the girl who had typed it. He ate his lunch at his desk, and his lunch 68
always consisted of a ham sandwich on rye bread, an apple, and a 81
small carton of skim milk. It took Henry exactly ten minutes to eat 94
his lunch. Since he was allowed an hour, Henry always read a library 108
book for the remaining fifty minutes. The library books, which he 121
borrowed three at a time, were historical novels, and none of them 134
contained any coarse words or immoral ideas. But Henry did have one 147
vice, and this was to prove his undoing. 155

Lesson 52

WARMUP

Rhythm   `a;qpa;slwosldkeidkfjrufjghtyghfjrufjdkeidkslwosla;qpa;slwosl`

Alphabet   `abcdefghijklmnopqrstuvwxyz abcdefghijklmnopqrstuvwxyz abcdef`

Numbers   `" on 2 # on 3 $ on 4 % on 5 _ on 6 & on 7 ' on 8 ( on 9 ) on`

Stroking   `far fare fat fate fee feet foe fought fight frighten freight`

Comma Guides

1. Use the comma to separate words or groups of words in a series.

2. Use the comma to separate two independent clauses joined by a conjunction such as "and" or "but".

3. Use the comma after a dependent clause which opens a sentence.

4. Use commas to set off appositives. Appositives are words which give additional information about a person or thing just mentioned.

5. Use the comma to indicate the omission of a word.

COMMAS ILLUSTRATED

Copy each sentence, noting the use of the comma.

1 `I did nothing but eat, sleep, read, and swim on my holidays.`
2 `We tried to be on time, but today our automobile broke down.`
3 `When we flew over the country, we saw many beautiful sights.`
4 `Mr. Doucet, our typing teacher, went to England this summer.`
5 `Jan read the novel; Fran, the play; and Ron, the manuscript.`

II. Following abbreviations, place a period, followed by one space.

III. In using decimals, a period is used to separate a whole number from a decimal fraction, with no space before or after the period.

IV. In outlines, a period is placed after the number or letter used to indicate a division in the outline. Do not use a period when the number or letter is accompanied by parentheses. E.g., (a)

V. Do NOT Use a Period--

1. After Roman Numerals, except in outlines. E.g., Part I; Chapter IX; Queen Elizabeth II
2. After display headings or titles.
3. After items in a list.
4. After metric symbols.

Job 2. A Bibliography is a list of publications which may contain the names of books, magazines, and articles. The following is one way of setting up such information. In the description of the publication, indent all lines but the first.

Avis, et al. Dictionary of Canadian English. Toronto: W.J. Gage Limited, 1967.

Type the following list of reference books for the typist from the handwritten copy. Save this list.

Reference Books For The Typist (Block Caps)

I Dictionaries and Word Books
1. Webster's New International Dictionary of the English Language, Third Edition, Springfield, Mass., G. & C. Merriam Company.
2. Roget's Thesaurus of the English Language in Dictionary Form, New York, G. P. Putnam's Sons, Inc. (How to find the word to fit an idea.)
3. Leslie: 20,000 Words, Sixth Canadian Edition, Toronto, McGraw-Hill Ryerson Limited. (A pocket-sized book for checking spellings and divisions.)

II Financial Information
1. Dun & Bradstreet's Ratings and Reports, New York, Dun & Bradstreet.

A In each of the following, the main clause opens the sentence. Retype the sentences making the dependent clause open the sentence.

E.g.   I shall have to catch an early bus if I wish to get there on time.
If I wish to get there on time, I shall have to catch an early bus.

1 You may go home at noon if you finish your work this morning.
2 Our telephone will be disconnected unless we make a payment soon.
3 The doctor will call you when the tests are completed and checked.
4 **The new manager closed the bank although it was only noon.**
5 He wrote the annual report while the meeting was in progress.

B Set up the following words in tabular form. Remove your paper from the typewriter and on another sheet type the words as they are dictated to you by your partner or your teacher. Check your words for correct spelling. Use each of the words in a separate sentence.

absence	lose	forty
disagree	accommodate	partial
fierce	receive	amateur
foreign	truly	enemies
occasionally	paid	villain

Lesson 53

WARMUP

Rhythm   `a;qpa;slwosldkeidkfjrufjghtyghfjrufjdkeidkslwosla;qpa;slwosl`

Alphabet   **`Pay quickly lest Max just seize our five white books and go.`**

Numbers   **`(10) (23) (47) (58) (69) (84) (65) (93) (72) (83) (62) (183)`**

Stroking   **`it in ill ice icon ideal ides idiom idle idol ignite ignore`**

Quotation Marks Guides

1. Quotation marks are used to set off the direct words of a speaker. When using quotation marks, refer to the following guides for correct punctuation and capitalization.

(a) At the end of a quotation, the period or comma is placed inside the quotation marks.
(b) If the quotation asks a question, the question mark is placed inside the quotation marks; otherwise, the question mark is placed outside the quotation marks.
(c) Precede a direct quotation with a comma.
(d) Capitalize the first letter of a quotation. Begin the second part of a divided quotation with a small letter unless it starts a new sentence.

2. The title of a book, song, or play may be set off in quotation marks. A comma should be used if the title is in apposition.

7. If two numbers form one item, one of them, usually the shorter, is spelled out. E.g., twelve 16-room houses.

II. Type numbers as figures —

1. In all statistical and tabular work.
2. When a large number occurs. E.g., 1827.
3. If several numbers occur in a connected group, including those under ten and round numbers.
4. For all dates. E.g., December 25, 1955 or 1955 12 25.
5. When writing amounts of money in business correspondence.
6. When expressing percentages. Use % sign in tabular work, but 8 per cent in context.
7. In correspondence for dimensions, measures, masses, degrees, distances, volumes, and market quotations. E.g., 8°C, 9 kg, 6 L
8. For house and street numbers.
9. For time, when the 24 hour clock is used. E.g., 08:30.

III. Use Roman Numerals —

1. For important divisions of literary and legislative material. E.g., Volume I; Part III; Chapter IX.

Lesson 109

WARMUP

Rhythm `a;qpa;slwosldkeidkfjrufjghtyghfjrufjdkeidkslwosla;qpa;slwosla`

Shifting `British Columbia Alberta Saskatchewan Manitoba Ontario Quebec`

Numbers `weepy 23306 witty 28556 wrote 24953 wiper 28034 writer 248534`

Job 1.   Read and study the following rules for the use of the period. Set and type the rules for your collection. Save your finished work.

RULES FOR THE USE OF THE PERIOD

I.   End of a Sentence--

1.   Place a period after a sentence that makes a statement or issues a command.
2.   Place a period after a condensed expression that represents a complete statement. E.g., Yes, by all means.
3.   Use a period, instead of a question mark, after a request that is phrased in question form out of courtesy. E.g., May we have a copy of your price list.
4.   Use a period after an indirect question.

Copy each sentence, noting the use of the quotation marks.

1 "I would like a word with all of you," bellowed the captain.
2 He turned and asked, "You aren't actually serious, are you?"
3 Did the owner of the band really say, "I have enough money"?
4 "And furthermore," continued the speaker, "they were right."
5 We wrote the play, "Once Upon a Time," for today's assembly.

THINK AS YOU TYPE

Type the following:

1 Mr. Schram said, "All that glitters is not gold."
2 Miss Venturini remarked, "A stitch in time saves nine."
3 Mrs. Rogers commented, "Out of sight, out of mind."
4 Hannah replied, "Absence makes the heart grow fonder."

Describe in your own words the meaning of each of the quotations used by the above speakers.

TIMED WRITING

In surveys made to find why some people do not succeed in their   14
jobs, the same answers keep cropping up time and time again. Em-   26
ployers value most highly a person who can be depended upon. What   40
does this mean? It means, simply, that the person who has been hired   54
to do a job will arrive on time, will do a good day's work without   68
wasting his own time or that of his co-workers, will not find excuses   82
to take a day off, and will put his best effort and skill into every task   96
that is given to him to do. He will be loyal to his firm, will not tell   111
all he knows about its inner secrets, and will strive to get along well   124
with those with whom he works. Will your employer be able to depend   138
upon you?   141

Lesson 54

WARMUP

Rhythm   a;qpa;slwosldkeidkfjrufjghtyghfjrufjdkeidkslwosla;qpa;slwos

Alphabet   Ezra Axel Vic Ike Joy Gwen Bea Quincey Pete Doris Faith May

Numbers   we 23 wet 235 wetter 235534 wit 285 wittier 2855834 rio 489

Stroking   go got gum gun gift get greet greed grease gave grave grade

II. Capitalize proper nouns and adjectives; that is, the names of persons, places, things, or adjectives derived from those names. E.g., Canada; Canadian.

1. Do not capitalize words that were originally proper names, but are no longer used in that sense. E.g., french dressing; india ink.
2. Capitalize official titles of honour and respect when they precede personal names. E.g., Professor McDonald; Pope John; Uncle Harry.
3. When a title follows the name in a sentence, do not capitalize the title.
4. In the inside address of a letter and on an envelope, capitalize all titles whether they precede or follow the name.
5. Capitalize names of firms, companies, associations, societies, commissions, committees, bureaus, boards, departments, schools, political parties, clubs, and religious bodies.
6. Capitalize trade names and brand names.
7. Capitalize names of countries, international organizations, national, provincial, and city bodies.
8. Capitalize names of definite geographic localities such as provinces, cities, mountains, rivers, parks, oceans, and streets and buildings.
9. Capitalize the names of the days of the week, months, holidays, and religious days.

III. Capitalize a common noun when--

1. Used alone as a well-known short form of a specific proper name. E.g., the Lakes (the Great Lakes).
2. The dictator of a letter refers to "the Company" in place of the full name of the concern.

Job 2. Read and study the following rules for the use of numbers in typed work. Type the rules on a full sheet of paper. Save your finished work.

RULES ON HOW TO WRITE NUMBERS

I. Type a number spelled out as a word —

1. If the number is below 10.
2. When the number is an approximate or round number. E.g., Send forty or fifty samples.
3. When a number begins a sentence.
4. If the number is used as an ordinal (first, second).
5. When the number is a fraction standing alone. E.g., give him two-thirds of the books.
6. If the number is the name of a century. E.g., the twentieth century.

Capitalization Guides

In addition to the first word of a sentence, the following proper nouns should be capitalized:

1. Names of people and titles used for specific persons.

2. Names of countries, provinces, states, and geographic areas.
3. Names of schools, universities, and colleges.
4. Names of historic events and holidays.
5. Names of races, organizations, and members of each.
6. Trade names.

CAPITALIZATION ILLUSTRATED

Copy each sentence, noting the use of capital letters.

```
1  If John and Mary can come early, Mother can look after them.
2  On your first trip to Canada, be sure to visit the Prairies.
3  You can get a course at the Ryerson Polytechnical Institute.
4  At Thanksgiving, they visited battlefields of the Civil War.
5  They discovered that many of the Eskimo boys are Boy Scouts.
6  Trade names like Thermos and Kleenex became household words.
```

THINK AS YOU TYPE

A Retype the following paragraph inserting capital letters where they belong.

The bus pulled out of wesley centre onto king street to give the people a view of the federal building. Nearby, the prime minister was giving a talk for the chamber of commerce who were gathered in gage park beside the east river bridge.

B Set up the following words in tabular form. Remove your paper from the typewriter and on another sheet type the words as they are dictated to you by your partner or your teacher. Check your words for correct spelling and capitalization.

Saint John	Charlottetown
Edmonton	Portage la Prairie
Fredericton	Sydney
Chicoutimi	Estevan
Nanaimo	St. John's

Use a map of Canada to help you discover the province where each of these places is located. Compose a sentence using each of these place names with its province. Try to discover an item of interest concerning each place.

E.g., The Reversing Falls are located in Saint John, New Brunswick.

One of the interesting characteristics of present-day Canadian society   14
is the increasing amounts of leisure time that are available to most   28
citizens. Over the past decade or two, the length of paid vacations has   42
increased steadily. Today, it is quite common for an employee with   55
ten or twenty years' service to receive four, five, or even six weeks of   69
vacation each year. The length of the work week is also being shortened.   84
For many years, the five-day week has been the accepted standard in   97
most parts of the country, and now in many industries the four-day   110
week is already a reality.   115

The increasing time available for leisure and recreation does raise   128
problems. Many of the facilities that are popular for leisure activities   142
are already being used to their full capacity, and it will be necessary   156
to expand them quickly. During the summer months, every camp   168
ground in the country is filled, golf courses are crowded, and tennis   182
courts have long waiting lists. Hobbies of every type are thriving.   195
More and more Canadians are collecting rocks, antiques, stamps, coins,   209
and works of art. Supplies of many of these items are becoming scarce,   223
and the beginning collector is faced with constantly rising prices.   236

Lesson 108

WARMUP

Rhythm a b c d e f g h i j k l m n o p q r s t u v w x y z a b c d

Shifting Ottawa Victoria Calgary Regina Brandon Peterborough Halifax

Top Row My mass is 70 kg; Melissa's, 62 kg; and the baby's, 3.5 kg.

Job 1. Read and study the following rules for using capital letters. Type the rules on a full sheet of paper. Keep your finished work.

RULES FOR USE OF CAPITAL LETTERS

I. Capitalize the first word of--

1. Every sentence or group of words used as a
    sentence.
2. Direct quotations.
3. Lines of poetry.
4. Each item in an outline.

Lesson 55

WARMUP

Rhythm   `a;qpa; slwosl dkeidk fjrufj ghtygh fjrufj dkeidk slwosl a;q`

Alphabet   `A b C d E f G h I j K l M n O p Q r S t U v W x Y z a B c D`

Numbers   `In 1950, Canada paid out $297 514 000 in family allowances.`

Stroking   `hot hat ham hand handle here hire hone home hope have helps`

Number Representation Guides

The following points will help you to decide whether to use figures or letters for numbers.

1. Spell out any number which starts a sentence.
2. Spell out any number below ten. However, if the number is used in a sentence with other numbers above ten, use figures for the sake of uniformity.
3. – Use figures when representing distances, dates, percentages, amounts of money, hours, and page numbers.
4. – Use figures to express exact age in days, months, and years.

NUMBERS ILLUSTRATED

Copy each sentence, noting how the numbers are expressed.

1. `Fifteen seconds are needed to allow the cement to take hold.`
2. `There were three boys and seven girls on the two committees.`
3. `Have you heard that 4 and 20 blackbirds were baked in a pie?`
4. `Supper is served around 19:00 daily so please come at 18:30.`
5. `We have owned the horse for 23 years, 7 months, and 10 days.`
6. `On May 3, 90 per cent of John's shots passed the 200 m mark.`
7. `Refer to the footnote on page 17 and the summary on page 99.`

THINK AS YOU TYPE

Using the following opening sentences, complete the stories to explain what is happening and why. The use of direct quotations stimulates the reader's interest. Remember to use correct spelling and punctuation marks in order to help clarify your meaning.

1. "Now listen, son," pleaded the officer who had climbed the great height of the tower, "don't risk your life on that." His pointed finger drew the youth's attention to

2. Frantically she leafed through the pages searching for the name "Starr" that would mean her code was complete. Time was running out, for at 24:00 her contact would

3. Nothing could stop the countdown. All the switches were thrown and a panel of green lights glowed at them. But still no one noticed the red flashes

10. Before and after a colon when expressing time.
11. Before the ¢ sign.
12. Following a period within a group of small letters.

II. TAP THE SPACE BAR ONCE--
1. After a comma.
2. After a semicolon.
3. After the period that indicates an abbreviation.
4. Before a constructed fraction.
5. Before and after the &.
6. Before and after the @.
7. Between the digits expressing year, month, and day.
8. Between a number and the following metric symbol.
9. Between groups of 3 digits to the left and right of the decimal.

III. TAP THE SPACE BAR TWICE--
1. After the period ending a sentence.
2. After the question mark.
3. After the colon.

Job 2.   Review the following rules about the use of quotation marks with punctuation marks. Set up and type the rules and examples on a full sheet of paper. Save your finished work.

USE OF QUOTATION MARKS WITH PUNCTUATION MARKS

1. The closing quotation mark goes after a period.
      I said, "Throw it away now."
2. The closing quotation mark goes after a comma.
      "Do come again," said Betty.
3. The quotation mark precedes a semi-colon.
      I said, "Do it"; so she did.
4. The quotation mark precedes a colon.
      Our "Motto": "We always try."
5. The quotation mark goes after a question mark if the quotation asks a question.
      I said, "When will it come?"
6. The quotation mark goes before the question mark if the question is not in quotation.
      Did she say, "Give it away"?
7. The quotation mark goes after an exclamation mark if the quotation is an exclamation.
      I shouted, "Yes, we scored!"
8. The quotation mark goes before an exclamation mark if the exclamation is not in quotation.
      How ridiculous to "quibble"!

It was a big thrill to climb aboard the giant plane that was to carry us two-thirds the way across Canada. We got on at Toronto International Airport where the sun was shining on a lovely summer day. As we were borne aloft, we could see the great sprawling city behind us and the wide expanse of Lake Ontario to our left. It seemed but a few minutes before we were passing over the vast wooded area of Northern Ontario dotted with lakes and rocks. Then we saw a very dark sky ahead of us, and there were flashes of lightning. The plane climbed higher. We seemed to be floating in a land of nowhere. All we could see was the sun above and a sea of clouds below. Later, as we winged our way over the prairie region, we could not quite believe that the world could be so flat. When we came to the mountains, we were equally dazed by the majesty of those snowy peaks. All too soon, we could see the ocean spread out in front of us, and we were coming down in Vancouver.

15
28
41
55
69
82
95
109
123
137
151
164
178
192
196

Lesson 56

WARMUP

Rhythm   a;sldkfjghfjdksla;sldkfjghfjdksla;sldkfjghfjdksla;sldkfjghfj

Alphabet   Queen Val Liz Axel Gwen Beth Fred Mary Joan Cupid Doris Kate

Numbers   120 394 586 379 465 960 245 378 931 405 210 340 415 617 8190

WORD FAMILIES

1 ard, bard card guard hard shard ward sward reward
2 ble, able table stable cable fable ramble capable
3 est, best guest jest lest pest quest rest nearest
4 not, notarial notable notices notch notify notion
5 ple, sample temple staple simple cripple disciple

Job 1.

On a full sheet of paper, make a copy of the illustration on the next page, "To Type a Short Essay." Follow the instructions given in the illustration.

Do you feel that you are becoming a competent typist? You should 14
now be able to handle your machine with ease. You are thoroughly 27
familiar with the keyboard and have gained in both speed and 39
accuracy. You have learned many skills such as centring, tabulation, 53
display techniques, letter set-ups, correction of rough drafts, and 66
doing some of your own composition at the machine. 76

To help you become more competent by adding auxiliary skills, 90
you are going to apply your knowledge of manuscript and display 102
typing to set up a series of notes on various aspects of punctuation, 116
capitalization, syllabication, and the use of numbers in relation to 130
typing. This series will be complete with the addition of a Table of 143
Contents and a Cover Sheet. 149

Lesson 107

WARMUP

Rhythm   asdfg ;lkjh asdfg ;lkjh asdfg ;lkjh asdfg ;lkjh asdfg ;lkjh

Accuracy   Six jovial antics of Becky quite amazed a large happy crowd

Numbers   I. II. IV. V. 1. 2. 3. 4. a) b) c) d) (i) (ii) (iii) (viii)

Job 1.   Review the following rules for using the space bar. Set up and type the notes on "Rules for Using the Space Bar." Save your finished work.

RULES FOR USING THE SPACE BAR

I.   DO NOT TAP THE SPACE BAR--

1. Before or after a hyphen.
2. Before or after a dash.
3. Between quotation marks and the words enclosed.
4. Between parentheses and the words enclosed.
5. Before or after a decimal.
6. Between the # symbol and numbers.
7. Before the % symbol.
8. Before the symbols ' and " to mean minutes and seconds
9. Between a key fraction and the number preceding it.

TO TYPE A SHORT ESSAY

How often have you wished that you might type out your English or history essays? It is really very simple. Note that all compositions, essays, or manuscripts, whether long or short, are double line-spaced. Be sure to set your line-space indicator at two. If your essay is very short, use a 50-stroke line. If the essay is longer, use a 60-stroke line. Since your work will be double spaced, you must indent for the beginning of each new paragraph. This means that you will need one tab stop, five spaces in from the left margin. Now, you are ready to begin.

Imagine your essay as a picture in a frame. You want to have good margins at the top, at the bottom, and on both sides. Centre the title on the twelfth line down from the top of the page. Remember always to leave two blank lines between the title and the body of any display typing. When your typing of the body of an essay is finished, type your name about five centimetres from the bottom of the page to balance the title. It looks more attractive if you backspace from the right margin before typing, so that your name ends at the margin.

Janet Williams

II. Enumerating and Indenting

    1. Use letters or numbers to separate the divi-
        sions and subdivisions in your notes. Roman
        Numerals are usually used to indicate the main
        divisions. Capital letters, small letters,
        and arabic numerals are used for further
        divisions.
        a) Follow each guide with a period or a
            right bracket sign.
        b) Space twice after the period or bracket.
    2. Indent further for each succeeding step
        in the outline.
        a) Set three or four tab stops each four
            spaces apart starting at left margin.
        b) Keep indentations the same for similar
            steps in the outline.
    3. If using Roman Numerals that take more than
        one space, use the margin release in order
        to backspace from the left margin.

III. Line Spacing

    1. Always leave two blank lines before the
        Roman Numeral indicating a main sub-division.
    2. Always leave one blank line after the Roman
        Numeral indicating a main sub-division.
    3. Single space all other lines.

Job 2. Read and review the following "Rules for the Division of Words." Set up and type these rules on a full sheet of paper. Keep your finished work.

RULES FOR THE DIVISION OF WORDS

1. Divide a word only when you cannot avoid it.
2. Divide between syllables. For example: men-tion. A good typist keeps a dictionary handy and consults it when he is in doubt about the proper syllables in a word.
3. Divide as close to the middle of the word as possible. For example: pronun-ciation, rather than pro-nunciation.
4. Words that are pronounced as one syllable are never divided. E.g., shopped, brought, string.
5. Do not split a word unless you can leave at least three strokes before the division (the third may be a hyphen). E.g., you may divide be-fore, but not alone or about.
6. Do not divide contractions such as wouldn't, couldn't, etc.
7. Never divide an abbreviation such as RCMP or YWCA.
8. Do not divide a number written in figures. An exception may be made for a very long number, using a space as the dividing point. E.g., 497 000-000 000.
9. Do not divide a proper name such as Canada, Susan, Macdonald, or Limited.
10. Divide after a prefix. E.g., contra-diction, rather than con-tradiction.
11. Divide before a suffix. E.g., reason-able. Where a consonant is doubled before adding a suffix, divide between the double consonants. E.g., ship-ping.

Job 2.

Follow the instructions given in the illustration for Job 1. On a full sheet of paper, set up and type the following short essay, entitled, "How to Write an Essay."

HOW TO WRITE AN ESSAY

A good essay is well organized and presents a logical arrangement of facts and ideas. Before starting to write, one should decide upon the purpose of the essay. Then, a brief outline should be prepared stating the purpose of the essay. This should be followed by a good arrangement of headings for the facts and ideas to be presented.

The next step is to make certain that the headings come in the proper order to provide a logical development of the theme of the essay. The writer must be sure to choose a very strong and effective point on which to finish the essay. It is also vitally important that he have a good opening paragraph, which will grasp the attention of the reader and lead him to read further.

Once the writer has his ideas on paper and a good plan outlined, it is a fairly simple task to do the writing and to expand his ideas with clarity. He can give examples and illustrations to reinforce the points he wishes to make. He must be sure of his facts, and he must prove his points. Any opinions expressed should be backed up by experience or by sound reasoning.

It takes practice to write a good essay. However, a well organized plan will help students to achieve the desired goal.

Your name and class.

Lesson 57

WARMUP

Rhythm   a b c d e f g h i j k l m n o p q r s t u v w x y z abcdefgh

Accuracy   Five wizards jumped over those fourteen green boxes quickly.

Top Row   #98 "65" $13 10% 567 & 390 (142) 08:30; 295* 9 @ $0.75 $185.

Centring

CENTRAL COLLEGIATE INSTITUTE

Job 1.

Type the following invitation on a half sheet of paper, inserting the longer edge in the machine. Use double line-spacing, and centre each line. The / indicates the separation of lines. Use *extended centring* for 'ANNUAL GRADUATION EXERCISES'. Remember that there is never any punctuation at the end of any centred line.

The Principal and Staff / and / The Home and School Association / of / DEEP GLEN DISTRICT HIGH SCHOOL / request the pleasure of your company at the / ANNUAL GRADUATION EXERCISES / to be held in the / Auditorium of the School / on Tuesday, June the Twenty-eighth, / at Eight o'clock.

As you read your daily newspaper, you can find many humorous items 13
that reveal the friendly rivalry that exists between various pairs of 27
Canadian cities. Although Victoria is the capital of British Columbia, 41
Vancouver, Canada's largest seaport, is more important commercially. 54
In Alberta, Calgary and Edmonton are old and traditional rivals, Cal- 68
garians boast of their world famous Calgary Stampede, and Edmon- 81
tonians participate enthusiastically in their Klondike Days. Saskatoon's 95
mayor once (in jest) announced that he felt he should take out a large 109
insurance policy on his life before making an official visit to Regina, the 124
"Queen City of the Plains". 129

Toronto and Montreal are the country's keenest rivals. Both are ports 143
and bustling industrial centres. Both are large metropolitan areas and 157
vie with each other in the fields of sport, entertainment, and culture. 171
Both can boast of their universities which are famous centres of learn- 185
ing. Both can claim much of Canada's early history in their back- 198
grounds. Both have modern subway systems, but they argue about the 211
efficiency of the subway cars and the beauty of the subway stations. 225

Each Canadian has his own reasons for choosing his favourite city. 238
What is your choice? What are your reasons for making it? 251

Lesson 106

WARMUP

Rhythm a;sldkfjghfjdksla;sldkfjghfjdksla;sldkfjghfjdksla;sldkfjghf

Speed It is very wise to count the seats after you open the door.

Numbers pure 0743 purr 0744 pore 0943 pout 0975 pyre 0643 poor 0994

Job 1.   Read and study the following article before typing it. Set up and type,
"Rules for Setting Up a Page of Notes," just as it appears below. Retain
your finished work.

RULES FOR SETTING UP A PAGE OF NOTES

I.   Placement and Margins

    1.   Centre the longest line, and set the margins
         to accommodate that line. Remember to allow
         for the Roman Numerals that indicate the main
         headings.
    2.   Centre the material vertically by counting the
         number of lines.

Job 2.

Type the invitation in Job 1 on a half-sheet of paper, inserting the shorter edge in the machine. Follow the instructions given for Job 1.

Job 3.

Use a full sheet of paper to type the following menu in an attractive style. Use as many devices for display typing as you can. Here are some suggested devices:

Where there are only two items in a course, these might be set against each margin — e.g.,
Consomme au Sherry   Cream of Mushroom

Where there are several choices in a course, these should be grouped together by single line-spacing the grouped items.

Some decorative typing (such as the use of asterisks) could be used effectively between courses.

NEW YEAR'S DAY DINNER / Hearts of Celery, Baby Sweet Gherkins, Radish Roses, Manzanilla Stuffed Olives / Chilled Fresh Fruit Cocktail / Consomme au Sherry, Cream of Mushroom / Baked Tendersweet Ham with Glazed Pineapple, Roast Young Turkey with Cranberry Orange Relish, Roast Sirloin of Beef au jus, Curried Jumbo Shrimps Carolina / New Green Peas with Mint, Glazed Beets, Creamed Whipped Potatoes Duchesse / Hot Mincemeat Pie with Brandied Hard Sauce, Old English Plum Pudding with Rum Sauce, Chocolate Grenadine Parfait, Orange Sherbet / After Dinner Mints, Assorted Fruit Tray / Tea, Coffee, Milk / January 1, 19 - -, Price $9.00 / For very special guests under 10 years of age $4.50.

THINK AS YOU TYPE

ATTRACTIVELY DISPLAY AN ADVERTISEMENT FOR A 1965 SECOND-HAND PINK CADILLAC.

Lesson 58

WARMUP

Rhythm   asdfg ;lkjh asdfg ;lkjh asdfg ;lkjh asdfg ;lkjh asdfg ;lkjh

Shifting   Black Byron Davies Foley Grant Jones Roux Quamme Wiley Zaph

Numbers   we 23 wet 235 were 2343 weep 2330 wort 2945 type 5603 we 23

SPEED SENTENCES

```
A jury ruled that the treasury had inflicted injury on them.
Those victims lived in the vicinity of the village vicarage.
A pantomime was part of the programme that the panel judged.
It is maintained that certain grains are unsuitable for use.
```

Composition Skills

We usually think of a verb as a part of speech that expresses action. There are several kinds of verbs and they may take various forms. So that the material which we compose will be clearly understood by the reader, it is important that we try to use the correct verb form at all times. Remember, the verb must agree with its subject. e.g.: The *Prime Minister*, as well as his advisors, *is going* to China. *One* of our calculators *does not work.*

Job 1.

Type the following sentences choosing the correct verb form.

There (is, are) dances every Saturday night.
The band (help, helps) us to buy new uniforms.
Accuracy and speed (is, are) both important to the typist.
Each of the boys (work, works) at the Steel Company of Canada.
None of the players (is, are) going to university.
Your father and I (am, are) growing old.
The laziness of the two helpers (were, was) unbelievable.
Neither the parents nor the child (was, were) watching the light.

Job 2.

Type the following sentences correctly. If necessary, use your dictionary to help you make the proper selection of the words in the brackets.

He came upon the (scene, seen) of the crime.
Ottawa is the (capital, capitol) of Canada.
He will (accept, except) the teacher's (advice, advise).
The electrician may (loose, lose) the (loose, lose) wire.
The poor weather may (affect, effect) their (assent, ascent) of the mountain.
The (sight, site, cite) of the building is in (sight, site, cite) of the lake.
The (principal, principle) upheld the school's (principles, principals).
The student had (excess, access) to the (stationary, stationery).

THINK AS YOU TYPE

Give the verb forms of the following words:

agreement, presentation, permission, remittance, insertion, renovation.

Consult your dictionary for the correct spelling and meaning of each word. Compose six complete sentences using each of your verbs.

The Use of Leaders in Typewritten Work

The use of LEADERS is a display technique which is effective, and sometimes necessary so that the eye can follow what is typed. This technique consists of joining up two points on the paper by the use of periods. For example, in a program such as the one below, the name of the characters in the play are joined to the respective names of the actors by a row of periods between the two names. Leaders may be made in one of two ways, either by filling every space with a period or by filling in every other space. The second way is more difficult because it is essential that the periods be lined up one under the other.

This is one type of work at which you are going to have to lift your eyes to see what you are doing. The name on the left margin is typed, then the name on the right margin is typed after backspacing from the right margin so that the name will end in line with all the other names. The leaders begin *one space* after the end of the name on the left, and must end one space before beginning the name on the right margin. If you are using the second type of leader, spacing between periods, you may have to space twice after the name on the left in order to align the periods. This will slow you down somewhat, but remember that it is a technique that is used only on special occasions to achieve an attractive piece of work.

Job 2. Set up the following program on a full sheet of paper. Use leaders between the character names and the names of the persons acting the parts. The names of actors will end on the right margin. Plan your vertical placement with appropriate spacing.

```
                THE DIARY OF ANNE FRANK
                     dramatized by
             Frances Goodrich and Albert Hackett
      (based upon the book, "Anne Frank:  Diary of a Young Girl")
       by special arrangement with Dramatists Play Service Inc.
                   Cast, in order of appearance
        Mr. Frank ......................... Robert Monk
        Miep .............................. Jane Brown
        Mrs. Van Daan ..................... Sheila Denton
        Mr. Van Daan ..................... Gordon Campbell
        Mrs. Frank ........................ Lana LaMarsh
        Kraler .......................... Walter Anderson
        Anne Frank ...................... Sandra Macdonald
        Peter Van Daan ...................... Bill Leslie
        Margot Frank ...................... Janet Duncan
        Mr. Dussel ........................ Frank Holmes
        German Soldiers .. Ross Black, Ron Davey, Ed Wiley
   THE SCENE:   Throughout the play the scene remains the same,
               the top floors of a warehouse in Amsterdam,
               Holland.
   THE TIME:    The story of "The Diary" is set in the period
               of World War II and immediately thereafter.
```

Compose complete sentences using each of the words in Column A.

THINK AS YOU TYPE

Form nouns ending in "ion" from the following words:

agitate, project, suggest, radiate, react, appreciate.

Check with your dictionary for the correct spelling and meaning of each word. Compose six complete sentences using each of your nouns.

ACCURACY PARAGRAPH

Type as often as time allows. Try to have one perfect copy to hand to your teacher at the end of the class period.

The home which we entered was a quaint, old-fashioned English dwelling. We found later that most of the village houses were alike. Nearly all had thatched roofs with great chimneys projecting high into the air. At first we were curious to know why there were four or five little smoke stacks to be seen on the top of every chimney. The reason for this became apparent, however, when we saw in the larger rooms of the house the great old English fireplaces, each one requiring a separate flue up the chimney. The fuel that was burned in these fireplaces was turf, dug from the low-lying lands, or "fen districts" as they are more familiarly called. The houses were lighted with candles. The floors, in many cases, were of brick. Antique pieces of furniture were to be found in every home; the great high bed curtained about with white; the grandfather's clock, solemnly ticking off the passing moments; the harmoniums and melodeons that help to while away many a long winter's evening. There were no streets and no sidewalks in the village; at least, not as we have them in Canada. Evidently the houses were built wholly at the pleasure of the owners, with no thought of conforming to any specified town plan. And yet the village presented an appearance of singular beauty.

Lesson 105

WARMUP

Rhythm a b c d e f g h i j k l m n o p q r s t u v w x y z abcdefgh

Top Row **Find the volume of a room 9 m long, 7 m wide and 2.5 m high.**

Attention .tuo sdrow evael netfo uoy fi uoy rof ecitcarp doog si sihT

More About Leaders

Leaders are frequently used in a Table of Contents. It is wise to include a Table of Contents with a long essay or report. Use the same margins as you used for the body of your essay. Either single or double spacing may be used when typing the Table of Contents.

Job 1.

Set up the following Table of Contents on a full sheet of paper. Centre the title on the twelfth line down from the top of the page.

TABLE OF CONTENTS

<table>
<tr><td></td><td></td><td align="right">Page</td></tr>
<tr><td>I.</td><td>Introduction ....</td><td align="right">1</td></tr>
<tr><td>II.</td><td>Investigation......................</td><td align="right">1</td></tr>
<tr><td></td><td>A. Sources of Information...........</td><td align="right">1</td></tr>
<tr><td></td><td>B. Organization of Findings.........</td><td align="right">1</td></tr>
<tr><td>III.</td><td>Findings..........................</td><td align="right">2</td></tr>
<tr><td></td><td>A. Outline Headings.................</td><td align="right">2</td></tr>
<tr><td></td><td>B. Page Arrangement................</td><td align="right">2</td></tr>
<tr><td></td><td>C. Table Arrangement...............</td><td align="right">3</td></tr>
<tr><td></td><td>D. References......................</td><td align="right">4</td></tr>
<tr><td>IV.</td><td>Summary...........................</td><td align="right">5</td></tr>
<tr><td></td><td>Bibliography......................</td><td align="right">6</td></tr>
</table>

THINK AS YOU TYPE

Prepare a list of ten Canadian place names and a product for which each place is famous. Use leaders to join the place name to its product.

E.g.	*Place*	*Product*
	Sydney	coal
	Hamilton	steel

Lesson 59

WARMUP

Rhythm fit die sit six and the aid for wit leg pay man men pen got
Alphabet Avis Ben Dick Fred Glen Joy Hugh Max Patsy Queenie Zoe Will
Top Row 10 mL 388-4013 100 km/h 191 East 35th Street 67 cm 10 g 8 L

Form nouns ending in "ment" from the following words:

settle, content, judge, acknowledge, arrange, govern.

Check with your dictionary for the correct spelling and meaning of each word. Compose six complete sentences using each of your nouns.

Lesson 104

WARMUP

Rhythm `a;qpa;slwosldkeidkfjrufjghtyghfjrufjdkeidkslwosla;qpa;slwosl`

Shifting `Quen Tex Kim Virve Thirza Peg Wayne Joy Duff Beth Clem Karen`

Attention `Bob's a_nt sa_d, "W_ m_st pay a bi_l of $89 _t 4_ int_r_st."`

ACCURACY SENTENCES

```
Only the elite are eligible; all the others were eliminated.
The council elected to have electrically operated elevators.
Half of the population recognize the hallmark of good paper.
There is a technique involved in recognizing a good antique.
```

Job 1. With the help of your dictionary, select the definition in Column B that most nearly describes the word in Column A. Set up in tabular form the words and their corresponding meaning.

Column A	Column B
trivial	a plan or outline of a journey
allay	ability to remember
rescind	of little importance
improvise	overused and commonplace
trite	repeal, cancel
itinerary	to make the most of what is at hand
prerequisite	sides or aspects
facets	required beforehand
retention	put at rest, quiet

Job 1.

Type the following sonnet on a half-sheet of paper. Remember to centre the longest line and set your margins for that line.

```
There is a greatness in the simple-hearted,
There is nobility in being kind;
This good man's life, in his full powers departed,
Still glows for all of us; within each mind
Something of his integrity has come to dwell;
Something of his example, like a flame
Is passed from hand to hand; its mystic spell
Lighting life's darker hours with his name. . . .
This man, our friend, was truly great of heart,
Modest and wise, forbearing in all things;
Dowered with humour, tolerant, apart
From any pompous littleness.  He truly led
By following humbly; and his high spirit's wings
Forever lift him high above the dead.
```

                                    --Nathaniel A. Benson

Job 2.

Type the following poem on a half-sheet of paper, inserting the shorter side of the paper in the machine. Note that every second line is indented.

```
                AULD LANG SYNE

    Should auld acquaintance be forgot,
        And never brought to mind?
    Should auld acquaintance be forgot,
        And auld lang syne?

    For auld lang syne, my dear,
        For auld lang syne,
    We'll tak a cup o' kindness yet
        For auld lang syne!

    And there's a hand, my trusty fiere,
        And gie's a hand o' thine;
    And we'll tak a right guid-willie waught
        For auld lang syne.

    For auld lang syne, my dear,
        For auld lang syne,
    We'll tak a cup o' kindness yet
        For auld lang syne!
```

Composition Skills

For clarity of expression, each of your compositions, whether they be letters, essays, or book reports, must contain complete sentences. A sentence is said to be complete when it contains both a subject and a predicate (verb) which are in agreement. Such a sentence must express a complete thought.

Complete sentence: John broke his leg.
Incomplete sentence: Because John broke his leg.
Complete sentence: Because John broke his leg, he cannot go skiing.

Job 1.

Rewrite the following incomplete sentences making them complete sentences.

The letter that had been carefully written.
Because the principal was sick.
Although Bernie agreed with the group.
Everyone who went to the hockey game.
The aeroplane flying over the city.

Job 2.

Consult your dictionary for the meanings of each of the following abbreviations. Set up in tabular form the abbreviations and their corresponding meanings.

p.m., LL.D., c.o.d., i.e., Ltd., Sr., e.g.

TIMED
WRITING

1 AND 5 MINUTES

A Canadian banker once said that how you look upon money and 13
how you manage it will have a lot to do with the amount of happiness 27
you will find in your life. He pointed out that it is important that 40
young people learn to get the best value for their money, and at the 54
same time, learn to be neither misers nor spendthrifts. Even on a 67
very small allowance, a student can learn to plan his spending so 80
that he can have the things that are most important to him. He can 94
learn not to fritter it away on trifles, so that he never has any saved 108
for a rainy day. 111
Thrift is an old-fashioned word about which people like to make 125
jokes. If you look in the dictionary, you will find that thrift means 139
"economy" or the "good management of money." Good management 151
of money involves regular saving, not for the pleasure of hoarding 164
money, but to be able to buy for cash the things that you need and 177
want, and to be able to cope with the unexpected emergencies that 190
arise in all our lives. If your savings grow beyond your needs, you 204
can find places to put them to work for you — you can invest them and 218
watch them grow. This will afford you a sense of well-being and 231
security that is much more pleasant than the frustrated feeling you 244
get when you just cannot imagine what you did with all your money. 257

Bibliography

A Bibliography is a list of books and other publications which is used for reference in the preparation of an essay or report. The list is arranged alphabetically according to the authors' surnames. Use the same margins as those used for your essay. The first line of each reference begins at the left margin, and the second line is indented. Double space between references. You have already discovered from the Table of Contents in Lesson 58 that the Bibliography is the last page of your essay or report.

Job 3.   Type the following Bibliography on a full sheet of paper. Note that when a book has more than one author, only the first author's name is typed with the surname first.

BIBLIOGRAPHY

McConnell, Jean M., and William L. Darnell, Building Typing Skills, Second Edition, SI Metric. Toronto: McGraw-Hill Ryerson Limited, 1978.

Rowe, John L., Alan C. Lloyd, Fred E. Winger, Typing 300, Canadian Edition Metricated. Toronto: McGraw-Hill Ryerson Limited, 1977.

Turabian, Kate L., A Manual for Writers of Term Papers, Theses, and Dissertations, Third Edition. The University of Chicago Press, 1967.

Wright, Shirley, The Personal Touch, Second Edition. Toronto: McGraw-Hill Ryerson Limited, 1976.

Lesson 60

WARMUP

Rhythm   they dish wish with such sick work turn sign duty city roam

Shifting   Gamow Lewellen Vergara Watson Swezey Wright Taylor Zim Reed

Numbers   500 504 509 583 523.1 523.7 523.8 539.77 540.72 541.2 551.5

Compose a letter announcing the Grand Opening of a new branch of
your sporting goods store. This letter is being sent to the Purchasing Agent
of your local school board. Try to use the "you" attitude.

My upbringing took place in a medium-sized city where my friends 14
were confined to a rather small group who were associated through 27
school, church, and the social activities of our parents. I had been to 41
fall church suppers which were fun. However, it was not until I went 55
out to teach in a small town on the prairies that I realized that great- 69
ness of hospitality for which the prairie provinces are famous. 82

The small town church supper was no small affair, nor was it con- 96
fined to the members of its own congregation. Each church entertained 110
and invited everyone in the town and the surrounding countryside to 123
attend; and everyone did attend. These affairs were part of the Harvest 137
Festival and Thanksgiving. Great succulent turkeys, golden brown 150
and fresh from the oven, were carved at every table. Spread upon the 164
groaning boards, vegetables, fruits, pies, cakes, and concoctions from 178
every housewife's secret recipe store, spoke of a bountiful harvest. It 193
was the pleasure of the hosts to watch every guest enjoy all the deli- 207
cacies he could eat. And what deep satisfaction was gained from being 221
a guest where one and all sat down to enjoy the best of food and the 234
most gracious hospitality together, regardless of race, colour, or creed. 249

Lesson 103

WARMUP

Rhythm a b c d e f g h i j k l m n o p q r s t u v w x y z abcdefgh

Top Row 292 "9" 63 #63 480 $80 579 79% 386 35 & 83 & 90 23.5 (100) 2

Attention .easy work makes here up drawn plan good a that fact a is It

WORD FAMILIES

cle cycle uncle circle muscle icicle cubicle miracle vehicle
pen penny pencil pending pension penguin peninsula penthouse
man many manage mansion manner management manuscript mankind
urn burn turns spurn return adjourn churns sojourn returning

Here is a list of books with brief descriptions, such as might appear in the Book Section of a large newspaper or be distributed by your school librarian. Set it up attractively on a full sheet of paper. Triple line-space before each new heading. Use your margin release to have the headings begin 5 spaces before the left margin.

HISTORICAL FICTION

SHIPLEY, N. - THE SCARLET LILY

This story concerns the opening of western Canada in 1860, as seen through the eyes of Ellen Nash - a musically talented young woman who marries a missionary Indian.

BUCK, P. - IMPERIAL WOMAN

This is a novel about the last empress of China--a young girl who became a brilliant strategist and finally a goddess.

GOUDGE, E. - THE WHITE WITCH

This story concerns the English Civil War and the men and women on both sides who committed themselves to a war they hated.

MITCHELL, M. - GONE WITH THE WIND

This novel brings the American Civil War and the Reconstruction Period vividly to life as it tells the story of spirited, selfish, but unforgettable Scarlett O'Hara.

CATHER, W. - SHADOWS ON THE ROCK

Through Cecile Auclair and her father, Euclide, the apothecary protected by Frontenac, the author recreates the atmosphere and historical events of old Quebec.

IRWIN, M. - THE GAY GALLIARD

In the furious turmoil of her Scottish Kingdom, Mary's aptitudes for statecraft and affection were constantly at war--only in Bothwell's courage and love did she find serenity and momentary happiness.

BRILL, E. - MADELEINE TAKES COMMAND

The memorable and beautifully told story of Madeleine de Vercheres and her two young brothers, who, with a garrison of seven people, defended their home fort against the Indians.

Lesson 102

WARMUP

Rhythm   abcdefghijklmnopqrstuvwxyz abcdefghijklmnopqrstuvwxyz abcdef

Top Row   Add 100 and 228 and 147 and 56 and 39 to get the sum of 570.

Attention   mr. jones went to oshawa to pick up his new buick on friday.

ACCURACY SENTENCES

My firm has confirmed a sound pension scheme for its infirm.
The demanding wife does not create an understanding husband.
The costs to most farmers are very heavy when frost strikes.
She fixed the situation by affixing a stamp to the envelope.

The "You" Attitude

When composing any business letter, you should adopt the reader's point of view rather than your own. This is often known as the "you" attitude and it is an essential ingredient of a good business letter. To write effective letters you should always keep in mind that to persuade others to do what you want, you must demonstrate that it is to their advantage to do it.

Job 1.

Type in good form:

THE "YOU" ATTITUDE

Avoid	*Use*
I would like to order	Will you please send
I wish to apply	Please consider my application
We will give good service	You will receive good service
We acknowledge receipt of	Thank you for

Job 2.

Rewrite the following sentences to make them more effective. Take into consideration the reader's point of view.

1. We have received your cheque for $25.
2. I am sending you a duplicate copy of the invoice.
3. We cannot ship your order because our workers are on strike.
4. Let me take this opportunity to tell you that we value your business.
5. I would like to have an interview as soon as possible.

Job 2.

Follow the instructions given in Job 1. Set up the following book list, MORE HISTORICAL FICTION, to match the one done in Job 1.

MORE HISTORICAL FICTION

ROBERTS, K. — ARUNDEL. Steven Nason of Arundel tells of his adventures while attached to the secret expedition led by Colonel Benedict Arnold against Quebec during the American Revolution. LANCASTER, B. — NIGHT MARCH. While engaged in the abortive attempt to free Union prisoners in Richmond, cavalry commander Kirk Stedman and his friend, Jake Pitter, are captured by the confederates. KINGSLEY, CHARLES — WESTWARD HO! This story of adventure and sea fights in the time of Queen Elizabeth gives an account of the Armada and introduces Hawkins, Drake, and other British naval heroes. MAUGHAN, A. — MONMOUTH HARRY. This is an interesting account of the brief and glorious reign of Henry V. We travel with the king through his boyhood days, to the splendour of Agincourt, and finally to his death-bed. COSTAIN, T. — THE BLACK ROSE. This exciting historical novel is the story of a young English nobleman who fights his way to the heart of the fabulous Mongol Empire. COSTAIN, T. — HIGH TOWERS. This is an historical romance chronicling the adventures of the LeMoyne family of Montreal who became the heroes of French Canada and founded the city of New Orleans.

Footnotes

Use a footnote to indicate the source of the material which you have used for your essay or report. From your reference material you may have used facts, opinions, and exact quotations. The footnote should appear on the bottom of the appropriate page but should not extend into the bottom margin.

Job 3.

Type the following material which illustrates the set up of typewritten material requiring a footnote. Use double spacing and margins appropriate for an essay.

If a writer uses another's exact words or ideas, a credit should be given in the form of a footnote. The credits in a report are numbered in the order in which they appear. Each must be explained in a matching footnote on the same page. Although the rules for typing reports and term papers vary from place to place, they are fairly well standardized. One would do well to consult a reference[1], which may be available in your school or library, if more detailed suggestions are required for the set up of your material.

————————

[1]Dorothy M. Newman and Jean P. Newman, _Canadian Business Handbook_, Second edition (Toronto: McGraw-Hill Ryerson Limited, 1967) pp. 635-644.

Job 2.

Retype the following sentences making the appropriate substitution for the business jargon.

1. During the course of the past two years, I have been secretary to the Student Council.

2. At the present time I am working part time as a librarian.

3. Enclosed please find my cheque in the amount of $25.

4. I am sure we can cooperate together on the new project.

5. My past experience includes the operation of duplicating machines.

6. In the event that there is a postal strike, the shipment will be sent by means of air freight.

Set a Goal

In the last 25 lessons, your typing technique has improved. Let us set our goal a little higher for the next cycle of lessons. For the timed writings in Lessons 101 to 105, try for not more than 3 errors in five minutes of typing.

TIMED WRITING

1 AND 5 MINUTES

When I was a child in Saskatchewan, one of the wonders of nature 14
that held my interest was the southern migration of birds as winter 27
approached. Great flocks of Canada geese and many species of ducks 40
darkened the sky as they flew over. The fields in which grain stood 54
in stooks, particularly if they were near a lake or river, became feeding 69
grounds where the flocks rested on their long journey. Many an hour 82
have I spent looking through field glasses and watching the birds as 96
they came to feed. 100

Twice, I saw whooping cranes, the birds that are now almost extinct. 115
The first time I saw them, they were in flight at the tail end of the 129
long V formation in which Canada geese fly. The characteristic whoop- 143
ing sound that the cranes make could be heard above the honking 155
of the geese. The second time I saw them was years later when I sat 169
and watched what I believed was a flock of geese feeding at Rice 181
Lake near Saskatoon. We were able to pick out nine of the tall stately 195
birds which have become known as the rarest bird in North America. 208
Today, the naturalists are putting forth every effort to save these 222
magnificent birds, whose worst enemy has been the hunter with his 235
gun. Nesting grounds discovered in the Northwest Territories and 248
the cranes' winter homes in Texas are now being protected by agencies 262
interested in the preservation of these rare and beautiful birds. 275

Lesson 61

Speed   Will you come to the hall when she is able to meet with you?

Top row   She feels that $7520 is too much for only a 34% share of it.

Alphabet   Frank jumped quickly to extinguish the very dangerous blaze.

TIMED WRITING

What time of the year do you like best? For many Canadians, fall   13
is the season that they enjoy most. In nearly all parts of the country,   27
the days tend to be sunny and warm, and the nights are crisp and   42
clear. The trees exhibit a riot of colour that is almost impossible to   56
describe and that strangers find hard to believe. Even the sounds of   70
fall have their peculiar appeal. The honking of the great flocks of   83
geese winging their way southward and the rustle of dry leaves being   97
crunched underfoot have no counterparts in the other seasons. It is   110
little wonder that, in the fall, Canadians stream from their cities and   124
towns to enjoy the sights and sounds so abundantly spread before them.   138

Job 1.

Read the personal business letter illustrated on the next page and then copy it. The illustration shows you how to arrange and type your personal business letters in an attractive way on letterhead paper.

Job 2.

Type the following personal business letter in the style illustrated in Job 1 and using today's date.

Dr. Lawrence Lyman, Department of Theatre Arts, York University, Toronto, Ontario M4G 3A7 Dear Dr. Lyman: A group of our students ranging in age from 15 to 19 years have recently organized a drama club. The members plan to prepare and produce several one-act plays which can be presented at student assemblies throughout the coming year.

Our immediate problem is to find suitable plays for our purpose, and Mr. Ivan Restoff, our faculty advisor, has suggested that you might be able to help us.

We would be most grateful if you could send us within the next week or two a list of one-act plays suitable for inexperienced actors and for which no royalty payments are required.

Anything you can do to help us will be much appreciated.

Sincerely yours, Clifford Sorenson

Lesson 101

WARMUP

Rhythm   `a ; q p a ; s l w o s l dkeidkfjrufjghtyghfjrufjdkeidkslwosl`

Top Row   `we 23 wet 235 were 2343 you 697 your 6974 pour 0974 yet 635.`

Attention   `.tcat fo kcal ruoy yb dedneffo saw eciffo ruo fo reganam ehT`

WORD FAMILIES

```
mel melts melon mellow melodic melancholy meliorates melting
cou could cough coupon cousin course council courage country
tow toward towel tower town township towhead towage tow-line
aut auto autocrat automobile automatic authorized autographs
```

Business English

Many people when composing business letters and reports use language that is awkward and unnatural. The trite and outworn expressions that they use are often called "business jargon", and you should learn to avoid them in your letters. Good Business English is the same English that you would use in a formal and polite conversation. To eliminate the useless phrases and unnecessary words from your business communications, ask yourself, "Would I say it this way if I were talking instead of writing?"

Job 1.   Set up in tabular form:

BUSINESS EXPRESSIONS

Business Jargon	Use Instead
in the amount of	for
enclosed please find	enclosed is
during the course of	during
past experience	experience
by means of	by
in the event that	if
cooperate together	cooperate
at the present time	at present

Student Council

Central Secondary School

Westview, Alberta
T8W 1M8

19-- 11 12

Miss Margaret Olsen
42 Columbine Drive
Toronto, Ontario
M4V 1F2

Dear Miss Olsen:

     This illustration shows you one way in which
you can set up your personal business letters in
a pleasing and attractive style.

     Because you are typing on letterhead paper,
you begin by typing the date. Usually the date
begins at the centre of the paper a few spaces
below the letterhead. Then move down six or eight
spaces and type the name and address of the person,
company, or organization to whom the letter is
being sent. The remaining parts of the letter are
separated by one blank line.

     Normally, for the body of the letter you will
use a line that is either 50 (pica) or 60 (elite)
strokes long. As illustrated here, you may indent
the first line of each paragraph five spaces.

     The closing lines begin at the centre of the
page, and you should leave four blank spaces for
your handwritten signature.

       Yours sincerely,

       William Macdonald

       William Macdonald

Job 4.

Suggested time: 10 minutes

Write a letter to Mr. Ferris telling him that you are pleased that he is the district representative for the Regina area and ordering a piece of lawn furniture of your choice. You would like this order to be charged to your account.

Job 5.

Suggested time: 20 minutes

Set up the following notice on a full sheet of paper.

EMPLOYEES' CREDIT UNION LIMITED ← Extended Centering
of
UNITED ALLOYS COMPANY - WINNIPEG DIVISION
← (4 spaces)
Notice Of Annual Meeting ← Underscore

The Annual Meeting of the Employees' Credit Union Limited of United Alloys Company - Winnipeg Division will take place on ~~Thursday~~, January 17 at 8 p.m., in the ~~employees~~ cafeteria at the plant.

The following slate of officers for the Board of Directors has been submitted by the Nominating Committee:

President - Mr. John X. Parker
Vice President - Mrs. Helen Ross
Recording Secretary - Mr. Wm. B. Handy
To Represent plant ~~workers~~ employees - Mr. R. T. Frame
Mr. J. P. White
To Represent office staff - Miss Jane Watt
Mr. Paul Gibson

All members are urged to be present to vote on incoming officers and to take part in an important discussion on the proposed new dividend rate.

Lesson 62

WARMUP

Addressing Envelopes in Blocked Style

Envelope Size	Small	Large
Begin Address	on line 12 10 spaces to the left of centre	on line 14 10 spaces to the left of centre

Spacing	Addresses should be single spaced.
Special Notations	Instructions such as "please forward," "personal," "confidential," etc., are typed 4 lines below the return address, or on line 9. Use initial caps and underscore. An attention line, if used, should be typed four lines below the return address, or it should be typed in the address block on the line following the company name. Mailing directions are typed in all capital letters below the return address as well.
Return Address	This is usually printed, but if it must be typed, use single spacing and start on line 3, 3 spaces in from the left edge of the envelope.
Punctuation	The style of punctuation used in addressing an envelope is the same as that used in the inside address of the letter that is to be inserted in the envelope.
Postal Code	When a Postal Code is known, it should be typed as *the last line of the address*, with nothing below it or to the right of it. The Postal Code must appear between 8 and 5 lines above the bottom of the envelope.

Job 3.

Suggested time: 15 minutes

Set up the following letter in the semi-blocked style. Prepare a large envelope for the letter.

March 16, 19 ....

Lyle & Jamieson, Ltd.
1872 Scarth Street
Regina, SK
S4P 2G2

Gentlemen:

You will be interested to know that on April 1, Mr. John E. Ferris will assume his duties as permanent district representative for the Regina area. His offices will be located at 1784 Broad Street and your orders may be sent to that address.

The opening of this office will enable us to give better service to our friends in Regina and will help us to maintain the personal contact which is so essential in our business.

A cordial invitation is extended to you to visit the new offices at any time after April 1.

Very truly yours,

Sherman S. Harkness
Managing Director

If time permits, type the same letter in blocked style and prepare an envelope to be sent to:

The Acme Supply Co. Limited
2342 Albert Street
Regina, SK
S4P 2Y5

```
Barbara A. Polk
39 Riverside Street
Calgary, AB
T2W 2P4


REGISTERED
Personal
```

Address area {

Ms. Olga Valchuk
Henderson & Company
107 Lake Avenue
SASKATOON, SK
S7L 1B2

11 lines

5 lines

TO FOLD LETTERS...

To Fold a Letter for a Small Envelope...

Bring bottom up to 1 cm from the top.

Fold right-hand third toward left.

Fold left-hand third toward right.

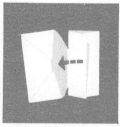
Last crease goes in envelope first.

To Fold a Letter for a Large Envelope...

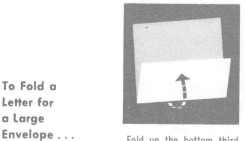
Fold up the bottom third of the paper.

Fold the top third over bottom third.

Swing paper so last fold is at left.

Last crease goes in envelope first.

Lesson 100 Test

Job 1.

Suggested time: 15 minutes

Type two 5-minute writings. Score and hand in the better one.

Canada has been richly endowed with minerals. Its mines and	13
related industries provide thousands of jobs and are a source of great	27
wealth. In addition to the mineral deposits already discovered, there	41
are more waiting to be found. There are still many opportunities in	54
Canada for the adventurous prospector to experience the thrill of	67
making a new find.	71
Modern science has provided instruments that make the work of	84
the prospector easier and more accurate. Already these are helping	98
to explore regions that up to now have been untouched.	108
Much of the country's mineral wealth lies in remote areas. The	122
cost of transporting men and machinery to these areas is so great	135
that it is difficult to develop the ore bodies. If they could be devel-	149
oped, the cost of getting the ore to its markets would be so high that	163
successful competition with other producers would be impossible.	176
However, there is no doubt that increasing demand and better methods	190
of transportation will make the use of these deposits necessary and	203
feasible in the future.	208
Although minerals are still being formed, the rate is so slow that	222
we can count on using only those minerals which already exist. It is	236
important, therefore, that wise use be made of our present resources.	250
Part of Canada's mineral wealth must be conserved for the future,	263
and unnecessary waste must be avoided.	270

Job 2.

Suggested time: 20 minutes

Set up in good tabular form.

Industrial Stock Quotations

Stock	Sales	High	Low	Close
Alberta Gas	3420	28¼	27½	28¼
Algoma Central	20	18½	18½	18½
Bank of Montreal	450	62¼	62	62
Central Porcupine	2000	12½	12½	12½
Inglis	100	450	440	440
International Nickel	595	65½	65¼	65¼
Salada	1945	14½	14¼	14½
Tamblyn	50	22	22	22
Texaco	75	61	60½	61
Westeel	100	10¼	10	10

Job 1.   Address a "large", a "small", and an odd-size envelope for each of the following addresses.

a. Miss Margaret Thurston
   2892 Cypress Avenue
   Vancouver, BC
   V1N 1B5

b. Mr. John Fraser, Credit
      Manager
   Alberta Steel Company
   1752 8th Avenue West
   CALGARY, AB
   T2N 1C5

c. Mrs. J. K. Blackstone, Office
      Manager
   Atlantic Canning Company
   2642 Centre Street
   Charlottetown, PE
   C1B 2A3

d. Ryder, Ryder, and Hastings,
   Attorneys-at-law,
   1752 Federal Building,
   Portage Avenue,
   WINNIPEG, MB
   R3G 2G6

e. Miss Janet Graham
   118 Haddington Blvd.
   Toronto, ON
   M8H 4C4
   confidential

f. Mr. Reginald Franklin
   Director of Public Relations
   Regency Oil Company
   Suite 6, Standard Building
   1042 St. Clair Avenue West
   Toronto, ON
   M5G 3M7

g. Plant Personnel Department
   Excelsior Plastics Limited
   3916 Dovercourt Road
   Saint John, NB
   G4N 6P3

h. Mrs. F. W. Wilson
   1621 Decarie Boulevard, #402
   Montreal, PQ
   H7S 2M9

Lesson 63

WARMUP

Rhythm We are sure that they can do this work in less than an hour.

Shifting Peter, William, John, Charles, Ontario, Hamilton, Burlington

Top Row 2672 King 1642 Main 1742 Tamarack 22 Granite 400 km April 23

Carbon Copies

You may wish to make one or more carbon copies of the material you are preparing. Usually, light weight paper is used for the carbon copy. Proceed as follows when preparing carbon copies:

1. Lay the copy sheet of paper on the table.

2. Place the carbon paper, glossy side down, on the copy paper.
3. Place the paper on which you will type the original on top of the carbon paper.
4. Pick up the pack, holding it on both sides; insert the top edge of the papers into the machine.
5. Type with a sharp, firm stroke to get a clean-cut copy.

Job 1. Set up in good form using a 50-space line.

Last Year's Performance of
Selected Common Stocks

Stock	High	Low	Close
Algoma Steel	37¼	32½	36¼
Argus Corporation	42½	35	41
Calgary Power	28¼	23	28¼
Canadian Pacific Railway	27½	25¼	26½
Dominion Stores	69½	63	68
Famous Players	19¼	17½	18¼
Imperial Oil	41	37½	40½
Moore Corporation	52	44½	50
Royal Bank of Canada	75¼	72¼	72½
Simpson's	32¼	28¼	30½
Standard Radio	38	29	37¼
Steel Company of Canada	24	21½	23
Triad Oil	13	10¼	11½
Union Gas	22	19¼	21½
York Knitting Mills	15	12½	14
Zellers	37¼	31	34½

Job 2. Set up in good form on a half-sheet of paper.

Executive Members
of
Maple Leaf Club

Office	Name	Address	Telephone
President	Harvey Linker	18 Aspen Dr.	694-3281
Vice-Pres.	John Frame	167 Farley Ave.	694-6287
Secretary	James Morgan	49 Golf Rd.	721-7746
Treasurer	Roy Linton	26 Fraser Ave.	281-6437
Programme	Ronald Best	41 Haddon Ave.	281-2660
Social	Frank Pinter	31 Linton Ave.	473-1180
Membership	Gordon Potter	16 Crescent Rd.	694-1692

1. Carbon paper has a dull side and a glossy side. The glossy side does the work.

2. Glossy side is put against the paper on which the copy is to be made.

3. You always have one more sheet of typing paper than of carbon paper.

4. Straighten sides and top of pack carefully before inserting it in your machine.

5. Hold pack with left hand; turn cylinder smoothly with right hand.

Erasing on Carbon Copies

1. Turn the sheets up a few spaces and lift the paper bail.
2. Move the carriage to the right or left to prevent crumbs from falling into the machine.
3. Put a protective sheet be⁺ween the carbon and the copy before erasing on the original.
4. Remove the protective sheet and erase on the copy.
5. Replace the paper bail, turn the cylinder back, and type the correction.

For the best results, use a typewriter eraser on the original, and a pencil eraser on the copy.

Job 1.

Set up the following personal business letter on a full sheet of paper. Prepare a carbon copy of the letter. Use school letterhead paper, or type the name and address of your school for the heading of your letter. Address an envelope for your letter.

O'Keefe Centre, Front and Yonge Streets, Toronto, ON M2R 3P4
Gentlemen: I am writing to inquire about special student rates for the spring performance of the Royal Winnipeg Ballet to be held at your Centre.

There are 32 students in our Theatre Arts class. We would like to attend an afternoon performance of the Ballet during the week of March 8. Is there a special matinee for students? Can you reserve a block of seats for 32 students and 2 teachers? What are the rates?

Our class is looking forward to visiting Toronto and to attending the Ballet. Please send the information which I have requested as soon as possible so that we can complete our plans. Sincerely yours, Your Name, Class Representative

THINK AS YOU TYPE

Write a letter to Pine Crest Lodge, 101 Mountain View Road, Banff, AB T0L 0C0 inquiring about their accommodation and rates. Ask for any literature they may have to offer, information on popular activities available at the time of year you wish to visit, and whether or not they have tours of the area. Use your home address for the heading. Make a carbon copy of your letter and properly address an envelope.

Job 1.	Account	Balance		Job 3.	Account	Balance
	Mr. Howard Haney Box 687 Markham, ON M8S 4K5	$32.50			Mr. John Phillips 418 Centre Street Cooksville, ON M3T 8L2	$72.90
Job 2.	Mr. William Lorenzo 627 Fairfield Avenue Oshawa, ON M5L 9R1	$46.85		Job 4.	The Home Grocery 678 Pine Avenue Sudbury, ON P1M 6S2	$89.25

Job 5. Address "small" envelopes for the letters you have just completed.

Lesson 99

WARMUP

Speed If you will send them your bill soon, they will order again.

Accuracy A negative uncooperative attitude alienated his subordinate.

Top Row My brother is 160 cm tall, but my father's height is 180 cm.

TIMED WRITING
1 AND 3 MINUTES

As you sit in front of your modern, stream-lined typewriter, have 14
you ever thought of the people who invented this wonderful writing 27
machine? 29

So far as anyone knows, the first person to think up the basic idea 43
of a typewriter was an English engineer named Henry Mill. On 55
January 7, 1714, Queen Anne granted Mill a patent giving him exclu- 68
sive rights to "an artificial machine or method for the empressing or 82
transcribing of letters singly or progressively one after another as in 96
writing." 98

There are no drawings of Mill's machine and some people doubt 111
that he ever built one. However, there is no doubt that he was the 125
first person to patent the idea of a typewriter. 134

Others invented and built typewriters after Mill, but it was not 148
until 1867 that the first practical commercial machine was built 161
by Christopher Latham Sholes. 167

Lesson 64

Speed   If you will do the job now, we can pay you more than he can.

Phrases   if you are, if you will, if they are, if they will, you will

Top Row   The 6% bonds sold at $101.35 for an effective yield of 5.845%

SENTENCES

A wishful person imagines that wisdom comes without labour.

To the sorrow of campers, lamplight is marred by lampblack.

An official in our office was offended by his lack of tact.

The maintenance of the wistarias has been sorely neglected.

Spirit Masters

You may be required to distribute copies of a group or individual project to all the members of your class. This will normally require more copies than can be made by using carbon paper. In this lesson you will learn how to prepare a master for a spirit duplicator. If you have a spirit duplicator in your school, your teacher or a senior student will demonstrate how to run off copies from the master.

Job 1.

On page 94 is an illustration of material typed on a spirit master. Instructions and related information about the production of spirit masters are contained in the copy. Read it carefully before you begin to type a master.

Job 2.

Obtain a spirit master for each group of five students. Each student in turn will type his name, address, and telephone number on the master. Arrange these five names in alphabetic order. You may wish to prepare a class roster on a master from the combination of names from each group.

THINK AS YOU TYPE

Compose a letter which will be sent to each of the members of your class advising them that the school Yearbook is now available. Be sure to include such necessary information as the price, and where and when the Yearbook may be picked up. Try to sell the publication by explaining why this is a once-in-a-lifetime opportunity. If material and facilities permit, prepare a master of your letter, run copies off on a spirit duplicator, and distribute copies to the members of the class. Refer to the roster prepared in Job 2 for a complete list of names.

Suggestion: If material and facilities are limited, choose one letter from each group to be duplicated.

Lesson 98

Speed   Will you go now while the sun is high and the air is so hot?

Concen-
tration   eW tnaw ot knaht uoy rof lla eht noitarepooc uoy evah nevig.

Top Row   Invoice #6280, amounting to $153.74, received a 3% discount.

TIMED WRITING

1 AND 2 MINUTES

The lake was calm that night. As our boat put out from the shore,   14
the pale moon rose over the hills and a lone bird voiced its plaintive   28
song. The tall trees, so friendly in the light of day, now loomed   41
dark and menacing. All of us knew that danger lurked in their thick   55
cover and that our lives depended on avoiding it.   63

Our leader, crouched in the bow of the boat, stretched out his   76
arm and pointed silently to the farther shore. There, we could find   90
help for ourselves and for those we had left behind. Could we reach   103
it before the light of dawn betrayed our purpose?   113

Jobs 1 to 4.

Using the semi-blocked style and mixed punctuation, set up and address the following form letter as indicated.

Dear Mr. ---- :
    We have sent you several reminders
about your past-due account for $
without receiving a reply from you.
    In fairness to yourself, we hope that
you will consider how valuable your credit
standing is. Certainly, it is worth far
more than the amount you owe us.
    You can protect this important asset
by telling us when you will make payment--
or better still, by sending us your cheque
now. Use the envelope that we are enclosing for your convenience--and mail it today
please.

                Yours truly,
                T. R. Evenson
                Credit Manager

TRE:URS

ORIGINAL ON WHICH YOU TYPE

INSERT THIS OPEN END,
NOT THE BOUND END

THE TYPING OF A MASTER SHEET

A "Master" is a sheet of special glossy paper, fastened at the bottom to another sheet that is coated with a layer of carbon containing a special reproducing dye. When you write on the master, carbon is transferred from the backing sheet to the back of the master sheet; then, later, when the master is placed on the duplicating machine, copies are made when other sheets of paper, dampened by a chemical in the machine, are pressed against the carbon on the back of the master.

Typing the Master. Follow these steps:

1. Prepare the copy--verify that it is correct.

2. Prepare the typewriter--clean the type.

3. Prepare yourself--read the directions on the box in which the master packs come.

4. Prepare the master pack--remove the protective sheet that separates the master page from the carbon page.

5. Insert the master pack, being sure to insert the open end first. Type with a very even touch.

6. Proofread your typing with extra care.

Correcting a Master. This is a matter of removing the carbon of the error and replacing it by the carbon of the correction, a process that can be done in many ways. The usual procedure:

1. Roll the paper up and bend the master toward you to expose the carbon that contains the error.

2. Using a blade (knife or razor), carefully scrape off the carbon that contains the error.

3. Place a slip of unused carbon (cut from another sheet of the carbon paper) between the backing sheet and the master in such a way that the new carbon will be at the point of the correction.

4. Roll the paper back to the typing position and type the correction without erasing the original incorrect typewriting.

5. Pause to remove the slip of carbon paper; then continue typing the rest of the job.

Related Information: Reproducing carbon is available in red, green, blue, black, and purple colors. Of these, only the purple serves for long runs (up to 200) of vivid copies, which explains why most spirit copies one sees are purple. The other colors are used for illustrating, ruling, and other special art effects.

When writing, drawing, or tracing on a master, use a ball pen with a very fine tip or a hard, sharp pencil.

PERFORATION PERMITS YOU TO DETACH CARBON EASILY
WHEN READY TO PUT THE MASTER ON THE DUPLICATOR

- -

The Roman system of numerals uses letters instead of figures to represent numbers. The seven letters used are I for 1, V for 5, X for 10, L for 50, C for 100, D for 500, and M for 1 000.

Each letter has a defined value when standing alone. In addition to this, its value may be added to or subtracted from other values depending on its position in a series of letters. The rules which govern their use are simple to follow.

1. Repeat a letter to repeat its value. I = 1; II = 2; III = 3; X = 10; XX = 20; XXX = 30. Note that today, the letter is never repeated more than three times, although the Romans did repeat more often.

2. Place a letter of less value before one of greater value, and the resulting value is the difference between the greater and the lesser. IX = 9; XL = 40; XC = 90; CD = 400.

3. Place a letter of less value after one of greater value, and the resulting value is the sum of the two values. XI = 11; LX = 60; CX = 110; DC = 600.

4. Place a bar over a letter to multiply that value by one thousand. $\overline{V}$ = 5 000; $\overline{X}$ = 10 000; $\overline{C}$ = 100 000. Note that a bar is never placed over I because we have M for one thousand. $\overline{V}$ = 5 000; $\overline{V}$M = 6 000; M$\overline{V}$ = 4 000.

Job 2.   Set up the following in four columns, using a full sheet of paper.

ARABIC AND ROMAN NUMERALS

Arabic	Roman	Arabic	Roman
1	I	30	XXX
2	II	40	XL
3	III	50	L
4	IV	58	LVIII
5	V	59	LIX
6	VI	60	LX
7	VII	80	LXXX
8	VIII	90	XC
9	IX	100	C
10	X	123	CXXIII
11	XI	400	CD
12	XII	500	D
13	XIII	600	DC
14	XIV	1 000	M
15	XV	1 012	MXII
16	XVI	4 668	M$\overline{V}$DCLXVIII
17	XVII	5 000	$\overline{V}$
18	XVIII	10 000	$\overline{X}$
19	XIX	1945	MCMXLV
20	XX	1812	MDCCCXII

Lesson 65

WARMUP

Speed   The boy was told to come as soon as he could. He will come.

Shifting   Windsor, ON; Charlottetown, PE; Vancouver, BC; Montreal, PQ.

Top Row   The 4's are faulty on model #87906; the 8's on model #88125.

Job 1.

Set up the following application letter on a full sheet of paper. Prepare a carbon copy of the letter. The heading will be your home address.

Mrs. A. Scherer, 191 West 35th Street, Belleville, ON K8N 4S9

Our neighbour, Mrs. Ratelle, has told me that you are looking for someone to accompany you to your summer home to look after your children for the month of July.

I am interested in obtaining summer work this year and I would very much like to have the opportunity to take care of your children and to do any other work required at your summer home. I will be 15 years old this summer, and I have done a lot of baby sitting in my spare time for the past three years. Last summer I looked after Mrs. Ratelle's little boy while she did part-time work in an office. I am fond of children and I hope to be able to work with pre-school youngsters when I graduate.

Mrs. Ratelle and my typing teacher, Miss Martineloo, have consented to provide references for me. If you would like to meet me in person, I would be pleased to visit you. My phone number is 588-6551. I am available any day after school. Sincerely yours,

Job 2.

Prepare an envelope for the letter in Job 1.

THINK AS YOU TYPE

A. Your local theatre requires an usher to work three evenings a week. The salary offered is $2.50 per hour. They state that the applicant must be reliable and punctual. Your friend, the cashier at this theatre, has told you about the opening for an usher. Compose an application letter for this job.

B. Compose your own letter of advice in answer to one of the questions sent to "Dear Abby" or "Dear Ann Landers."

Nature, usually the farmer's friend, sometimes plays dreadful tricks. 15
One such happened in my part of the West in the fall of 1903. Early 28
in September, all the crops had been cut and stocked, and everywhere 42
around us there seemed to be prospects of a bountiful harvest. A few 56
machines were in readiness to begin their long season of threshing. On 70
the morning of the thirteenth, we awakened to a blinding blizzard. 83
Never before at that season of the year had the oldest settlers seen 97
anything like it. All day the storm continued, and the farm houses 110
were isolated as though it were the middle of winter. Schools were 124
closed, and people kept within-doors all day. The next morning we 137
awakened to a white world and a cold one. It was a day in which to 150
take account of our losses. 156

The cattle had been the worst sufferers. One herd in our neighbour- 170
hood had huddled on the railway tracks, and a train had ploughed 183
into them during the worst of the storm. Another herd, drifting 196
before the storm had come to the shore of a lake. Those ahead, 209
unable to stop because of the pressure from those behind, plunged 222
into the icy waters of the lake, and many were drowned. 233

The fields were covered with snow, and the stooks were just mounds 247
of snow in a white world. I still remember the job it was to clear 260
the snow from those stooks to hasten the drying process. 272

Lesson
97

WARMUP

Rhythm   asdfg ;lkjh asdfg ;lkjh asdfg ;lkjh asdfg ;lkjh asdfg ;lkjh

Shifting   XLIX 10.05 DCCCLXXIII 20.038 MCMLXXIII 30.46 MCMXXXIX 40.79

Top Row   138 900 & 745 6.045 #3 $5.00 4½% (100) 283* 45 - 10 = 35 (a

Job 1.   Study the following information on the use of Roman Numerals. Type
it, complete with enumeration of points. Try for a neat, accurate and
well set up piece of work. Use a 60-stroke line and single line-spacing.
Remember to double space between the paragraphs. Begin the heading
on line 14, and remember that we always leave two blank lines after a
heading.

THE USE OF ROMAN NUMERALS

We often forget that many of the things we use in our
everyday life have come down to us from ancient times. One
of these is the Roman system of numerals. While these
numerals are never used for mathematics or computing, they
are frequently used in printing and in manuscripts. Hence,
a typist must know how Roman Numerals are made and what they
represent.

Jock was a born fisherman. From the time he could just toddle, 14
he would sit, silent and patient, waiting for the fish to bite. This fish- 29
ing was done in a muddy stream on the prairies. The rest of us could 43
not understand his passion for the sport because it was often hot, 56
dry, and dusty, and there were few fish biting. Then, we moved to 70
rural Ontario to live. Jock was in a seventh heaven. He could fish all 85
summer long beside a quiet, sparkling stream, and the fish were as 99
enthusiastic as he was. To make Jock's joy complete, his eastern grand- 114
father loved to fish, too. The old man and the young boy spent many 127
a tranquil day, being lazy or energetic as the spirit moved them — or 141
more truly as the fish moved. Jock is grown now and has become a 155
very busy man, but when he feels tired or in need of recreation, he just 169
puts his rod and reel in the back of his station wagon and heads for 183
the peace and quiet to be found along the banks of his favourite stream. 194

Lesson
66

WARMUP

Speed From where she sits she can see the red jug but not the jar.
Hyphen My brother-in-law is red-faced, bow-legged and loose-framed.

SENTENCES

The forecast was that the banks would foreclose on the loan.
It is common for a submarine to submerge in the deep waters.
Perhaps you will let us know the amount of the discount now.
A man who misinforms others on any subject may be miserable.

Lesson 96

Rhythm   `a;sldkfjghfjdksla;sldkfjghfjdksla;sldkfjghfjdksla;sldkfjghfj`

Shifting   `Hazel Quentin Peg Tex Beth Clif Gwen Roy Jean Dick Mavis Guy`

Top Row   `201 "7" #94 $56 878 39 & 20 4.7 (126) 251* 96 - 13 = 83 125%`

Concentration Drills

When you mark your work, do you find a number of errors that you feel you should not have made? Do you repeat words? Do you omit words? Do you sometimes switch from one line to another? If you do any of these things, you are not concentrating on the copy. You need to practise concentration. Future lessons will include concentration drills of different kinds. Examine each drill and use it to help you improve your accuracy. Here are some examples of concentration drills. Try them – each three times.

1. Insert the missing letters, without marking this copy.

`Sh_ l_st th_t boo_ _n t_e street _n fr__t _f the n_w sch__l.`

2. Type each line backwards.

`Ed. of aid the to come to boys good all for time the is Now`
`.pu gnikool fo tibah eht kaerb ot yaw a si sdrawkcab gnipyT`

3. Spell words correctly.

`Deer Jeen:  Wee shal bee veri pleezed too see yu nex munth.`

4. Insert capitals where required.

`i was to meet mr. o'connor at the alberta hotel in calgary.`

THINK AS YOU TYPE

Prepare a set of directions which clearly describe the route you would take if you were driving from your home to your school. Centre your heading and enumerate each of your directions. It will be helpful if you indicate approximate distances.

Job 1. Set up in good form on a half-sheet of paper.

THREE LETTER WORDS

a's	b's	c's	d's	f's
and	bay	cab	dad	far
art	bat	cad	dam	fad
arm	ban	can	day	fan
arc	beg	cap	dog	fat
awe	bet	car	dot	fed
aft	boy	cat	den	few
ail	bow	cow	dew	fig
aim	box	cod	did	fit
aid	bid	cop	dig	fix
all	big	cot	dim	fog

Job 2. Using the title MORE THREE LETTER WORDS and the headings: g's, h's, j's, l's, and m's, arrange the following words in good tabular form.

gay, gag, gap, gas, get, god, got, gun/ had, ham, has, hat, hay, hot, how, hub/ jar, jab, jam, jaw, jet, job, jog, joy/ lay, lad, law, led, leg, let, lot, low/ mad, man, may, mob, mow, men, met, mud.

THINK AS YOU TYPE

There are 51 states in the United States of America. Without consulting any reference books, list as many of the states as you can. If you are unable to list at least 30 of the states, you should review your North American geography. After you have reviewed the names of the states, set them up in two columns on a full sheet of paper. Check your work with your partner to make sure that you each have a complete list.

Lesson 67

WARMUP

Speed **Did you tell him that if he wins, he will not be able to go?**

Apostrophe **Malcolm's class has trouble with the 4's, 5's, 6's, and 7's.**

Job 1. Set up the following tabulation on a full sheet of paper using a 60-stroke line.

SELECTED CANADIAN HOTELS

City	Hotel	No. of Rooms
Calgary	Calgary Inn	554
Edmonton	Macdonald Hotel	455
Vancouver	Bayshore Inn	522
Victoria	Empress Hotel	416
Winnipeg	Fort Garry Hotel	265
Fredericton	Lord Beaverbrook Hotel	150
Halifax	The Lord Nelson Hotel	325
Hamilton	Royal Connaught Hotel	250
Montreal	The Queen Elizabeth Hotel	1200
Saskatoon	Bessborough Hotel	226

Job 2. Set up the following tabulation attractively on a full sheet of paper.

NEW BOOKS
PUBLISHED THIS YEAR

Author	Title	Month	Price
Ballantyne, John	The Copper Kettle	Apr.	$11.50
Dunton, Mary	Nova Scotia Trails	Sept.	9.95
Francis, Jean	Summer Homes	Feb.	12.50
Gregory, Rita	Maritime Ships	Mar.	16.95
Jalnick, Albert	Prairie Skies	Jan.	8.95
Molnar, Marie	Quebec Furniture	Oct.	29.50
Pelczar, Kenneth	Mammals of Canada	Nov.	14.95
Rae, David	Easy Gardening	May	12.95
Tanger, George	More Wood Carving	July	8.50
Wenger, Helen	Country Cooking	June	12.50

Job 3. Set up on a full sheet of paper a table entitled First Quarter Sales using the headings: Territory, Jan., Feb., and Mar. and listing the following sales: Vancouver, $11 500, $10 675, 12 480; Calgary 9 720, 10 460, 11 375; Regina, 10 870, 11 940, 10 270; Winnipeg, 15 650, 15 890, 14 820; Toronto 60 740, 72 190, 69 875; Montreal 42 780, 44 670, 39 875; Moncton, 8 180, 9 125, 10 180; Halifax 11 890, 10 620, 9 470.

Columns Containing Numbers

When typing a column containing numbers it is customary to align the *units* column.

When no whole number precedes a decimal marker, type a zero.

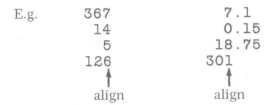

The tab stop for the column is set at the most frequently occurring line-beginning. The backspace key or the space bar is used to arrive at the starting point of lines which do not conform to the tab stop.

```
              E.g.          $4.56
                             3.75
                             6.45
                             0.75
                             5.15
                             3.20
                               ↑
              Set tab stop here
```

Job 1.   Set up in good form on a half-sheet of paper.

NEW BOOKS

Author	Title	Price
Bowman, T.	Treasure Trove	$1.69
Denton, A.	Black Gold	2.45
Gaynor, T.	Desperate Hours	3.50
Karon, S.	Daffy Definitions	0.89
Lyons, J.	Jungle Journeys	3.25
Moore, F.	Summer Fun	1.85
Stevens, L.	Tall Tales	0.75
Tallman, C.	The Old West	4.15
Trenton, D.	Pioneer Days	3.85
Warner, K.	Pacific Isles	2.90
Wilder, L.	Queen's Quest	0.95
Yarnton, W.	Royal Command	1.60
Yolles, S.	Dangerous Flight	2.65
Zaner, J.	Whaling Days	3.25

Job 2.   Set up the following information about School Clubs in tabular form.

1. The Science Club meets on Monday in Room 18. The president is John Mathers and the yearly fee is $2.

2. The French Club has a yearly fee of $2.50. It meets on Wednesday in Room 26 and the president is Jean Graham.

3. Marvin Leahy is president of the Stamp Club which meets on Friday in Room 19. The annual fee is $1.50.

4. The yearly fee for the Business Club is $2.50. The president of the Club is Mary Angman and meetings are held on Monday in Room 29.

5. Louise Everson is president of the Girls' Athletic Club which meets on Tuesdays in Room 20. The yearly fee is $3.

6. The Boys' Athletic Club under their president, John Forbes, meets on Tuesdays in Room 1. The annual fee is $3.

Lesson 95

WARMUP

Speed   They said that they will soon work with new tools and staff.
Accuracy We emphasized the extreme importance of productive capacity.
Top Row The man's shirt should fit a 38 cm neck and an 84 cm sleeve.

TIMED WRITING

1 AND 3 MINUTES

Bob and Tom had long cherished the dream of making a trip by canoe   13
through the dense forest country that lay beyond their summer home.   26
This year all the conditions for the trip were right, and all their elaborate   41
plans had been completed and checked. The trip was to last for four   54
weeks, and the necessary supplies had been purchased. Long hours   67
had been spent in wrapping the supplies in small convenient packages   81
that would be safe from damage by water or sun. The packages them-   94
selves had been carefully labelled and numbered.   104

The boys had experienced some difficulty in finding accurate maps   117
of the area that they were to traverse. By sheer good luck they had met   131
an old prospector who had made several trips through the region. On   144
each trip he had made neat and detailed maps and had kept notes which   158
explained and described the terrain. The old veteran had been willing   172
to give his maps and notes to the boys and had added some advice that   186
was to prove very useful.   191

Job 2. Review the rules in Lesson 45 for centring a column heading which is longer than the longest item in the column.

NOTE: In typing a column in which the items are sums of money, it is usual to type the $ sign in front of *only* the first item in the column.

Set up on a half-sheet:

Quantity	Item	Unit Price	Total
24	Steel Chairs	$12.50	$300.00
6	Filing Cabinets	45.00	270.00
2	Coat Racks	17.50	35.00
3	Bulletin Boards	18.50	55.50
			————
			$660.50

Job 3. Set up the following personal-business letter on a full sheet of paper. Prepare a carbon copy of the letter. The heading will be your home address. Leave 6 spaces between each column in the tabulated section of the letter.

The Ski Loft, 4857 Main Street, Vancouver, BC V3N 9D4
Gentlemen: Will you please send me the following items from your current sports catalogue.

Quan.	Item	No.	Page	Price
1 pr.	Hockey gloves	6B3	52	$12.95
1	Hockey sweater	5C2	57	5.29
1 pr.	Ski glasses	2D9	61	5.99

Please send this order C.O.D. Sincerely yours,

THINK AS YOU TYPE

Compose a letter to be sent to The Modern Fashion Shop, 79 Dupont Street, Montreal, PQ H2R 7D3 ordering three items of clothing which you would like to have sent to you C.O.D. Prepare a carbon copy of the letter, and a properly addressed envelope.

Job 3. Arrange on a half-sheet the following order in tabular form under the headings, Quantity, Description, Price, and Total:

2 gross, No. 2 Pencils @ 7.50, 15.00; 3 doz., Desk blotters @ 1.50, 4.50; 5 boxes, #8 Staples @ 0.55, 2.75; 2 doz., Black ribbons @ 15.00, 30.00.

Lesson 94

WARMUP

Speed   This week send them your bill with each item that they want.

Accuracy   His unsolicited testimonial influenced the group's decision.

Spelling   niece independent seize already receive forty rhythm occurred

Job 1.   Type the following rough draft in good tabular form.

Auditorium Bookings
for February

	Date	Time	Organization	Fee
arrange in chronological order	15	20:00 – 22:30	Kiwanis	$12.50
	04	19:30 – 22:30	Boy Scouts	15.00
	12	14:30 – 16:30	I. O. D. E.	10.00
	07	20:00 – 23:00	Red Cross	15.00
	21	20:30 – 23:00	Rotary	12.50
	19	18:30 – 22:00	Canadian Club	17.50
	14	20:00 – 23:00	Chamber of Commerce	15.00
	27	13:30 – 16:00	Y. W. C. A.	12.50

Lesson 68

WARMUP

Speed   When I go, it will be time to tell them what he came to do.

Quotes   "When?", "Where?", "How?", and "Why?" are adverb questions.

Job 1.   Set up on a half-sheet.

STAFF LIST

Name	Address	Telephone
Armstrong, Mary	84 Elm St.	221-6240
Corning, John	216 Maple Dr.	486-7128
Fenson, Ida	418 Ridge Road	732-7678
Hanson, Fred	17 Pine Ave.	483-2246
Jenkins, Ron	64 Cedar Dr.	222-2168
Manning, Helen	121 Cypress St.	926-4421
Pinder, Grace	72 Princess Rd.	197-2615
Ryan, George	618 Regent Ave.	924-6892
Stevens, Iris	26 Oxford Cres.	192-2189
Terry, Marion	118 South Dr.	484-2196
Vernon, Fred	18 Park Blvd.	924-6621
Watson, Beth	621 Brook Ave.	221-4836
Yates, Cora	43 Court Pl.	483-9972

Job 2.   Use a half-sheet of paper.

TEAM STANDINGS

Rank	Team	Captain
1	Giants	Fred Jones
2	Bombers	John Parker
3	Tigers	Les Fraser
4	Lions	Joe Phillips
5	Panthers	Roy Mackenzie
6	Eagles	Pete Lewicki

Job 3.   Refer to Lesson 64, Job 2. Arrange the names of the students in your class in alphabetic order. Set up these names together with the addresses and telephone numbers in tabulated form similar to Job 1 on this page. Centre the main heading, "CLASS LIST." Use a full sheet of paper.

Lesson 93

Speed   They will send your bill for this fine item when they like.

Accuracy   Suffering was alleviated by generous foreign contributions.

Numbers   If we add 3 and 4, or 5 and 2, or 6 and 1, we always get 7.

Job 1.

CLUB SCHEDULE

(Fall Term)

Club	Day	Room	Sponsor
Athletic	Tuesday	15	Mr. Courtney
French	Friday	24	Miss Pinay
Drama	Monday	12	Miss Kerns
Camera	Tuesday	27	Mr. Shuter
Printing	Thursday	18	Mr. Pressman
Dance	Wednesday	16	Miss Foote

Job 2.   (Use a 60-space line and arrange the items in alphabetical order.)

District Sales
(by units)
for
The First Quarter

District	Jan.	Feb.	Mar.
Windsor	9 850	7 325	8 460
London	7 410	7 015	7 360
Niagara	9 925	8 860	8 730
Hamilton	9 875	9 220	9 385
Toronto	10 105	9 875	9 925
Sudbury	6 340	6 125	6 275
North Bay	5 325	5 975	6 025
Lakehead	6 020	5 875	5 925
Ottawa	7 750	6 825	7 040
Kingston	5 275	5 300	5 625

Lesson 69

Speed He should go as soon as he can; are you able to go with him?

% Sign 25% of 96 is 24; 30% of 50 is 15; 40% of 25 is 10; ¼ is 25%.

Ruled Tables

The ruled table is "dressed up" by the use of horizontal lines made from underscores. These lines are called *rules* and two lines typed close together are called a *double rule*.

1. Type a double rule above column headings.

2. Type a single rule under column headings.

3. Type a single rule at the bottom of a table.

4. Leave a blank line above and below all rules.

5. The rules should be exactly as wide as the table.

To Type a Double Rule:

1. Type the first "rule."

2. Draw the carriage back by hand to the start of that rule.

3. Bring the ratchet-release lever forward and advance the paper about 0.25 cm.

4. Type the second rule under the first one.

5. Return the ratchet-release lever. It will automatically return the cylinder to the original line of writing.

Job 1.

TEAM STANDINGS

(as at December 6)

Team	Won	Lost	% Won
Cougars	8	2	80.0
Panthers	7	3	70.0
Wolves	7	3	70.0
Bearcats	3	7	30.0
Tigers	3	7	30.0
Beavers	2	8	20.0

Job 1.   (Use a 60-space line.)

COMPARISON OF ANNUAL SALES

District	This Year	Last Year
Halifax	$12 450	$11 619
Truro	9 210	8 415
Yarmouth	10 618	10 971
Charlottetown	7 067	6 924
Moncton	12 463	11 383
Saint John	9 813	9 926
Fredericton	7 214	7 034
Campbellton	7 754	6 986
Bathurst	4 453	4 207

Job 2.   (Use a 60-space line.)

TRIAL BALANCE

Account	Dr.	Cr.
Cash	$ 1 225	
Merchandise Inventory	5 000	
Furniture & Fixtures	1 575	
Delivery Truck	2 000	
Land & Buildings	9 000	
Supplies on Hand	60	
Accounts Receivable	650	
Accounts Payable		$ 575
Mortgage Payable		4 000
Capital		14 935
	$19 510	$19 510

"Boxed" Tables

A "boxed" table is one with both horizontal and vertical ruled lines, as shown in Job 2 below.

1. Type the table as you did in Job 1. Omit all rules *but leave space for them.*

2. All rules are drawn with pencil or pen after the typing is completed.

3. Vertical rules are drawn to separate the columns and the headings.

4. The sides of the table are not closed in.

5. Extend the horizontal rules slightly beyond the width of the table (0.5 cm is acceptable practice).

Compare Job 1 (a ruled table) with Job 2 (a boxed table).

Job 2.

TEAM STANDINGS

(as at December 6)

Team	Won	Lost	% Won
Cougars	8	2	80.0
Panthers	7	3	70.0
Wolves	7	3	70.0
Bearcats	3	7	30.0
Tigers	3	7	30.0
Beavers	2	8	20.0

Job 3.

Set up the following table on a half-sheet of paper leaving six spaces between columns. Rule in horizontal and vertical lines to make a 'boxed' table.

SPELLING DEMONS
(Words Commonly Misspelled)

A - E	F - M	N - T
analysis	foreign	niece
anxiety	frivolous	ninth
beginning	fulfilled	occurred
eighth	library	rhyme
embarrass	mortgage	tragedy

THINK AS YOU TYPE

Have your partner or your instructor dictate to you the words in Job 3. Type them in four columns on a half-sheet of paper. Check the spelling and use each word in a sentence.

Job 2.

Set up the following information in either a "ruled" or a "boxed" table form:

DISTRICT SALES
for the month of January

District	Sales	Quota	Per Cent of Quota	Rank
Winnipeg	$10 000	$9 000	111	1
Regina	9 000	8 500	106	3
Saskatoon	8 500	7 750	110	2
Calgary	8 750	9 250	95	6
Edmonton	8 500	8 750	97	5
Vancouver	9 500	9 250	103	4

THINK AS YOU TYPE

Prepare a "ruled" or "boxed" table describing five of your best timed writings. Suggested headings are: Date, Time, Gross Speed, No. of Errors. Compose a suitable heading.

Lesson 92

WARMUP

Speed   **Your bill will be sent later if you send your new order now.**

Accuracy   **This judicial inquiry terminated in acrimonious controversy.**

Top Row   **The 420 men consumed 1893 sandwiches and 850 cups of coffee.**

Table with Leaders

In typing many tables, particularly financial tables, the columns of figures are placed at the right side of the typing space, separated from each other by *two* spaces. The explanatory material is placed at the left side of the typing space and is joined to the figure columns by *leaders* (rows of periods). One blank space is left before and after the line of periods. Sometimes one blank space is left between the periods.

To set your tabulator stops, *pivot* from the right margin. To do this, set your right margin and then backspace through the figure columns or the column headings, whichever is longer. Set a tabulator stop for each column. Whatever space is left is used for the first column.

Remember:
1. Set your left and right margins first.
2. To set your tabulator stops, backspace from the right margin.
3. Leave two spaces between figure columns.
4. When inserting the leaders, leave one blank space before and after your line of periods.

Lesson 70

Speed **You can see this end of the red car, but she can see it too.**

$ Sign **Gifts of $1, $2, and $5 were common; gifts of $10 were rare.**

Technique Pointers — Typing on Lines

A typist often has to type on a printed line.

The problem is, how to adjust your alignment to get your typing in just the right place.

Your Name	~~Elisabeth Totten~~	Too low!
Your Name	Elisabeth Totten	Too high!
Your Name	Elisabeth Totten	Just right!

Before typing on the line, check the alignment by tapping the underscore key. It should strike right on the printed line. Put your ribbon-control in the stencil-cutting position while you do your checking. Don't forget to put it back afterwards. You will have to use your line disengaging lever to move up or down as necessary. Your teacher will explain these two mechanisms. For practice, draw 10 lines on a piece of paper (have them unevenly spaced) — then, type your name on each line.

Job 1.

Using lined note paper, type one page of your class notes from your own handwriting.

Technique Pointers — Making Insertions

The typist often finds, after he has taken a sheet from the machine, that there is a letter that needs to be inserted. The difficulty lies in getting the letter in the exact place where it belongs. For example:

typ st often finds,	letter missing
typist often finds,	insertion is wrong
typist often finds,	insertion is right

On most machines, the marks on the aligning scale point to the exact centre of each letter. Before typing an insertion, use the paper release to slide the paper to the left or right to line up the other characters in the word. This will ensure that the missing letter is properly aligned. PRACTICE — Type "typ st often finds" in 10 or 12 different places on a sheet of paper; remove and reinsert the paper each time before typing the missing "i".

Lesson 91

Speed   Send them your new order now and you may pay the bill later.

Accuracy   The banquet programme is organized by a competent committee.

Top Row   On April 17 we sent you $147.30 in payment of invoice #2085.

TIMED WRITING
1 AND 3 MINUTES

This is the age of numbers. Almost every aspect of our daily living   15
has a number involved in it. We live in numbered houses, often on   28
numbered streets. We drive our cars with their numbered licence   41
plates on numbered highways. We communicate with one another   53
by dialling telephone numbers and we buy our clothes by quoting   65
a size number. If we are so unfortunate as to land in jail, we are given   80
a number instead of a name.   85

For the typist, the lesson in all this use of numbers is very obvious.   100
In today's world, any typist must be proficient in the use of the top   114
row of keys. The skill of typing numbers quickly and accurately is   128
attained only through frequent and serious practice.   138

Tables

Review the instructions found in Lesson 69 for setting up "ruled" and "boxed" tables.

Job 1.

Set up the following "ruled" table:

SALES QUOTAS
for the month of January

District	Manager	Quota	Increase
Winnipeg	Hearn	$9 000	$500
Regina	Jorgen	8 500	250
Saskatoon	Fraser	7 750	750
Calgary	Beston	9 250	500
Edmonton	Maxwell	8 750	250
Vancouver	Ord	9 250	750

Job 2. Copy exactly the following sentences on lined note paper. Remove the paper from your machine. Reinsert and carefully realign the paper. Insert the missing letters.

1. When did he rece ve the award?

2. She is an excell nt typ st.

3. I saw a l ama in the zoo.

4. They will as end on the escalat r.

5. He omit ed the first sent nce.

Lesson 71

WARMUP

Rhythm   `a;sldkfjghfjdksla;sldkfjghfjdksla;sldkfjghfjdksla;sldkfjghfj`

Shifting `Queen Avis Jay Ben Dick Zoe Max Fred Will Hugh Patricia Glen`

Top Row `Bob's aunt said, "We must pay a bill of $90 at 4% interest."`

SENTENCES

1 `Adopt this "motto":  you will feel bright when you do right.`
2 `Lincoln's jump measured one metre in the school's high jump.`
3 `When I return from British Columbia, I hope to travel South.`
4 `I said, "The Welland Canal links Lake Erie to Lake Ontario."`
5 `We will leave school at 15:30 on January 4 with $8 to spend.`

THINK AS YOU TYPE

A Type the following paragraph inserting the necessary capital letters and punctuation marks.

My friends father is an excellent doctor. He attended dalhousie university and mcgill university in the 1940s. After he graduated from university my friends father worked in a hospital in halifax nova scotia. After working in the maritimes he decided to go west. I guess he believed in the saying go west young man. He says that he loves the salt water. One day he said to me I hope to retire on an island in the pacific because there is something very basic about the ocean. What do you think his remark means?

Form Letter

A *form letter* is a letter which, with minor changes, can be sent to more than one person. The jobs in this lesson are good examples of the use of a form letter. By observing the following steps, you will be able to speed up your typing of such letters.

1. Type your first copy very carefully.
2. Note carefully how the other copies will differ from the one you have just typed.
3. Using your *first* copy as a model, type the necessary additional copies.
4. Check each copy to see that *all* the necessary changes have been made.

Jobs 1. to 4. Set up in semi-blocked style, the form letter in Job 1. For Jobs 2 to 4, repeat the letter addressing it as indicated and making any other changes that are necessary.

Job 1.

```
Mr. Peter Grant
2672 King Street
Hamilton, Ontario
N5S 3T4

Dear Pete:
        The April meeting of the Hamilton
Sales Club will be held in the Crystal
Room of the Connaught-Sheraton Hotel on
Wednesday, April 23, at 8 p.m.
        At this meeting, we shall have short
reports from all committee heads. As
chairman of the Membership Committee, you
will be allotted five minutes in which to
report on the activities of your group.
        We are looking forward to seeing you
at the meeting and to hearing your report.
                        Sincerely yours,
                        Fred R. Hammond
                        Corresponding Secretary

    FRH:URS
```

Job 2.

Mr. William (Bill) Warner
1642 Main Street
Hamilton, ON
N5S 1A1
(chairman of Education Committee)

Job 3.

Mr. James (Jim) Plady
1742 Tamarack Drive
Burlington, ON
N6A 8P2
(chairman of Social Committee)

Job 4.

Mr. Charles (Charlie) Swinton
22 Granite Road
Stoney Creek, Ontario
N6A 9V3
(chairman of Program Committee)

Job 5.

Address "small" envelopes for the letters you have just completed.

B   Answer each of the following questions with a complete sentence.

1   How much money would you like to make in your life?
2   How many courses are you taking this year?
3   How many days are there in a week?
4   Some months have 31 days, some have 30; how many have 28 days?
5   A farmer had 17 sheep. All but nine died. How many were left?
6   We all know there are 12 one-cent stamps in a dozen, but how many two-cent stamps are there in a dozen?
7   How many minutes does it take you to get to school from your home?
8   What is the speed limit on the street outside your school?

TIMED
WRITING

We all know that most of Canada's birds fly south when the days   13
grow short and the winter winds begin to blow. What happens to those   27
winged beauties, the butterflies? There is one species, the Monarch   41
butterfly, which finds its way to a certain pine grove in California.   55
This is just another of the unsolved mysteries of nature. Hundreds of   69
thousands of these Monarchs arrive in the same grove each November,   82
and yet, no Monarch exists long enough to return a second time. Some   96
of them have winged their way a great distance coming from Canada   109
or even Alaska. What unknown instinct leads them to this particular   123
zone? Man, with all his wisdom, has no answer to this question.   136

Lesson 72

WARMUP

Rhythm   `a;sldkfjghfjdksla;sldkfjghfjdksla;sldkfjghfjdksla;sldkfjghfj`
Shifting `Dixon Adams Black Franz Potter Quigley Walsh Jarvis Robinson`
Top Row   `127 "38" #96 45% $5.00 75% 823 62 & 73, 12:30 (2000) *No. 19`

TIMED
WRITING

In the modern office practically everyone is called upon to use the   14
telephone. When you speak over the telephone, your voice represents   28
your firm to the customer. Whether or not the impression of the firm   42
is a favourable one, depends upon your voice. Any business managers,   56
interested in their firm's standing in the community, will insist that 70
their workers please the listening public. An interesting, sparkling   85
voice is easily acquired through training so see to it that you have the 99
kind of voice business people want to hire.   107

Job 1. Study the model letter on page 135 and then copy it. It is a "medium" length letter.

Job 2. Type this short letter in the semi-blocked style using the mixed pattern of punctuation.

Today's date.
Mr. Carl Peterson, Executive Secretary, Canada Safety Council, 1822 Carling Avenue, Ottawa, ON K2A 1E2. Dear Mr. Peterson:
Our group is making a study of driver education programs in Canadian high schools. It is our understanding that your association has recently issued a report on such programs and their effect on road safety.
We would appreciate receiving as soon as possible three copies of the report together with any other relevant information.
Thank you for your co-operation and assistance.
Very truly yours, C. Henderson, Secretary

THINK AS YOU TYPE Mr. Peterson, to whom you wrote in Job 2, has complied with your request. Write to him thanking him for sending the copies of the report on driver education programs. This information has been of great help to your committee which is planning this type of program for your school.

Use the semi-blocked style, today's date, and, if possible, your school letterhead.

Lesson 90

WARMUP

Postal Cards

Postal Cards are frequently used for advertising purposes, making an announcement, or sending a brief message. One side is used for the address and the other side for the message. To use one for a message, the typist should allow a 3-stroke margin on all sides of the message. With ruler and pencil, outline four postal cards on a sheet of letter-size paper.

To use the address side, follow the instructions in Lesson 40 for addressing envelopes.

Job 1.

On one of your outlined postal cards, display the following announcement attractively. Centre each line. You will not likely have room to double space throughout. Use your judgment as to grouping of lines.

THE EATON OPERATIC SOCIETY / Presents / THE STUDENT PRINCE / book and lyrics by Dorothy Donnelly / music by Sigmund Romberg / EATON AUDITORIUM / February 7th to February 11th / at 20:20.

Job 2.

On your second postal card, type the following message.

NOTICE OF MEETING

There will be a meeting of the full executive of the Hi-Y Club on Thursday, January 17, at 20:00 in the Club Rooms at Central YMCA. Our Spring Prom is the important item on the Agenda. All members are urged to be present.

Allan Hughes,
Secretary.

Job 3.

On your third postal card, type the following advertisement. Follow the instructions given for Job 1.

PHOTOGRAPHS / PUBLIC RELATIONS / PERSONNEL AND / EXECUTIVE PHOTOGRAPHS / George Robert McGregor / A.E.B.P., A.R.P.S. / MCGREGOR PHOTO STUDIOS LTD. / 482 College West

THINK AS YOU TYPE

On your fourth postal card, compose a message to be sent to the Red Cross Blood Donor Clinic advising them that you cannot keep your appointment to give blood on Tuesday because you have a cold. Ask them to give you a new appointment for next week. Address the postal card to the Red Cross Blood Donor Clinic in the Town nearest you. Type your return address in the appropriate place.

Commonwealth Products

KNOWN THROUGHOUT THE NATION

Executive Offices .... 220 Berkeley Street, OTTAWA, ONTARIO K2L 8D4

December 20, 19--

Mr. Ronald Whiting
124 Maple Boulevard
Hamilton, ON
N5L 4G7

Dear Mr. Whiting:

This letter is typed in the semi-blocked style which is a style used frequently in Canadian office correspondence.

The only difference between this style and the blocked style which you studied previously is that the first line of each paragraph is indented. The usual indention is five spaces, as illustrated in this letter, but some typists prefer to indent ten spaces or more. Your own preference or the stated practice in your office will determine which indention you will use.

To save time, you should set a tab stop at the paragraph indention point. This will enable you to make the indention quickly and effortlessly.

Yours very truly,

William L. Hartnell

William L. Hartnell
Supervisor of Training

WLH:URS

SEMI-BLOCKED
Mixed Punctuation

Lesson
73

Speed   `Dear Mr. Lyle:   Thank you for the last order that you sent.`

Shifting   `Saskatchewan, Manitoba, Ontario, Newfoundland, Nova Scotia.`

Top Row   `The list price of the #6 desk is $94.75 less 30%.   Buy now.`

TIMED WRITING

One of the marks of a good office worker is your ability to organize   14
your work and your time. You must develop work habits which enable   28
you to do the most possible work in the least possible time.   40

This ability is one that you have not been required to show in school.   55
There, your work has been organized for you. The day has been con-   68
veniently divided into periods, and specific activities have been   81
assigned to each period. Your teachers have directed your work and   95
assigned your duties. Your textbooks have been carefully organized so   109
that you have derived maximum benefit from the time you spent with   122
them.   123

In the business world you will be called upon to do much of this   137
organizing for yourself.   142

Job 1.

Set up the following personal business letter and address an envelope for it.

March 16, 19--   Lyle & Jamieson, Ltd.   1872 Scarth Street, Regina,
SK   S4P 2G9   Gentlemen:

An announcement appeared in our local newspaper which stated
that you will soon be opening a new store at 1784 Broad Street in this
city.

The opening of this store will make it much easier for me to arrange
to have my motorcycle serviced. In the past, I had to drive to the other
side of the city and it was always difficult to get transportation back
home.

I hope you will let me know when you are open for business. I am
anxious to see the new models for this year which I hope you will have
on display.   Very truly yours,   Leon Plante

THINK AS YOU TYPE

Compose a letter to Lyle & Jamieson, Ltd. They have just notified you that
their store will be open as of the first of next month. You would like them
to send you literature, specifications, and price lists on the latest model
**of Honda Trail 70 cm³ motorbike. You would like to look over this literature
before visiting the store and seeing the new models.**

Job 2. Take 1½-minute timings on the following closing sentence of a letter, complimentary closing, signer's identification, and initials. Follow the procedure outlined in the previous lesson.

```
We are looking forward to meeting you and to hearing your
message.

                                  Sincerely yours



                                  Edward J. Watson
                                  Convention Chairman
EJW:URS
```

Job 3. Take a 5-minute timing on the letter on page 130. Your objective is to be able to complete the letter in 5 minutes with less than 5 errors.

THINK AS YOU TYPE

Compose a short paragraph on each of the following topics: (1) The importance of conserving energy (2) The viewpoint of a giraffe in a zoo.

Lesson 89

WARMUP

```
Speed      You can see all of the old cars at the far end of the road.
Accuracy   Rex quickly jumped off the hazardous big van without Brian.
Numbers    3 and 6 and 9 and 12 and 15 and 18 and 21 and 24 and 27 and
```

The Semi-Blocked Letter

On the next page you will find a model letter set up in the *Semi-Blocked* style. The only difference between this style and the Blocked style that you have been using is that the first line of each paragraph is indented. You will need to set a tab stop for this paragraph indention; otherwise, you can proceed as before.

Lesson 74

Speed   She can see the end of the car, and you can see the end too.

Top Row   John's brother-in-law asked for 20% of Kenneth's $87.35 fee.

TIMED WRITING

Canada's most important natural resource is water. Without it, the   14
high standard of living that we now enjoy would not be possible.   27

The St. Lawrence River and the other mighty waterways of Canada   41
enabled our early settlers to penetrate into the vast interior regions   55
of the country. Today, those rivers still carry a large share of our trade   70
and commerce.   73

Much of the electricity which turns the wheels of our industries   86
and services our homes is generated by water power. The waterfalls   100
and swift-flowing streams which hampered the journey of our early   113
settlers have been harnessed for the benefit of all Canadians. Our lakes   127
and rivers provide the millions of litres of water that are used daily   142
in our homes and in our industrial plants.   150

Job 1.

Arrange the following book order in tabular form under the headings, Quantity, Title, Price, Amount:

24, Lost in the Woods, $1.75, $42.00; 5, Home Cookery, $3.25, $16.25; 3, Golf for Duffers, $3.15, $9.45; 12, Square Dancing, $4.20, $50.40.

Job 2.

Arrange the following VACATION SCHEDULE under the headings, Name, Department, Start, Finish:

Browne, T. L., Sales, July 2, July 23; Cochrane, F. N., Accounting, July 16, July 30; Davis, M. R., Shipping, July 2, July 16; Farmer, E. F., Service, July 5, July 19; Gray, P. R., Sales, July 16, August 6.

THINK AS YOU TYPE

Copy the following material leaving six spaces between the columns. Use the necessary capital letters as you type.

on new year's day   the toronto maple leafs
the english and typing courses   an air canada flight
the board of education   on main street
the red river valley   a visit to the rockies
the indian culture   at the education centre
my father's aunt   the supervisor of the factory

Lesson 88

WARMUP

Speed   To do that will make it bad for the men who are on the job.
Numbers Remember June 6, 1944, December 7, 1941, November 11, 1918.
Shifting #98 "56" 908 13' 10% 567 & 380 (136) 08 20 $30 54 m $85.00.

TIMED WRITING

1 AND 3 MINUTES

```
We are delighted to hear that you can attend our annual      11
meeting and that you have agreed to speak to our members.    22

You will be given one hour on Thursday morning, and we       33
should like you to tell our members about the use of gas     44
in Canadian industry.  So that you may be suitably intro-    55
duced, we would appreciate receiving an information sheet     66
outlining your background and experience.  A photograph      77
which we can use in our printed program would also be        88
helpful.  We are looking forward to meeting you and to       99
hearing your message.                                        103
```

Job 1.   Set your margin for a 60-stroke line. Set a tab at the centre. Take 1½-minute timings on the following inside address and salutation. Follow the procedure outlined in the previous lesson to increase your production rate.

```
Mr. Arnold Frisbee
Alberta Gas Company Ltd.
665 Eighth Avenue West
Calgary, AB
T2B 1B4

Dear Mr. Frisbee
```

Lesson 75

Test

Job 1.

Suggested time: 15 minutes
Type two 3-minute writings. Score and hand in the better one.

> One of the springtime delights of children living in Eastern Canada   14
> is to walk through the sugar bush and listen to the soft ping of the   28
> maple sap dripping into the metal buckets. Long before white peo-   41
> ple came to America, the Indians had discovered how to draw off   54
> the sap of the maple and to make syrup and sugar from it. There is   67
> a legend that the Indians boiled venison in sap instead of spring water.   81
> The early settlers made sugaring a time of social activity, and the   95
> sugaring-off party has become a tradition. After the boiling, some of   109
> the hot clear maple syrup is poured on clean snow. It hardens quickly   123
> into a sweet, sticky mass that is a delight to eat. Is it any wonder that   137
> children and adults alike look forward to this special springtime treat?   151

Job 2.

Suggested time: 15 minutes
Set up the following material on a full sheet of paper. Before you type,
read the material and follow the Typing Suggestions in Section B for the
proper set up.

GUIDE FOR WRITING A BOOK REPORT

A.   MAIN SECTIONS TO BE INCLUDED

    1.   Title of book
    2.   Name of author
    3.   Name of persons reviewing the book
    4.   Summary of the story
    5.   Opinions and comments on the book

B.   TYPING SUGGESTIONS

    1.   Top margins of 12 line spaces.
    2.   Book title centred in capital letters
    3.   Main section headings at left margin in capital
       letters
    4.   Report single spaced, with double spacing between
       sections
    5.   Side margins set for a 50-space line
    6.   Allow an extra 5 spaces at left margin for binding
    7.   Bottom margin of at least 6 line spaces

Job 3.

Step 1. Type the following inside address beginning at the left margin.

```
Mr. Arnold Frisbee
Alberta Gas Company Ltd.
645 Eighth Avenue West
Calgary, AB
T2B 1B4
```

Step 2. Practise for one minute the lines which you found most difficult.
Step 3. Type the inside address as many times as you can in one minute.
Step 4. Repeat Step 3 for greater speed.
Step 5. Repeat Step 3 for greater accuracy.

Job 4.

Step 1. Practise the most efficient way of using the carriage return on your machine.
Step 2. On a 1½-minute timing start typing the date at the centre, space down 10 lines, and type the inside address in the proper place. If you complete the inside address in the time given, return your carriage, tab to centre and repeat the exercise.
Step 3. Repeat Step 2 for greater speed.
Step 4. Repeat Step 2 for greater accuracy.

Job 5.

Step 1. Using a blank sheet of standard letter paper, take a 1½-minute timing on the following:
(a) insert paper and space down to line 15
(b) tab to centre and type date
(c) space down 10 lines and type inside address.
Step 2. Repeat the above procedure for greater speed.
Step 3. Repeat the above procedure for greater accuracy.

Your objective is to type and set up the date and inside address in 1½ minutes with a maximum of two errors. Practise this exercise daily until you have reached your objective.

THINK AS YOU TYPE

Compose a paragraph explaining (1) how you felt when you were typing the above jobs and (2) what suggestions you might follow to improve your production rate.

C. GENERAL SUGGESTIONS

1. Use correct spelling and punctuation for clarity.
2. Edit and retype for best possible form.
3. Support your comments by using specific examples from the book.

Job 3.

Suggested time: 15 minutes
Compose a personal-business letter to be sent to your local bus company. Advise them that your class would like to charter a bus for a trip to a neighbouring city which is 50 km from your school. You are planning to visit the new Science Centre in that city on the afternoon of May 15, and return to your school that same evening. There are 34 students in your group. You would like to know if a bus is available on that day and what the cost would be.
Type an envelope for your letter.

Job 4.

Suggested time: 20 minutes
Set up the following information in the form of either a boxed or a ruled table.

Title: Practice Schedule (fall term)

Headings: Day, Time, Activity, Supervisor

Information: Monday, 16:00, Basketball A, Mr. Jeeves

Tuesday, 15:00, Volleyball, Miss Canton

Tuesday, 16:30, Badminton, Mr. Coates

Wednesday, 15:30, Basketball B, Miss Graham

Thursday, 15:30, Table Tennis, Mr. Fraser

Thursday, 16:30, Tumbling, Mr. Gregory

Friday, 16:00, Basketball C, Miss Lawrence

Friday, 16:30, Curling, Mr. Jasper

Saturday, 09:00, Bowling, Mr. Peters

Lesson 87

WARMUP

Alphabet gray zoom oxen five quip jury bike came stay cold down half
Spelling bibliography, accommodate, reference, periodical, precedes,
Numbers   1827 1836 1852 1887 1895 1910 1914 1923 1949 1952 1968 1972

TIMED WRITING

1 AND 5 MINUTES

One of the most enjoyable aspects of taking a trip is the planning 13
for it. Some of the seasoned travellers that I know start their planning 26
months and even years ahead. 32

Having decided where they want to go, these travellers begin to 45
collect information about the places they will visit. They write for 58
travel folders and maps and guide books. They compile lists of 71
hotels and inns and guest houses. They read about the history and 84
the customs and the people of the region. When they have absorbed 98
all this information, they are ready to draw up a day by day 111
itinerary for their trip. 116

To these travellers, the planning has a double value. The collecting 129
of the information is enjoyable and stimulating, and the possession 142
of it enables them to make the best possible use of their travelling time. 155

Production Typing

Your production rate on business letters will increase if you can type each of the parts of a business letter quickly and accurately, and if you can move from one part to another without hesitation. To do this you must make efficient use of the service keys, such as Tabulator and Carriage Return.

The following exercises are designed to help you to improve your production rate. You may wish to use this plan to improve your rate on any of the material in the text.

Job 1.

Step 1. Using a 60-stroke line, and starting at the left margin, practise typing today's date. E.g., October 19, 19--.
Step 2. Type today's date as many times as you can in 15 seconds.
Step 3. Repeat Step 2 for greater speed.
Step 4. Repeat Step 2 for greater accuracy.

Job 2.

Step 1. Clear all tabs; set a tab at the centre.
Step 2. Tab to the centre and type today's date as many times as you can in 15 seconds. Tab to centre each time you type the date.
Step 3. Repeat Step 2 for greater speed.
Step 4. Repeat Step 2 for greater accuracy.

Lesson 76

WARMUP

Rhythm   `a s d f g f ; l k j h j asdfgf;lkjhjasdfgf;lkjhjasdfgf;lkjhj`

Alphabet   `exit wry equal baby cat fine vote saw dam have jet keg prize`

Numbers   `Add 274 and 385 and 1490 and 1637 and 1935 and 2986 and 100.`

Technique Review

Do you get tired when typing? Do your wrists, arms, shoulders or neck ache before the class period is finished? Are you making too many errors?

Have a Posture Check-up!

Team up with a classmate; watch each other type, and using the chart given below, find out your weak points. Make an effort to improve your posture, and hence your typing.

Posture Check-up Chart

Straight back
Lean forward from hips
Head erect
Shoulders relaxed
Elbows in; arms hanging loosely
Wrists level and off the frame
Fingers curled over guide row
Feet planted firmly on the floor
Copy to right of typewriter
Eyes on copy

SPEED SENTENCES (double letters)

```
The abbot addressed them on the books in that
ancient abbey.
Telling that odd riddle seems to leave poor men in
a muddle.
He gave a peerless account of each odd event which
occurred.
Each occasion was accented by the addition of a
yellow jeep.
```

SPELLING PRACTICE

One word in each of the following sentences is spelled incorrectly. Locate the words and correct them when typing the sentences.

```
Your priviledge to use the library was cancelled.
I had to cancell the appointment with my dentist.
There were fourty customers who had not yet paid.
They seemed truely sorry for their lengthy delay.
```

THINK AS YOU TYPE

Type a paragraph on "Traffic Safety." What rules should drivers of vehicles observe? What rules should pedestrians observe? How can we make our highways and streets safer for all citizens?

Commonwealth Products

KNOWN THROUGHOUT THE NATION

Executive Offices . . . .   220 Berkeley Street, OTTAWA, ONTARIO K2L 8D4

November 21, 19--

Mr. Arnold Frisbee
Alberta Gas Company Ltd.,
645 Eighth Avenue West
Calgary, AB
T2B 1B4

Dear Mr. Frisbee

We are delighted to hear that you can attend our annual
meeting and that you have agreed to speak to our members.

You will be given one hour on Thursday morning, and we
should like you to tell our members about the use of gas
in Canadian industry. So that you may be suitably introduced, we would appreciate receiving an information sheet
outlining your background and experience. A photograph
which we can use in our printed program would also be
helpful. We are looking forward to meeting you and to
hearing your message.

                    Sincerely yours

                    Edward J. Watson

                    Edward J. Watson
                    Convention Chairman

EJW:URS

```
┌─────────────────────┐
│   BLOCKED STYLE      │
│   Open Punctuation   │
│   60-stroke Line     │
└─────────────────────┘
```

In the present group of lessons on Skill Building, we begin 5-minute timed writings for the first time. We have been trying to develop good typing technique so that what we produce is done rapidly and accurately. Controlled, speedy typing is our ultimate goal! For this group of timed writings, set yourself an immediate goal of not more than 5 errors in five minutes of writing. *Remember*, no more than 1 error for each minute of writing.

TIMED WRITING
1 AND 5 MINUTES

There was a boy in our typing class whose name was Don. He	13
was a tall, good-looking boy who did well in all his classes except	26
typewriting. When his teacher stood over Don to see what the trouble	40
was, he could find little to criticize. Don had good typewriting	53
techniques. His stroking was excellent. He was an athlete, and he	66
displayed the same smooth rhythm when he typed as he did on the	79
gym floor. What was the matter? The answer was simple. As soon	92
as the teacher walked away, Don slid down on his chair until he was	105
sitting on the end of his spine. Perhaps it was comfortable, but it	119
surely did things to his typing. The teacher begged, lectured, coaxed,	133
and teased. Don was quite sure that he would never qualify for his	147
certificate because his tests were full of errors. He was also sure that	161
it was much too hard to sit up straight. The teacher finally made a	175
promise. He told the class that the day Don got his certificate, he	188
would also receive a rubber chair cushion as a present from the	201
teacher. The teacher also promised Don that if he would sit up straight,	216
the cushion would be his in a very short time. It worked! In just a	229
few weeks, Don received the coveted certificate, and with it, a cushion	244
to make good posture all the more comfortable.	253

Lesson 77

WARMUP

Rhythm   `aa ss dd ff gg ff ;; ll kk jj hh jj aassddffggff;;llkkjjhhj`

Shifting   **Kim Tex Virve Iza Joy Squire Peg Wayne Duff Beth Clara Karl**

Numbers   `weep 2330 were 2343 ripe 4803 true 5473 your 6974 wipe 2803`

Technique Review

Do you move your hands and arms when typing? Do you over-reach or miss a stroke because your hands are out of position? Do you use up a lot of energy and time with waste motions that you should not be making?

Check-up on Stroking

Team up with a classmate. Check these points and concentrate on correcting any weakness in your stroking of the keys.

1. Arms steady but relaxed.

2. Hands level and quiet.

3. Fingers well curled, so that any required key can be struck by just a quick reach and a sharp stroke of the finger only.

Commonwealth Products

KNOWN THROUGHOUT THE NATION

Executive Offices . . . .

September 15, 19--

Miss Elsie Blackburn
3284 Poplar Crescent
Regina, SK
S4S 2E9

Dear Miss Blackburn:

This letter is typed in the blocked style
which is often used in Canadian business
correspondence.

Observe that all lines begin at the left
margin except the date line and the closing lines. These lines usually begin at
the centre of the paper.

When you are using this letter style, set
a tab stop for the centre of your paper.
This saves you time and effort in typing
the date line and the closing lines.

Very truly yours,

Richard R. Henderson

Richard R. Henderson
Director of Training

RRH:URS

BLOCKED STYLE
Mixed Punctuation
40-stroke Line

CAPITALIZATION AND PUNCTUATION

Capitalize and punctuate the following sentences wherever necessary.

john ross sr president of ross & sons will retire next year
a box 10 cm x 10 cm x 10 cm contains 1000 cm³ of space doesnt it
although the buick is for sale it is not operating properly
this year i am taking typing french science english and art

THINK AS YOU TYPE

Complete each of the following sentences. Compose a paragraph using one of your sentences as an opening.

```
Hidden in the dead leaves
On a visit to Nova Scotia
Twenty days out of Singapore
The mayor quietly lowered
```

PARAGRAPH

Ottawa, the capital city of Canada, has many attractions for summer visitors. One of the most colourful spectacles that takes place daily during the tourist season, from June to September, is the changing of the Household Guard on Parliament Hill. Hundreds of people gather every morning to watch the ceremony, which has quite an air of old-world pageantry about it. The precision and symmetry of the soldiers in scarlet tunics, their faces almost hidden under bearskin shakos, are a source of delight to children and amazement to adults. Somehow, the contrast between the stately grey buildings and the colourful ceremony of the changing of the guard leaves one with a deeper sense of history in the making.

Lesson 78

WARMUP

Rhythm `abcdefghijklmnopqrstuvwxyz abcdefghijklmnopqrstuvwxyz abcdef`

Numbers `123 456 789 101 767 843 923 462 597 835 130 628 319 705 4821`

Stroking `Extra care must be taken to avoid loss of items in a letter.`

The Modern Trend

The modern trend is to use a uniform length of line for all letters, regardless of the number of words in the body. Usually, the line length is 50 strokes.

If you are using a uniform length of line for all letters, it is advisable that you adjust the space between the date and the inside address to provide a better balanced page. For example, if your letter contains less than 100 words, use a 50-stroke line, and leave up to 12 lines between the date and inside address.

Punctuating the Business Letter

The punctuation in the body of any business letter conforms to the usual rules of good English. However, the punctuation used after the date line, the inside address lines, the salutation line, the complimentary closing line, and the signer's identification lines does vary. For these lines, there are three patterns of punctuation in common use in today's offices.

1. The Mixed Pattern, which is the one most commonly used, requires a colon after the salutation and a comma after the complimentary closing. All other display lines require no punctuation after them.

2. The Closed Pattern, which is now rather old-fashioned, requires that *every* display line be ended with some punctuation mark.

3. The Open Pattern, which is gaining wider acceptance, eliminates punctuation marks after *all* display lines, including the salutation and the complimentary closing.

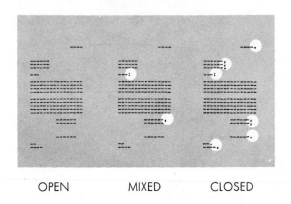

OPEN   MIXED   CLOSED

Job 1.   Copy the letter on page 129.

Job 2.   Copy the letter on page 130.

Technique Review

Do you make errors just after throwing the carriage? Do you sometimes feel that the machine has got out of position? Maybe you are out of position or thrown off balance.

Check Feet Position

Have a classmate check the position of your feet when you are typing. They should be planted firmly on the floor to give you complete balance and erect posture. Good typing depends on good posture.

SPEED SENTENCES

```
You can appreciate the need for accuracy in all bookkeeping.
The foolproof arrangement was approved by an office manager.
A trooping of the colours is a happy event for the children.
The tooth was extracted in error, much to the lady's sorrow.
```

NUMBER REPRESENTATION

In the following sentences, choose the correct way to represent the numbers. Type each sentence correctly.

(Forty, 40) tickets were ordered for each of the (two, 2) games.
Accommodation for (six, 6) boys is available on March (ten, 10).
I can bring the (twelve, 12) girls home by (twelve, 12) o'clock.
Claudia has packed (fourteen, 14) dresses and (six, 6) sweaters.

THINK AS YOU TYPE

Type a short paragraph describing a recent event at your school, such as an assembly, a game, or a dance.

TIMED WRITING

1 AND 5 MINUTES

Years ago, digging potatoes by hand was one of the annual jobs on | 14
the farm. Today a trim machine moves up and down the rows, and | 27
the potatoes are bounced up a conveyor belt and dropped in long | 39
rows along the field ready to be picked up. In the old days, the digger, | 54
armed with a potato fork, attacked the ridged hill and from beneath | 67
each plant pulled out the potatoes. The work was hard, but there | 81
was a sense of accomplishment in the digger's mind as the rows of | 94
potatoes lengthened and lengthened. In the back of his mind, how- | 107
ever, each digger had thoughts of further labour he was preparing | 120
for himself. Each potato that he pulled from beneath the frozen | 133
and withered plant was a potato that would have to be picked up | 145
later in a basket and then dumped into a burlap bag. Digging was | 158
the job for the morning and picking and bagging the afternoon's | 171
task. Each day's work was usually finished by four o'clock, and the | 184
bags of potatoes were carried to the woodshed. There they were | 197
spread to dry for a few days before being stored in the cellar for use | 211
during the winter months. | 216

Lesson 86

WARMUP

Rhythm	`a;sldkfjghfjdksla;sldkfjghfjdksla;sldkfjghfjdksla;sldkfjghfj`
Numbers	**November 21, 1972; December 23, 1954; August 20, 1949; 1900;**
Shifting	**K6L 5B2; S7T 8X0; R3P 4N9; V5M 7F8; H5P 7R9; ON; PQ; YT; AB;**

The Parts of a Business Letter

Letterhead ▶

Date Line ▶

Inside Address ▶
Salutation ▶
Body ▶

Complimentary Closing ▶

Signer's Identification ▶
Reference Initials ▶

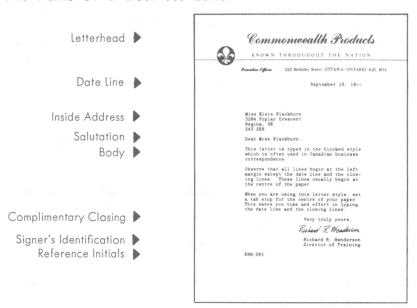

Separate the parts of a letter by 1 blank line, except —

◀ 1. Put extra space between the date and the inside address — see the table below.

◀ 2. Put extra space above the signer's identification, to provide room for his signature — leave 3 blank lines for it.

Placing the Letter on the Page

Step 1: Drop to the dateline position which is line 15 or 2 lines below the letterhead, whichever is lower.

Step 2: By estimating the number of words in the body of the letter, decide whether the letter is *short* (under 100 words), *average* (100-200 words) or *long* (over 200 words).

Step 3: Set the margin stops for a 40 or 50-stroke line (short letter), 50 or 60-stroke line (average letter) or 60 or 70-stroke line (long letter).

Step 4: Type the date and then drop 8 lines (short letter), 6 lines (average letter) or 4 lines (long letter) to the inside address.

Length of Letter	Short	Average	Long
No. of words in body	under 100	100-200	over 200
Length of line pica type elite type	 40-stroke 50-stroke	 50-stroke 60-stroke	 60-stroke 70-stroke
Date to inside address	8 lines	6 lines	4 lines

Lesson 79

Rhythm a b c d e f g h i j k l m n o p q r s t u v w x y z a b c d

Numbers 100 "3" #42 $53 69% 878 90 & 78 250 (126) 138* 82 - 10 - 72

Stroking jam jet jot job jib jog join jolt joy joyful judge judgment

Technique Review

Is your typing skill showing steady improvement? Is your speed increasing? Do you sometimes lose your place in the copy?

1. Copy should be to the right of the machine and should be propped up at the top for easy reading.

2. Eyes should remain steadily on the copy.

SENTENCES

A better attitude is a sure way of getting better attention.
The typist was helpless when it came to addressing a letter.
The puzzled dog was muzzled because he nuzzled the children.
Guests wear formal dress when attending these jazz concerts.

CAPITALIZATION AND PUNCTUATION

Capitalize and punctuate the following sentences wherever necessary.

jake has been in london england since february 29 1972
the principal said return at noon tomorrow and she did
how many cartons did mr thomsons manager receive today
this book a long night is available at any coles store

THINK AS YOU TYPE

Type a short paragraph (as if it were a paragraph in a personal letter) telling a friend about some place you have visited or something you have seen recently, e.g., a zoo, a museum, a good movie, a circus.

Job 1. Type the following extract from the Canada Year Book, entitled, "The Public Libraries of Canada". Use a 60-stroke line, double line-spacing, and make any corrections indicated. Type the title on line 8.

The Public Libraries of Canada *(BLOCK CAPS)*

The citizens of Canada like to read. Today, public library services are available to over 80 percent of the people of Canada. All Canadian cities of over 40 000 population have municipal libraries, and most smaller cities enjoy the same services. Regional libraries bring library service to smaller communities. Provincial library services in nine provinces provide limited facilities for those in sparsely-settled areas by mail, bookmobile, boat, and plane.

The problem of bringing library services to new suburban developments and to rural areas continues to receive attention, and various solutions have been tried. Among these are the extensive use of mobile units, and of rental units, instead of permanent, publicly-owned buildings.

Public library service to the business community is becoming increasingly important. Five large libraries--in London, Ottawa, Toronto, Windsor, and Vancouver--now have separate business sections in charge of full-time specialists.

Children 5 - 14 years of age continue to be the most frequent visitors to public libraries, and borrow 46 percent of the books circulated. Children's librarians also provide story hours, plays, and puppet shows, organize clubs, and appear on radio and television, to the delight of a receptive clientele.

Special libraries serving government, professional, business, and technical organizations and the universities, assist research workers and administrators to keep abreast of new developments in science and technology.

--Canada Year Book

Job 2. Type the following recipe on a piece of paper cut to the size of a file-card to fit a recipe file box.

WALDORF SALAD

250 mL diced apples
250 mL diced celery
125 mL broken walnuts

French dressing
Lettuce leaves
Mayonnaise

Fold together the apples, celery and nuts with French dressing and serve on lettuce leaves with mayonnaise. Do not allow to stand long before serving, as the nuts will discolour the fruit.

No person should be expected to provide complete details on any 14
subject at a moment's notice. People often are unable to furnish 27
data on even commonplace topics. The educated person does not 39
necessarily have at his fingertips all the facts that he needs, but he 53
knows where to go for these facts. There are many sources of informa- 67
tion for him or for anyone else and one would be much wiser if he 80
made continual and intelligent use of these sources. 90

Your typewriter cannot select and spell correctly the best word, 104
but a good English dictionary can provide the answer. You may 117
forget a friend's telephone number or his address. A telephone direc- 131
tory is always within reach and will put you right. Details of the 144
history or science course that you took last winter may escape your 157
memory; reference to a good text or to an encyclopedia will bring 170
them back to mind. If you are asked to write an essay about the 183
Federal Cabinet, you should realize at once that an almanac or the 196
current Canada Year Book will furnish you with the details you 209
need. Be alert! Know the good sources of information, and do not 222
hesitate to use them. 226

Lesson 80

WARMUP

Rhythm   a s d f g f ; l k j h j asdfgf;lkjhjasdfgf;lkjhjasdfgf;lkjhj

Shifting   Quentin Joy Liza Val Alex Mac Hugh Pat Beth Gwen Frank Doris

Numbers   10 26 39 48 57 10" 26L $39 48% 57 & 10 & 260 (39) & (47) 100

Centring   Jig Saw Puzzle
                 J I G   S A W   P U Z Z L E

Technique Review

Are you slowing yourself down by a poor "carriage-return" technique?

Check-up on Your Carriage Return

Have your typing partner check you on the following:

1. Eyes remain on the copy — no peeking to see how you are doing and no looking up at the sound of the bell.

2. Carriage is tossed back with a quick throw — not dragged and not slammed.

3. Left hand returns to position immediately and resumes work on the keys.

4. If you are faulty on these points, ask your teacher for some carriage return drills.

**THINK AS
YOU TYPE**

In the time allotted to you by your teacher, try each of the following:

Type as many words as you can think of that begin with "be."   e.g. before
Type as many words as you can think of that begin with "in."   e.g. income
Type as many words as you can think of that end in "ing."   e.g. acting
Type as many words as you can think of that end in "tion."   e.g. action

**TIMED
WRITING**

1 AND 5 MINUTES

Joyce was a peculiar girl. She was pretty to look at and was always   15
very well-groomed. In fact, the boys turned around to have a second   29
look at her lovely hair and her trim figure. She was quiet and soft-   42
spoken and had a ready wit that made us all like her. She was intelli-   55
gent and learned easily. She was an expert typist and a whiz at short-   69
hand. Yet, there was something wrong. During the four years that she   83
was in my class, she never learned to follow instructions as they were   97
given. She always managed to have things mixed up and in a turmoil.   111
Wherever Joyce was working, a job never got quite properly done,   124
and in some strange way, she kept others from doing their work. After   138
she left school, this trait, which her teachers had tried so hard to   152
correct, was her downfall in every office in which she worked. It is   166
sad to relate that, in spite of the fact that Joyce was liked by all who   180
knew her, no employer could afford to keep her very long.   191

Lesson 85

WARMUP

Rhythm `asdfg ;lkjh asdfg ;lkjh asdfg ;lkjh asdfg ;lkjh asdfg ;lkjh`
Speed `They were able to work well with any type of girl who came.`
Numbers `682-2950, 594-7786, 385-9968, 929-0370, 764-2443, 843-2664.`

THINK AS
YOU TYPE

Prepare a list of the groceries you would like to buy for the week-end. Show the amount of money you expect to pay for each item. Supply appropriate headings for each of your two columns.

SPEED SENTENCES

```
The shrewd man shrank from the shrill noise of the children.
There was a quality of sincerity in their giving to charity.
The beautiful and wonderful things in life make men hopeful.
The manager criticized them on the size of the organization.
```

WORD PRACTICE

Copy and complete the following sentences.

```
The capital of New Brunswick is
The plural of datum is
A synonym for ancient is
The verb form of practice is
The feminine form of duke is
```

THINK AS YOU TYPE

Write a paragraph describing good typewriting techniques. The last five lessons have emphasized a review of these techniques. What are they?

TIMED WRITING

1 AND 5 MINUTES

The poets have written much of the delights of the open road. 13
Many have sung the praises of the path winding through the green- 26
sward, the rutted trail zig-zagging across the bald prairie, the concrete 41
ribbon cut straight through hill and valley, and the super-highway 54
filled with speeding automobiles rushing on to unknown destinations. 68

Much less has been written, however, of the annoyances of these 81
same roads, the winding path with its mudholes or dust, or the rutted 95
trail which seizes your car wheels and compels them to follow all 108
its windings. Very few have extolled the charm of the concrete ribbon 122
where always there is a truck which is just starting up the hill ahead 136
and which chugs to a crawl long before the top is reached, forcing 149
all behind it to a snail's pace, or the super-highway streaming with 163
cars and trucks all madly seeking to be first in line and driven 176
by drivers seemingly bent on self-destruction. 185

Our insane craze for speed has produced a race of drivers who 199
are incapable of appreciating anything along the road except the 211
road signs which call attention to the dangers of excessive speed and 225
unwise passing; even these are usually regarded as something placed 239
there for the edification of other drivers. 247

Lesson 84

WARMUP

Job 1. Type the following essay, entitled, "Books are Windows Through Which We View the World." Use a 60-stroke line and double line-spacing. Make the corrections as indicated. Type the title on line 8.

```
     Books Are Windows Through Which We View The World   (BLOCK CAPS)

                     and
     Thousands -of- thousands (of) books have been written, and more
are being written all the time. They deal with many topics in
many fields, but every one helps us to gain a better understanding
of the people, history, and science of the world in which we live.

   History books, historical novels, and biographies take us into the
past.  By reading a biography, we can know an exciting, colourful
character such as Alexander the Great.  Through history books we
can see, because we are not involved in the same critical situ-
ations, the lasting effect of the accomplishments and errors of
                  past
the leaders of centuries ago.  An historical novel is primarily
entertaining, but (is there) usually an underlying lesson in it.

     Many of the books about the modern world contain pictures of
foreign lands and people.  By looking at these, we can see what
other parts of the world are like today.  We may see Buckingham
Palace in London, Saint Peter's Church in Rome, the Eiffel Tower
in Paris, or the Clock Tower in Berne, Switzerland. Other books
about foreign places may not contain pictures, but they do paint
in our imaginations  vivid descriptions with words.  Books written
about our modern world present conflicting thoughts and ideals.
To read them is unlike reading history books because we are pre-
sented with biased opinions.  Nevertheless, we gain understanding
and tolerance of others from these opinions.

                                            our
     Books, in general, give us a picture of this world, whether
it be clear or confused, as it appeared in the past, appears in
the present, and may appear in the future.
                                         - Your name.
```

Lesson 81

WARMUP

Rhythm   me ma my am an on is us so to by of or he ha by do if ah pa

Shifting   Quenton Lex Kim Jack Virve Hazel Bud Wayne Peggy Fritz Stan

Accuracy   Emphasize to Jack Fred that a big yellow quilt is expensive.

Job 1.   Using a half-sheet of paper, set up and type the following notice for the students' bulletin board of your school.

TO ALL STUDENTS

Your Students' Council wishes to announce the following events, scheduled for the Winter Term. It is hoped that all students will plan to attend and participate in these activities.

January 15:   Sock Hop
February 1:   Annual Sports Night
February 16:   Valentine Dance
February 23:   Tri-Swim Meet
March 2, 3, 4:   Music Nights — Operetta — "The Mikado"

March 16:   St. Patrick's Dance
April 7, 8:   Drama Nights — Three-Act Play — "The Heiress"

Art Brown,
President, Students' Council

Job 3. Cut a sheet of paper into three pieces, postcard size, or use real post cards if they are available. Your teacher wants the following message typed on each. You are to address them (on the other side of the card) to the people listed below. Make the necessary corrections as you type.

NOTICE — ~~O.C.T.A.~~ *O.B.E.A.* EXECUTIVE

5] The Research committee of the ~~O.C.T.A.~~ *O.B.E.A.* will hold an important meeting on Saturday, April 12, at 2:30 p.m. at the King George hotel in Toronto. A matter of concern to all typewriting teachers will be discussed. Your presence is urgently desired. Please telephone me if you will ~~not~~ *stet* be able to attend.

G. Reeves,
Chairman

Address to:

Mr. W. R. Statton
Secretary,
Rideau ~~High~~ School
St. Laurent Boulevard
Ottawa, ON N7D 8E7

Mr. George D. Steele
61 Amesbury Avenue
Hamilton, ON N4T 3F2

Mr. D. W. Chambers
Eastern High School of Commerce
16 Phin Avenue
Toronto, ON N9G 4H9

Job 2. Set up and type the notice prepared in Job 1 incorporating the following changes:

a) Change heading to read —

— TO MEMBERS OF THE STAFF —

b) Change the preamble to read —

The Students' Council wishes to announce the following events scheduled for the Winter Term. We sincerely hope that members of the Staff will be able to attend and participate in these activities.

Job 3. On paper approximately 20 cm x 20 cm, prepare a Production Staff list for your school production, "Early Frost." Choose students from your class to fill the following production jobs: Director, Set Design, Stage Manager, Master Carpenter, Furnishings Design, Lighting, Sound, Costumes, Properties, Make-up, Script Assistant, Program Design and Layout, Publicity.

Complete your assignment using the following format. You may wish to review Lesson 58 for an explanation of the use of "leaders."

                    PRODUCTION STAFF

                    for "Early Frost"

Director . . . . Scott Olmstead

Set Design . . . . Jim Mitchell

Lesson 83

Rhythm   the and for fit sit wit did aid leg man men pay pen die via

Shifting   CCXIV L9C 5L1 CDXCIX 1980 MCMIX $37.40 MCMXXVIII 1923 07 17

Numbers   1066 1492 1508 1603 1759 1763 1842 1867 1914 1921 1945 1967

Job 1.   Type the following poem on a half-sheet of paper.

My Heart Leaps Up

My heart leaps up when I behold
   A rainbow in the sky:
So was it when my life began;
So is it now I am a man;
So be it when I shall grow old,
   Or let me die!
The Child is father of the Man,
And I could wish my days to be
Bound each to each by natural piety.

                    William Wordsworth

Job 2.   Set up and type the following program on a half-sheet of paper. Insert the short edge of the paper in the machine. Centre each item, and separate the items by using double line-spacing.

Program (Block Caps)
Grace
Toast to the Queen
National Anthem
Dinner
Introduction of Head Table Guests
Greetings from Provincial Executive
Speaker: Mr. J. A. Brown, M.A. Ph.D.
Presentation to Mr. Nathaniel L. Barrett
Presentation of President's Gavel
Introduction of Past-Presidents
Adjournment

Much of the work you may be required to do in an office will come 14
to you in a very rough form. This is called, "typing from a 'rough 27
draft'." Your employer or superior may hand you a piece of work, 40
such as a report or a letter, already typed but full of corrections marked 55
with pen or pencil. You will be required to produce a perfect copy 69
ready for use. On the other hand, your employer may scribble a 'rough 83
draft' of a letter and expect you to bring back a perfect specimen 96
ready to be mailed. The penmanship may not be the best in the world, 110
but you will be expected to decipher it without making errors. This 123
is a skill that requires much practice before you can do a quick and 137
efficient job without floundering. 144

There are standard markings that are used by editors, writers, and 158
typists to show the changes that are required in a rough draft. It will 172
be necessary for you to become thoroughly familiar with these so that 186
you can work well on any rough draft. By now, you should have 198
become convinced that there is more to being an expert typist than 212
meets the eye of the casual beginner. 219

Lesson 82

WARMUP

Rhythm `a;sldkfjghfjdksla;sldkfjghfjdksla;sldkfjghfjdksla;sldkfjghfj`

Shifting `I 20 III 30 V 40 IX 50 XIII 60 XIX 70 XXXV 80 XLVI 90 CX 100`

Top Row `1. 2. 3. 4. 5. 6. 7. 8. 9. 10. (a) (b) (c) (i) (ii) (iv) (v)`

PARAGRAPH PRACTICE

Type the first paragraph of the timed writing from Lesson 81. Attempt a perfect copy in one typing only.

Correction Markings for Rough Draft

Editors, proofreaders, and others frequently use certain markings to indicate corrections to be made on a piece of typed work. The following table gives some of the more common markings used. Study them so that you will know what they mean when you have to make a revised copy of a rough draft.

∧ Insert word	and∧is *(it)*	/Small letter	A̸nd he came
Insert space	and i̸t is	—Delete word	and s̶o̶ he
or #	and i̸t is	⌒ Close up	p.⌒m.
∧ Start		⑤ Indent	⑤I came home
⌐ Paragraph	⌐Mary went	⌒ Reverse order	and (the⁀so)
≡ Make capital	m̲a̲ry went	.... Stet (let it stand)	
O Make period	he came;̸	*stet*	and s̶o̶ he *stet*

Job 1.   The following item of news has been prepared and typed by one of your school reporters for the school yearbook. An English teacher has made some revisions. You are to type it on a full sheet of paper. Follow all handwritten instructions.

Senior Student Makes Headlines/. (BLOCK CAPS AND CENTRE) *60-stroke line double space*

⑤Sheila McGowan, a Member of this year's graduating *commercial* class, brought honours

to our school by ~~capturing~~ the *winning cup for the highest net speed in the* Provincial Typewriting Contest held at

Easter. ⌐Sheila scored a first with a net speed of 83 words per minute on

a ten-minute test. She competed against top-ranking students from (over⁀all)

the Province. When the cup was presented to Sheila, it was announced that

she had made only three errors on her test.

⑤This young lady has been an outstanding student. A member of the Honours

Club in each *of her four* year, *at our school,* she has found time for basketball, badminton, and track

and was a member of the swimming team. She is an accomplished pianist and

took one of the lead parts in last year's operetta, "The Mikado." Sheila

was secretary of the Students' Council this *p* Past year. She did *an* outstanding

job in that position as she did the previous year ~~as~~ *when she was* President of the

Commercial Club.

⑤Congratulations ~~to~~ Sheila! We wish ~~her~~ *you* every success and happiness as ~~she~~ *you*

takes ~~her~~ *your* outstanding skill*s* into the business world.